The Dyslexic Adult
in a non-dyslexic world

The Dyslexic Adult

in a non-dyslexic world

Ellen Morgan

Dyslexia Support Service, University of North London

and

Cynthia Klein

London Language and Literacy Unit, South Bank University

Consultant in Dyslexia
Professor Margaret Snowling, University of York

W

WHURR PUBLISHERS

LONDON AND PHILADELPHIA

© 2000 Whurr Publishers
First published 2000 by
Whurr Publishers Ltd
19b Compton Terrace, London N1 2UN, England and
325 Chestnut Street, Philadelphia PA 19106, USA

Reprinted 2001, 2003 and 2004

British Library Cataloguing in Publication Data
A catalogue record for this book is available from the British
Library.

ISBN: 1 86156 207 1

Printed and bound in the UK by Athenaeum Press Ltd,
Gateshead, Tyne & Wear

Contents

Foreword

As scientific knowledge of the nature and causes of dyslexia has grown, researchers have turned their attention to the characteristics of dyslexia in adults who have compensated for their earlier reading difficulties. However, very few studies have considered the impact dyslexia can have on the lives of those who have struggled through school and not had their dyslexic difficulties diagnosed until later in life. This book does just that.

Drawing on evidence from a series of semi-structured interviews, the authors uncover the experiences of dyslexic adults in the context of their everyday lives, the effects it can have on their emotional and behavioural development and on their family life. The book discusses the all too common feelings of isolation, loneliness, frustration and aggression that can become associated with dyslexia if it is not understood, and highlights the plight of dyslexic children from disadvantaged backgrounds whose parents may not be in a position to 'fight for their right' to appropriate teaching and support. In doing so, it emphasizes the importance of diagnosis as a turning point in an adult's self-perception and the beginnings of a reframing of negative school experiences. It is here that the authors' experience as educators of dyslexic adults is important in outlining guidelines for good practice that can take account of both the cognitive style and the sensitivities of the students they have supported so successfully over the years.

The book is a fascinating exploration of the under-researched personal experience of dyslexia and how this can affect adjustment and learning in education and in the workplace. It will make salutary reading for investigators who primarily view the problem from a language-based perspective and should generate new issues for research.

Margaret Snowling
York, October 2000

Acknowledgments

We owe much to the generosity, openness and courage of all those dyslexic adults who have contributed to this book, both directly and indirectly. We are also grateful to the many colleagues with whom we have worked over the years who have shared with us their experiences with students, as both teachers and learners. Their stories have enriched the book. Our thanks go also to all our students, both past and present, who taught us how to teach dyslexic learners, and who gave us the joy of witnessing their growth and achievements.

We very much appreciate the help of Liz Ahrends, Lesley Ayres, Erica Hunningher, Sharon McCabe and Helen Sunderland who kindly read chapters in progress and provided both affirmation and ideas for improvement.

We give special thanks to Ellen's husband, Wally, and Cynthia's partner, Ron, for their endless patience, support and many invaluable suggestions during all the stages of writing this book.

Ellen's Personal Acknowledgments

I extend particular thanks to my mother, Sylvia, whose creative approach to teaching served as my inspiration to become a teacher and my husband, Wally, for encouraging me to write. I would also like to acknowledge the support of the Research Committee at the University of North London, who granted me a one semester sabbatical to devote to writing this book.

Cynthia's Personal Acknowledgments

I would also like to thank my family who always encouraged me, and my teachers, past and present, who taught me how to learn.

Introduction

An elephant belonging to a travelling exhibition was stabled near a town where no elephant had been seen before. Four curious citizens went to see if they could get a preview. When they arrived at the stable they found there was no light and therefore had to investigate the elephant in the dark.

One, touching its trunk, thought the creature must resemble a hosepipe; the second felt an ear and concluded that it was a fan. The third, feeling a leg, could liken it only to a living pillar; and when the fourth put his hand on its back he was convinced that it was some kind of throne. None could form the complete picture; and each could refer to the part he had felt only in terms of things that he already knew. The result was confusion. Each was sure that he was right and none of the other townspeople could understand what the investigators had actually experienced (adapted from Shah, 1964).

Descriptions of dyslexia often seem a bit like the descriptions of the elephant by the men experiencing it in the dark: attempts to put together a comprehensive picture from limited perspectives. These create the contentions that surround issues in diagnosis and the disagreements among professionals about what it is and whom it affects.

There seems to be an 'essence' of dyslexia that eludes definition. This has variously been referred to as the 'feel' of dyslexia or its 'signature'. The ability of adults to articulate their experience offers a wealth of information that contributes to our understanding of the essence of dyslexia. Many dyslexic adults report 'knowing' when a close relative or friend is also dyslexic. Certainly what they tell us can help develop our knowledge about dyslexia and how it affects perception, information processing, thinking and behaviour. The information they provide can give us a fresh perspective on our non-dyslexic world. This book is an attempt to uncover and discover dyslexia through the experience of dyslexic adults in the broad contexts of their lives.

The book is based on the authors' extensive experience in diagnosing and teaching adult dyslexic students and in training specialist teachers. The material was collected from students and colleagues (both dyslexic and non-dyslexic) over the years, from teaching records, through interviews recorded on paper, tapes and video as well as from documents written by dyslexic adults. We also used reports and written information from colleagues working with dyslexic adults in a variety of settings.

In addition to the above sources of information, we conducted in-depth interviews of 14 dyslexic adults to gain a personal perspective of how dyslexic adults feel about life in a non-dyslexic world. Interview subjects were chosen to represent a range of backgrounds, and included people aged from 19 to 73 (with one ten-year-old who formed part of an intergenerational study). In addition to the broad age range, interviewees included native speakers and those who speak English as an additional language, men and women, those with university (and postgraduate) educational backgrounds and those with vocational training, and representatives from different ethnic and class backgrounds. Selection was intended to represent 'telling cases' (Mitchell, 1984); i.e. adults whose experiences might reflect that of others from similar backgrounds. The choice of informants from less privileged educational and economic backgrounds was intentional; we wanted to provide a voice to those dyslexic people who are rarely offered a platform.

The ethnographic approach used is premised on the notion that it is necessary to understand the way of life of a people before trying to explain their behaviour; hence semi-structured interviews were conducted. The ethnographic model often underlies the concept of 'practitioner research' such as that employed by teachers who use their own classes as communities to study. This approach is consistent with that described by Hammersley (1994) who points out the advantage of using small samples which allow for depth rather than breadth of information: '. . . one may study a small selection of cases that are designed to represent key dimensions in terms of which the population is assumed to be structured.' Hammersley makes the important point that much research may serve the powerful because the researcher is in the position of making decisions about what is to be studied, how and for what purpose. This often results in findings which are irrelevant and inaccessible to the people studied since they are decided by social science disciplines and do not necessarily address problems defined by the subjects themselves.

Our concern in this book was to give dyslexic adults an opportunity to identify the issues which most profoundly affect their lives. We hope the contents will be illuminating not only to those professionals who teach, counsel, advise or work with dyslexic adults, to work colleagues and family members, but also to dyslexic adults themselves, whose experiences often leave them feeling isolated. The book is intended as an opportunity for dyslexic adults to have a 'voice' and to have their experiences heard. We hope that it will offer its readers new insights and understanding in an area that is still fertile ground.

All the individuals referred to in the book were living in England at the time of interview. However, several of them migrated to London from other parts of the world, as in fact did the authors, both of whom are originally from the US. Although the book has a 'UK bias', much of the research cited in the literature comes from the US. It should be noted that there is a distinction in the terminology used in the UK and the US. In the former, the term 'dyslexia' is commonly used both to identify a particular specific learning difficulty (SpLD) and as an umbrella term encompassing other specific learning difficulties such as dyspraxia, dysgraphia and dyscalculia. In the US, the term 'dyslexia' refers primarily to a reading disability and, as such, tends to be much narrower in its use, while the preferred umbrella term is learning disability (LD). Many people who in the UK would be considered dyslexic are categorized as 'learning disabled' in the US. For the purposes of this book, the term 'dyslexia' is used in the British context except when direct reference is made to American research.

We have considered 'adults' to refer to anyone over 16, although most of the people whose stories have contributed to the book are mature adults over the age of 21. Throughout the book, when we have made general reference to students and tutors, we have varied the use of the personal pronoun, often referring to tutors as 'she' (based on actual fact) and using either 'he' or 'she' to refer to unnamed dyslexic adults. The distinction between further and higher education is that between students on vocational or pre-degree courses, where the main provider is further education colleges, and those studying for higher awards such as Higher National Diplomas (HNDs), degrees or postgraduate qualifications, usually in a university setting. We have discussed educational issues affecting those in adult basic education classes through to those studying at undergraduate or postgraduate level.

The book aims to examine a range of issues relating to dyslexia in adults and to present the reader with the implications of relevant current research in the field, along with practical examples of how dyslexia affects individuals' lives. It focuses primarily on people whose dyslexia was not diagnosed until adulthood, since through their eyes we feel we can gain insights about how it feels to be dyslexic in a non-dyslexic world. Although some of their perceptions mirror those of dyslexic people who knew about their dyslexia in childhood, their earlier lack of knowledge and understanding about how they learned, coupled with a lack of support, affected them in profound ways.

The book is divided into three sections, beginning with *Starting Points*, which focuses on the dyslexic cognitive style and the impor-tance of diagnosis, since these are the central issues for dyslexic adults themselves. Chapter 1 introduces the cognitive style of dyslexic adults, as one of the major themes is how dyslexic individu-als may develop their strengths to achieve success in their work, study and personal lives. Chapter 2 explores the significance of diag-nosis for previously undiagnosed dyslexic adults along with a discus-sion of some of the controversies concerning the definition and diagnosis of dyslexia in adults.

The second section, *Living in the Non-dyslexic World*, consists of Chapters 3 to 9 and is devoted to a discussion both of the difficulties faced by dyslexic people living in a non-dyslexic world and of the solutions and support which enable them to participate more fully and successfully in education, work and the wider context of their personal lives. Chapter 3 looks at the emotional and behavioural implications of dyslexia, particularly through the reflective accounts of adults who relate their early and current experiences and describe how their lives were and are affected by their dyslexia. Chapter 4 explores the impact of dyslexia on the family and discusses the find-

ings of an intergenerational study. Chapter 5 examines the consequences of dyslexia in the workplace, raising questions about appropriate guidance for course and job choice and support for dyslexic
employees in light of existing legislation. Chapter 6 describes
creative solutions to some of the barriers facing dyslexic people at
work and addresses issues of disclosure. In Chapter 7 we look at the
issues surrounding changes in the education system for adults and
raise questions regarding how dyslexic students can be accommo-
dated in response to widening participation and inclusive learning
initiatives. Chapter 8 attempts to illuminate teaching and learning
issues, considering particularly how best to support dyslexic learners
through developing strategies to encourage autonomous learning.
Chapter 9 presents an in-depth case study of a dyslexic adult whose
life is detailed from school experiences through basic literacy classes
to a university degree and beyond. His story touches on many of the
themes raised throughout the book.

The final section, *Turning Points*, consists of Chapter 10, which
looks ahead at some of the challenges and changes taking place at
the beginning of the twenty-first century, their effects on dyslexic
individuals and the contributions that dyslexic people can make to
our changing society. It considers some ways forward in making our
non-dyslexic world more dyslexia-friendly.

We have tried to present a comprehensive overview of the experiences of dyslexic adults. We hope the book will offer new insights to
all those non-dyslexic people who may benefit from a fresh perspective on the non-dyslexic world. We are particularly grateful to the
many dyslexic individuals who have willingly shared their experiences with us and hope that their stories will contribute to broader
understanding, greater tolerance of their weaknesses, more appreci-
ation of their strengths and increased opportunities for them to
contribute to the non-dyslexic world.

Interviewees

We are indebted to the following people for their willingness to share
their stories by volunteering their time to be interviewed. All interviews were taped and transcribed and, when requested, names were
changed to protect anonymity. Following each name, the first
number refers to age at diagnosis; the second to age at interview.

Lee (6, 10)

Son of Isobel, grandson of Catherine, contributed to intergenerational study; receives specialist help at school.

Isobel (24, 28)

Mother of Lee, daughter of Catherine, part of intergenerational study; final year student on teacher-training course, raised in London of Irish working-class parents, diagnosed while on an access to higher education course.

Catherine (n/a, 46)

Mother of Isobel, grandmother of Lee, part of intergenerational study, emigrated to London from Ireland; not dyslexic.

Graham (30, 33)

Raised in London, worked for many years in music industry before entering university, where he was diagnosed and is now in the final year of a degree in Business Studies.

Jackie (29, 31)

Raised in Hampshire in working-class family; received remedial support at school which never addressed her problems; after several years unemployment, enrolled on an access course and progressed to university where she is in the final year of a degree in Sports Science. She was diagnosed just prior to entering university.

Jenny (42, 48)

Born in Australia, raised in England in working-class family. Failed her 11+ examination and attended a girls' secondary modern school. Trained originally as a hairdresser and eventually became Head of School at a large further education college. Now works as an educational consultant. She was diagnosed at the college.

Lorraine (35, 37)

Born and raised in London from a Caribbean background; trained and worked as a beauty therapist after school; was diagnosed at university where she studied leisure and tourism management; has been accepted onto a Master's degree in Entrepreneurship.

Mac (71, 73)

Born and raised in Merseyside; left school with no qualifications, worked in many trades, including sales, gardening and as a greengrocer. Entered basic education classes as a mature adult of 71, where his dyslexia was diagnosed by a specialist trained tutor. Currently doing a pre-GCSE course in English and Local History.

Mark (22, 43)

Recently completed a Master's degree in Social Work; raised in a new town in Hertfordshire; working-class Irish background. Worked as graphic artist before entering adult literacy classes in a further education college, where he was diagnosed. Went on to study law at A Level and entered university, from which he graduated with a 2.1 degree in politics.

Martin (38, 53)

Born and raised in north London in working-class family; left school at 15 barely able to read and write. Gained employment making medical instruments, which he did for 26 years before being made redundant. Entered adult basic education classes at age 35; his diagnosis three years later by a specialist-trained tutor spurred him on to an access course and eventually to complete a degree in Social Policy with a 2.1. Currently works as a care assistant in a home for the elderly.

Michaela (15, 21)

Currently studying for BA in Human Resources and Business Law; worked in hotel and catering industry, raised in Suffolk, working-class family. She was diagnosed privately at the instigation of an employer. Was awarded a Young Achiever's Award at a ceremony at Buckingham Palace in 1999. This was in recognition for her ability to combine volunteer work in conflict resolution with 16–19-year-olds excluded from the education system while she was studying for her own degree and coping with her dyslexia.

Rob (9, 21)

Raised in London, middle-class family; diagnosed privately; attended special secondary school for dyslexic boys, completed GNVQ in catering, currently works as a chef in small restaurant in London.

Patrick (22, 26)

Born in Ireland and raised on a farm; came to London at age 16 where he worked in the building trade before beginning an apprenticeship in engineering. Diagnosed at university where he graduated with a 2.2. degree in Electronics and Marketing. Currently employed by a lift engineering company as a quality and safety advisor.

Veronica (15,19)

Emigrated to London from Angola at age 11; difficulties recognized by teachers in secondary school where she was both diagnosed and given specialist support. Has reading and writing difficulties in all four languages she speaks (Lingala, Portuguese, French and English). Completed Advanced GNVQ in Personal Care, with grade of Merit; currently works as a personal care assistant in home for the elderly.

In addition to the above individuals who were interviewed specifically for this book, Janet, Helen and Jean, whose stories contribute significantly, were all diagnosed in the 1980s, while in their 30s. They received specialist tuition and attended a group for dyslexic students over a period of several years. Their quotes were transcribed from a video made in 1992 in addition to other records. We are indebted to them for all they taught us. The quotes from Tony are taken from a transcript of a video made by The Manchester Adult Education Service.

We are especially grateful to Emma Elliott and Ross Cooper for contributing personal writing which has offered considerable insight into the dyslexic cognitive style and experience.

Finally, there are many other adults whose stories have enriched this book, but have been used primarily to exemplify particular points. In many cases, names have been changed, but the anecdotes recounted came either from direct teaching contact or from stories shared by colleagues in the field.

We extend our thanks to all those who contributed and hope their stories will serve as an inspiration to the many other dyslexic adults still trying to make sense of the non-dyslexic world.

PART I
Starting Points

Chapter 1
The dyslexic
cognitive style

Dyslexia is complex, subtle and eludes easy definition. It appears in varying degrees of severity and affects people in different ways. Critchley (1970) called it a 'veritable syndrome of language impairments.' Its most obvious feature is usually a profile of discrepancies yielding a distinct pattern of strengths and weaknesses. Dyslexic people can often perform a range of complex tasks, such as solving complicated problems in science or design, yet cannot do the seemingly simple: learn to read and spell, order and organise writing, copy from the board, remember instructions, tell the time or find their way around. One way to look at this pattern of strengths and weaknesses is as a 'cognitive style'. In adults, the cognitive style is especially apparent as the strategies they have developed for dealing with many aspect of their lives clearly reveal this pattern.

Almost all existing definitions of dyslexia are based on identifying one or more deficits in cognitive skills. On the other hand, many dyslexic people themselves experience their dyslexia as a *difference* – in how they think or learn.

Rieff et al. (1997) give a number of definitions offered by successful dyslexic adults which focus on processing difficulties, functional problems with reading and writing, discrepancies between their abilities and achievements; while others express a sense of difference rather than deficit. One of their subjects summed it up as 'Not a learning disability, but a teaching disability.' Another respondent stated, 'Mind operates differently than the normal. Does not mean that it doesn't work right, just different.'

Many of our own dyslexic students and colleagues have also emphasised this awareness of a difference in the way they think.

Many also feel that their dyslexia has endowed them with unusual gifts or talents along with the difficulties, and that it is a determining factor in defining who they are.

Recent definitions, particularly in the USA, are beginning to consider dyslexia from the perspective of difference. For instance, The International Dyslexia Association (2000) defines it the following way:

> The word dyslexia is derived from the Greek "dys" (meaning poor or inadequate) and "lexis" (words or language). Dyslexia is a learning disability characterized by problems in expressive or receptive, oral or written language. Problems may emerge in reading, spelling, writing, speaking, or listening. Dyslexia is not a disease; it has no cure. Dyslexia describes a different kind of mind, often gifted and productive, that learns differently. Dyslexia is not the result of low intelligence. Intelligence is not the problem. An unexpected gap exists between learning aptitude and achievement in school. The problem is not behavioral, psychological, motivational, or social. It is not a problem of vision; people with dyslexia do not "see backward." Dyslexia results from differences in the structure and function of the brain. People with dyslexia are unique; each having individual strengths and weaknesses. Many dyslexics are creative and have unusual talent in areas such as art, athletics, architecture, graphics, electronics, mechanics, drama, music, or engineering. Dyslexics often show special talent in areas that require visual, spatial, and motor integration. Their problems in language processing distinguish them as a group. This means that the dyslexic has problems translating language to thought (as in listening or reading) or thought to language (as in writing or speaking).

Deficit or difference?

The 'difference' model centres on the specialization in processing styles of the left and right hemispheres of the brain. Without over-simplifying the complexity of the functions of parts of the brain involved in various processes, it is generally agreed that the left hemisphere is specialized for processing language, handling sequential thought and functioning in an analytic, step-by-step manner; while the right hemisphere is specialized in processing visual-spatial information and utilises an holistic approach, responding to patterns and images and preferring synthesis to analysis. Current research (Galaburda, 1999, Frith, 1999) suggests that left hemispheric deficits or differences in processing language are prevalent among dyslexic people, while anecdotal reports and personal histories support the view that many dyslexic people tend to have a right hemispheric processing 'style'. They may be particularly gifted in areas that rely on - or are more suited to – right hemispheric functioning.

Is there any evidence for this view of difference rather than deficit? Do these 'gifts' just sometimes co-exist with the deficits or are they intrinsically linked?

There is certainly some indication that dyslexia has effects beyond 'low level' language or perceptual processing difficulties. Research into brain functioning is providing increasing evidence for the complex nature of dyslexia. Galaburda describes the 'multilevel' effects of the anatomical changes in dyslexia, based on human autopsies and animal research. These changes include areas of the brain involved in both perceptual processing and cognitive and metacognitive tasks.

> Moreover, there appears to be, at least in part, a causal relationship between the involvement at different levels and pathways, such that during development - a time of great plasticity - changes at one level or pathway propagate to affect other levels and pathways. It may be inferred from this research that dyslexia represents a complex interaction of both low-level and high-level processing deficits affecting language and perhaps visual performance.
>
> (Galaburda 1999)

If dyslexia involves a difference in high as well as low level processing, then the thinking of dyslexic people may indeed be different from that of non-dyslexic individuals. This suggests that differences in cognitive style are intrinsically bound up with deficits in processing language.

But is it merely a question of more complex deficits? Galaburda's findings show two distinct features of brains of dyslexic people; they contain malformations in the cortex and they show less cerebral asymmetry than 'normal' brains. He also (1990) suggests that there is a difference in the connections between hemispheres and that *therefore the pattern of communication between hemispheres is also different*. This may support the notion that dyslexic people think differently - and it may also allow for claims that the difference is linked to a special ability.

There is some evidence to suggest that dyslexic brains may be more specialised - or at least more able - in some right hemispheric processing tasks. Springer & Deutsch (1998) point out that Galaburda's research showed that asymmetrical (i.e. non-dyslexic) brains tended to have a larger temporal plane in the left hemisphere than in the right hemisphere, whereas symmetrical brains, a common feature of dyslexic people, tended to have a large right as well as a large left temporal plane. This difference in brain structure might result in increased development of right-hemispheric skills, such as visual-spatial skills.

The notion of a gifted side to dyslexia is still contentious; however, some experts in the field do acknowledge a positive side to dyslexia. For example, Shaywitz noted the ability to 'conceptualise on a broader scale' and often to 'see the whole before others do' (Coyle 1996). However, as Miles (1993) noted, there is a great deal of research into dyslexic weaknesses, but 'virtually none into the question of whether they have distinctive strengths'. It is certainly difficult to listen to dyslexic people in a number of fields and from a range of backgrounds – and not only those who are highly successful – without wondering if there is indeed an 'ability side' to the disability.

Tony, a self-employed joiner in his mid-30s describes his difficulties:

> My spelling's a problem, particularly with words where I have no vision of them. Like if someone says the word 'other' to me, it has no visual side at all. . . . I would have no concept about what it actually began with. . . . I've actually learned the word and I do know how to spell 'other' now, but I have lots of other things to remind me how to spell 'other', rather than knowing how to put 'other' together. It has no – it has no picture to it.

He then goes on to describe what he's good at:

> I'm good at hands-on things – mechanical and things that you can see things moving in and out, changing direction, internal things like combustion engines or gadgets, how they work. . . . I can see principles of engineering quite easy and understand stresses and strains in an object – And design – I can appreciate and see quality of design, things like plans. I can work from plans because I have a kind of like 3 D mind - I can actually get inside something just from looking at something in 2 D.

How do we explain the seeming contradiction between a poor visual memory for words – or sequences of letters – and 'a kind of 3D mind', without reference to the difference between right and left hemispheric processing? The link between language and sequence and the lack of meaning, or arbitrariness, of letters constituting words is difficult for the dyslexic person. However, a complex visual system where every part is meaningful in relation to its function and to every other part is processed differently and is often easy for the dyslexic person to grasp.

Many dyslexic people have described their ability to 'see the whole'. Baruj Benacerraf, an immunologist and Nobel laureate observes that:

> compared to others he has 'a much greater perception of space and time' and that he can readily 'visualise in three dimensions', special abilities he has found of particular advantage in his scientific research (West, 1991).

Jenny, formerly a head of department in a large further education college, described why she was successful as one of the first to set up a college wide learning support system:

> I don't know how to explain it but I see the whole thing. I see what will be the finished product of whatever I'm working on. I can see the final product and I have lots of ideas. . . It's like a picture that I have that I think everybody else should be seeing. I don't even know how the picture gets there, I don't even know how the bits and pieces get there. So I use other people to actually put the bits and pieces in, but I know the end result.

She now works as a successful educational consultant and says:

> I'm the one who has the ideas. I see that something will work immediately, but I don't always see how to get there - I need my partner to fill in the 'how'.

Ross Cooper, head of inclusive learning at another further education college, and himself dyslexic, has described his thinking process:

> Thinking, for me, is primarily a creative experience involving visual patterns, colour, shape and the movement of shapes (or objects) within and through space.
> I remember first coming across the strange idea that we could only think of things for which we have words, and realising, with something of a shock, that this did not describe me at all.
> From a very early age, I developed a colour coding system for sounds, feelings and ideas. When trying to make sense of the knowledge that other people claimed to hear beginning, middle and ends to even one-syllable words, I used my perception of the shape of sounds and the colour of sounds (and meanings) to 'see' what they were talking about. This experience had an impact on the development of my encoding system for symbolising visual meaning. Now sounds, words and letters resonate with colours. These can be overlaid without diluting the colours. Several distinct colours can emanate from the same source without needing to interfere with each other.

He goes on to explain visual thinking:

> . . . the ease with which one can ignore sequence (or logic) . . . allows me to focus on meaning without the encumbrance of sequence, detail or logic. . . . [I can]

for example, consider the experience of being inside two neighbouring semi-detached houses simultaneously, without the need to think about them one at a time as different objects, . . . to play, almost physically, with the nature of the space. This ability of visual images to play with meaning is very powerful. When I am thinking about how things can be understood, and represented, I can take a number of concrete and abstract images that represent the elements and the relationship between the elements and make them more meaningful by ignoring the confines of sequence, direction and 3D space. For example, I can do this visually by deciding that meaningful connections between elements in the 3D model will now be in the same place in space (even though this would be physically impossible). Just like, when I was younger, I allowed myself to 'see' words that I couldn't spell, or to 'see' colours which take up the same space; I allow myself to 'see' impossible shapes.

This is difficult to describe in words, or pictures. I only became aware of what I do when I tried to sketch out a drawing of a thought image that represented how a course for students with learning difficulties worked, and I realised that it could not be accurately modelled in two or three dimensions. However, this way of visualising connections between ideas and actions is a powerful way to conceptualise how things work, and how they can become a reality.

When I am problem-solving, the experience usually begins with a visualisation of the whole problem. At a certain point, I 'know' that I will find a solution. This is a distinct feeling. At this point . . . it's more like staring into the space between images. I am aware of the imagery, but I'm not looking at it. I concentrate on the feeling that I have a solution (which I can't yet see). Usually, quite rapidly, the solution appears with a resolving of the images into the pattern that represents the solution (along with intense pleasure). Once this has occurred, I can begin to examine the elements, details and logic implied by the solution, and begin to think of ways of communicating it to others.

He sums up:

I find words themselves lock thinking into pre-described patterns. . . The way I think is the defining characteristic of who I am, and in this respect, I would not choose to be any different.

(personal communication, 2000).

Is there a 'gift' of dyslexia?

Though many dyslexic writers, most notably Tom West (1991, 1992) and Ronald Davis (1994) claim there is a 'gift' of dyslexia, research into dyslexic strengths has been minimal, and largely disappointing. However, there are a few recent studies that encourage undertaking further research.

John Everatt et al. (1999) investigated the relationship between dyslexia and creativity using a range of tasks. They found that in comparison with non-dyslexic adults, dyslexic adults consistently demonstrated greater creativity when performing tasks which required insight or innovative approaches. The findings were unable to confirm that this creativity is related to enhanced right hemispheric functioning, although creativity is generally associated with the right hemisphere, which responds to pattern and is 'intuitive' in its style. As Everatt notes, the question also remains as to whether this heightened creativity is constitutional in origin or results from the need for the dyslexic person to develop compensatory strategies to deal with the deficits, thus leading to increased practice in creative thinking. However, Everatt did not find evidence to support anecdotal reports and claims of superior performance among dyslexic adults in visual-spatial tasks.

Bozena Wszeborowska-Lipinska (1998) used the Tower of Hanoi task, a non-verbal problem-solving task involving means-end analysis, with dyslexic and non-dyslexic children and adults. She found that the dyslexic subjects solved more difficult tasks than the controls and "took less time to find the algorithm which constitutes a solution to that problem." Dyslexic subjects also tended to study the task and arrive at the correct solution, whereas non-dyslexic subjects tended to take a more trial and error approach. Though dyslexic learners struggle with sequences, this study illustrates that they are often quick to pick out patterns.

Tony described how he would use a pattern to remember a telephone number if he had to use a dial phone.

> I would get a piece of paper, draw on it the digital numbers in the order they would be on a digital phone and punch them out as I would say the numbers.

Ross Cooper has been researching visual and verbal thinking with students at a further education college using interactive tasks. He found that dyslexic students showed a significantly greater preference for visual thinking. From a sample of 64 previously diagnosed dyslexic students, 87 per cent had a preference for visual thinking as compared with 65 per cent of the general sample of 468 students (personal communication, 2000). As most were on vocational courses, the general preference for visual thinking is in itself interesting, raising a wider question of the mismatch between much of the current curriculum with the learning styles of not only dyslexic students, but many others.

There are also many anecdotal reports suggesting a high incidence of dyslexia among artists, architects, engineers and others in fields requiring visual thinking. When one of the authors ran her specialist dyslexia training course for tutors at several art colleges in London, one tutor spoke for the rest when she declared that there were so many dyslexic students at her college that it would be better - and cheaper - to aim all teaching methods at dyslexic learners and have special support classes for non-dyslexic students!

Jane Graves, a former dyslexia support tutor and lecturer at an art college, asked all the students she assessed as dyslexic if they see in three dimensions. She says:

> of the 72 students I assessed [as dyslexic] last year, only three didn't understand what I meant. For those that did, it triggered off a flood of descriptions, such as: 'From the first moment, I see every detail of the final product'; 'I don't see words as "words" but as symbols of what they mean. It conjures up an image immediately, and that is very distracting when you're writing."
>
> (Appleyard, 1997)

Peter Fowler, head of a university multimedia unit, noted that most of the successful students in his unit come from art and design backgrounds with poor academic skills, and "a staggeringly high percentage are dyslexic", some severely so. He comments that many of them are dedicated, work well in a team and are able to think visually, laterally and creatively. One of them was told by an educational psychologist at 16 that he should consider applying to the local supermarket for a job. Another, now 27, had a report from an educational psychologist while studying for his A levels which said he had 'not yet developed a realistic attitude to his disability' (Fowler, 2000).

Dyslexic adults themselves can be very illuminating about the notion of giftedness, if asked the right questions. They are often aware of an 'excelling aspect' and when they are not, it is frequently because their abilities are neither valued nor nurtured. Richard, a plumber and builder, describes how in school, he was very quick at carpentry and good at making things.

> While the others were still working on joints, I was building a writing table. But no one ever encouraged me. They just said I was slow.

He still sees himself as 'a bit thick' despite his ability to renovate an entire house to extremely high standards as well as to devise creative solutions to plumbing problems.

Jenny, when asked what she was good at in school, said:

> I don't think I was particularly good at anything – oh I was good at mending things. I used to take – if the Hoover broke, I'd take it to bits. I'd have it all over the kitchen floor and then I'd put it all back together again – and the tumble dryer to bits – this is when I was at school - and it worked afterwards.
>
> I don't know why, but I remembered where all the bits went back to. And I used to like taking watches to pieces and putting them back together as well.

Many dyslexic people are surprised to find that not everyone shares their visualising abilities. One dyslexic artist said 'I see images for everything, for every word - doesn't everyone?'. A dyslexic musician explains how he gets along without being able to read music: 'I see music in patterns – every note has a different shape, like triangles and rectangles.'

Lack of success in efforts to identify this 'special gift' may be partly because of problems in devising appropriate research tools. One dyslexic artist said of a spatial rotation test, 'But that isn't how I see it - they give you a sequence of possible choices but I see all the possibilities at once'. There are questions to be asked about the sophistication and appropriateness of design of tests for visual-spatial thinking. Dyslexic people tend to function at a much higher level when they are doing something meaningful. It may be that they would perform better on three dimensional rotations related to visualising buildings or complex systems. It may also be that researchers who have themselves succeeded in primarily language-based areas may not be the best people to design tests for visual-spatial processing. Perhaps when dyslexic people devise such tests, we shall get closer to the truth.

Rieff et al. (1997) ask the pertinent question: 'to what extent are learning disabilities just a difference in style that becomes a disability because of our lack of understanding about individual learning differences?' If teachers were able to respond better to different learning styles we might erase the notion of 'disability.'

Emma, who is now a writer and has a BSc Honours in computer technology, has illuminated this perspective:

> I'm severely dyslexic and have struggled with literacy all my life. I was taught in a traditional way using phonics. I've completed five separate courses with five different tutors.

I'm a dynamic person, who thinks in pictures and uses three dimensional images in my head to understand concepts, yet I was being taught using a method that was rigid, structured, and two dimensional. I'm an experiential learner and learn best when the information presented is as real as possible. Unfortunately, many of the subjects I was taught at school were not taught using this approach. When words are used in isolation to impart knowledge, I find it difficult to grasp even simple concepts. I learn simple concepts within the context of more complex ones. However, the education system expected me to learn the simple concepts before moving on to the more complex ones.

. . . Learning was hard work for me because I was fighting my natural processing, which was very different from the one I was being encouraged to use. . . . Not only was this method inappropriate, it was also damaging. I was born with talents that my dyslexia had given me, these talents disappeared slowly, because I was being trained to think in a way that was alien to my very being.

My learning style could have been an advantage at school, if it had been identified, respected and developed. I retain far more information in pictures than I ever can with words. Receiving information in this form provides an understanding that has not been narrowed down by words. Seeing a problem within a picture in space gives me the advantage of approaching a problem from many different angles.

It is worth reminding ourselves that the non-dyslexic world has determined the place of written language and the value of academic success in our society. In fact, many of those who have contributed greatly to both our culture and economic life have not been academically successful. We may thus be advised to adopt a bit of humility in commenting on other people's deficits and being dismissive of their abilities. Perhaps some of the skills we most value are not as important as those we accord lower status. The following tale puts it even more starkly:

Nasruddin was ferrying a scholar across some rough water. When the scholar asked him a question, Nasruddin said something ungrammatical to him.
'Have you never learned grammar?' asked the scholar.
'No', replied Nasruddin.
'Then', said the scholar, 'half your life has been wasted.'
Nasruddin said nothing and they went on in silence. A few minutes later, Nasruddin said to his passenger, 'Have you ever learned to swim?'
'No,' said the scholar. 'Why?'
'Then all your life is wasted – we are sinking!'

(adapted from Shah, 1964)

The dyslexic cognitive profile

In the diagnostic process, the individual's learning style is an important indicator of dyslexia. Turner (1997) notes that 'there is no single experience better agreed than that non-dyslexic retarded readers are easy to teach! Response to intervention remains an important criterion. . . for a diagnosis of dyslexia'. The failure of the dyslexic learner to respond to 'traditional' teaching methods may be explained on the basis of a difference in learning style.

Most professionals working with dyslexic adults will agree with Rieff and his colleagues that 'learning disabilities in adulthood affect each individual uniquely' (1993 quoted in 1997). However, there are certain features that seem to be common to most dyslexic adults. These have been variously described as the 'pattern of difficulties' (Miles, 1993) and also as the 'clinical feel' of dyslexia. (Beaton et al., 1997).

Whether or not dyslexic individuals have a special 'ability' as the other side of the 'disability', these 'typical' features of the dyslexic cognitive style are likely to be intimately linked with their language processing and other characteristic difficulties.

It is commonly agreed that dyslexia is at least in part a weakness in language processing, with most dyslexic individuals experiencing difficulties in phonological coding, and some in visual and/or motor processing or a combination of the three. These weaknesses result in a range of problems with reading and writing, including an inability to recognise familiar words or to recall their spellings, difficulty discriminating or segmenting sounds or working out unfamiliar words in print, and forming letters or writing automatically.

These difficulties in storing and retrieving auditory or visual symbolic representations of language mean that dyslexic people often rely heavily on semantic coding; that is they rely on *meaning* to learn and remember. This has been confirmed, for example, by Brooks and Weeks (1998) in their research into spelling strategies, where they found that dyslexic 11 year olds responded better to visual/semantic strategies, such as words within words. We have also found this to be true of many of our students. Jean, for instance, when trying to learn "father" said in exasperation, "I just can't get this 't-h' sound - why can't I just learn it as 'fat' 'her'?"

One of the common indicators of dyslexia is a weakness in short-term or working memory, particularly with storing and retrieving verbal information. According to commonly used models (e.g. Baddeley, 1986) short-term memory relies primarily on auditory rehearsal; there is also a 'visuo-spatial scratch pad'. Dyslexic people may have weaknesses in one or both of these aspects, most commonly in using an auditory rehearsal strategy. At least some dyslexic adults also demonstrate weaknesses in visual memory for words and letters, finding it difficult to recognise even familiar words. McLoughlin et al. (1994) place great emphasis on the inefficiency of short-term memory as being a defining characteristic of dyslexia.

Mark proposes a useful analogy in describing his memory problems:

> My memory is like a bridge going across a deep ravine and if I load too much on it, the bridge will break. That's what it feels like.

Dyslexic learners may be described as 'quick forgetters' as they often seem quick to grasp something but fail to retain it, as opposed to slow learners who may only learn in small painstaking steps. Because of their short-term memory problems, they rely heavily on their long-term memory, which is commonly agreed to be based on association and understanding. Typically, dyslexic people perform poorly in recalling names, facts, dates or other relatively non-meaningful information. Dyslexic adults will often state that they couldn't learn something by rote, such as their multiplication tables, because they 'didn't understand it.'

Many dyslexic adults agree with Janet when she says:

> My long-term memory is fantastic - I think that's the only compensation I've got from being dyslexic, my long-term memory. It's much better than other people's. It's the short-term memory that lets you down, and other people can't understand it, they really can't.

Dyslexic people are able to remember information more successfully if they form a personal relationship with that information, both because they are motivated and because the information is then meaningful. This can sometimes have unforeseen consequences. Jenny describes her last session on a ten week counselling course when slips of paper with everyone's name were passed around, and each person was expected to write a positive comment about the others. Jenny wrote nothing. When later asked why by the tutor, Jenny explained that she didn't know anyone's name. The tutor expressed amazement that she hadn't learned anyone's name in ten weeks, to which Jenny replied, 'They weren't important to me, they were just other students on the course that I'd probably never see again. But you are my teacher, you're important so I remember your name.'

Poor short-term memory and phonological processing also affects the ability of dyslexic individuals to use and manipulate language. This may show up in a variety of expressive or receptive language problems such as difficulties with word retrieval, awkwardness of expression or misuse of words and difficulties understanding figurative language, words with multiple meanings or grammatical tenses (see H Klein, 1985).

Janet describes her problems with word retrieval:

> What happens quite a bit is that you know something and you want to say it – it's in the head but you can't actually say the word. And you lose it completely and you're sort of stuck up in the air with this conversation and it's here, it's all in the head, but you can't get it out. . . . You know what you want to say but you can't get it out at all, you're just stuck.

Another difficulty for dyslexic learners is their ability to remember and apply rules with regard to spelling or grammar. They often ask for and seem reassured by rules, and teachers can be misled into thinking these are useful. They may be helpful, but only in that they give sense to something seemingly arbitrary; they do not help the person to *remember* whether to double the letter or where to put an apostrophe. A rule must be searched for, then 'held' in the memory, then compared with others (is this the 'right' rule?) and then applied to the individual circumstance, by which time this is likely to have been forgotten if the rules haven't already been confused. Tony describes it this way:

> One of the things is remembering what the rules are. . . . The rules don't seem to have any kind of logic, they don't fall into a kind of pattern that I can recognise and to learn them becomes a big problem because then whenever I do come across a word where there's something to be changed, I'm thinking, well, is it this word or not this word and why is it this word and not any other word? The rules confuse the issue rather than actually kind of like help it.

Many dyslexic people have directional problems, particularly in remembering left and right and following a sequence. Some find they get lost frequently, even going to places they have been many times before. As one young dyslexic woman put it, 'I can get lost in a square room.' However, some others have a superb memory for landmarks, a kind of visual-spatial map in their heads.

Many have visual-motor processing difficulties which may affect planning and organising as well as handwriting, proof-reading and presentation. For some, handwriting is a particular problem as it never becomes automatic, or there is a lack of motor integration which results in omitted or unintended letters or words. They may have to press hard to control the pen. Jenny describes her difficulties:

> My hand gets very tired—it's really heavy...it's as if my hands belong to someone else.

Not being able to express themselves because they have to concentrate on forming the letters creates enormous frustration, as they are unable to demonstrate their knowledge to others. Frequently when they are able to use a computer, the level and complexity of their written work bears little relation to their poor handwritten efforts. Those who have difficulties with physical co-ordination may also find it difficult to do more than one thing at once.

Other typical difficulties include problems with sequencing, direction and time (see Krupska and Klein 1995, McLoughlin 1994, Miles 1993). These, together with difficulties with written and sometimes spoken language, may be seen as constituting a pattern of left-hemispheric weaknesses or, at least in some cases, a bias for right-hemispheric processing. In our experience, dyslexic people find it difficult to acquire the conventions of written language; they have most difficulties with those aspects which are arbitrary and abstract, including knowing what to put in and what to leave out, using linking words and understanding the conventions of spelling, punctuation and paragraphing.

However, there is also the issue of how these are taught and how the dyslexic person learns. Emma was unable to understand the principles of punctuation when she was taught at school. She began to understand it only through gaining feedback on her own writing by using voice recognition and voice synthesis technology. She says:

> The computer will talk back to me, enabling me to hear my mistakes. If a sentence doesn't have the emphasis expected, I insert a comma and get this software to read the sentence back to me. This process is repeated until I'm happy with the way the sentence sounds. I never understood commas until I used this software. I now know they give a sentence dimension.

Though dyslexic people struggle with sequences, they are often quick to pick out patterns. Charlotte, a student on a science foundation course, explained that she could remember numbers only when she 'sees' a pattern. This presented problems for her in her earlier education since she never had sufficient time in exams to recall the patterns she had learned.

> I was always frustrated because I knew the maths, but there wasn't time to show them what I knew.

An art and design student evolved a system of two and three dimensional patterns for managing time by visualising the days of the week and months of the year in a ring and placing herself at any point in order to calculate her position in time.

Meaning has a key role in the cognitive style of the dyslexic person. Richard Branson, the successful entrepreneur and businessman, noted that maths only made sense to him when he went into business and was 'using real numbers to solve real problems.' He recalls

> sitting in front of an IQ test and just looking at these questions and my mind going completely blank. I handed the paper in without a mark on it.

He goes on to say,

> I found that if I used my brain in a different way I could excel in other areas. When I turned my attention to the wider world and things which I could see a reason for, then I suddenly found I was beginning to flourish. When I started exploring what interested me I had no problems at all (Warren, 1999).

It is therefore important to realise that the dyslexic learning style is such that students develop literacy and learning skills most effectively when these are context-bound, especially in a personally meaningful context. This affects ability as well as motivation. Jenny described her difficulties with reading:

> I could learn all the specialist words – I never had a problem with those. But I couldn't make sense of the words around the specialist words.

Research with highly successful dyslexic adults in a range of fields has shown that they are able to read at a much higher level in their own subject than when reading texts of a general nature such as a newspaper. Fink (1995) found that nearly all her sample of successful dyslexic adults had learned to read through a passionate interest in their subject.

Fink (1998) also noted that although participants with dyslexia used decoding strategies along with context clues, they were not necessarily effective in using these strategies, no matter at how high a level they were reading. Many felt that in spite of explicit phonics instruction, their ability to decode through the use of phonological strategies remained poor. On the basis of her research, Fink recommends interest-driven instruction to develop fluency and automaticity for dyslexic learners. This was confirmed by a dyslexic student who, when asked what advice he would give to a dyslexic young person to improve his reading and writing responded, 'Find something you're interested in and the reading and writing will come from there.'

Implications of the Dyslexic Cognitive Style

An understanding of the dyslexic cognitive style may overcome the mismatch between how dyslexic people learn, remember and process information and the ideas, expectations and assumptions of their non-dyslexic teachers, colleagues, employers, friends or spouses.

For example, with sequences, there is an issue of how the dyslexic person is taught and how the non-dyslexic teacher assumes they learn. Dyslexic people typically have a right-hemispheric or global learning style; they need an overview and a context to learn. Cooper (1997) tells of one of his dyslexic students who was unable to learn a sequence on her computing course. Her IT teacher felt that she would not be able to do computing if she couldn't learn sequences. Cooper suggested that her learning style was such that she needed an overview and context and that if she had this, she would be able to learn the sequence. When the IT teacher then introduced the overall context into which the sequence fitted in such a way that the student was able to grasp it visually, the student was not only able to learn – and remember – the required sequence, but to teach it to fellow students who were finding it difficult.

Dyslexic people do not generalize and apply generalizations, but rather learn from experience and make connections through meaning; this has significant implications for how they learn, as Emma showed in the way she learned punctuation.

An understanding of the conventions of language must not be assumed; rather these must be made explicit. Martin, at 47, had never observed how to address an envelope properly; he placed the address in the top left-hand corner. Once his support tutor showed him the appropriate convention, he finally changed the habit of a lifetime.

As dyslexic individuals tend to take language literally and have difficulties with understanding multiple meanings, they are likely to have a continuous struggle to make sense of what is expected of them. One student proudly turned in her first essay at university and was devastated when she failed it; when asked to 'illustrate her argument', she had taken the instructions literally and drawn a picture. The inability to appreciate nuances in language can also impact socially when dyslexic people misconstrue irony and humour.

Problems processing oral language may also take their toll. Jenny describes her difficulties on a recent course:

> There were times I couldn't hear the teacher and it was because I could hear the people moving things next door. I could hear all these noises going on around me – like I can hear this actual tape going round and I can hear the noise over there from the computer – and eventually all these noises take me over and I don't hear the teacher. They dominate even if it is a really interesting session. And I find that really, really tiring – so tiring, in fact, that I could even fall asleep sometimes.

This example of problems in filtering noise is also mirrored in difficulties filtering excess visual stimuli. Some people indicate the need to sit at the front of lecture halls to avoid the visual distraction of others.

Dyslexic people are also likely to suffer from expectations to learn or perform skills according to conventional procedures. A student on an electronics course who was unable even to begin the required written description of a procedure was able to 'put the writing in' when given the opportunity to draw the procedure first. Emma describes how she learned to read from using voice recognition technology in conjunction with speech synthesis:

> When I read using this system, I'm reading from my context, words that are spelled and read back to me correctly. Words read in this environment provide a very clear shape, enabling me to recognise and read them. Initially it appeared strange to me that I was attempting to write a book before I was able to read one. Now this approach to reading does not seem so strange, for I need to understand my own thoughts on paper before I can understand the thoughts behind someone else's writing.

The cognitive style of dyslexic people may have both positive and negative effects on them and the non-dyslexic people in their lives. The potential positive contribution of dyslexic people is often not realised because of lack of understanding. On the other hand, the dyslexic person may feel frustrated because he does not fit the expectations of the non-dyslexic world.

For the dyslexic person there is also the shock, as Cooper describes, of finding out that he does not do things the way everyone is 'supposed to'. This not only isolates him, but he is likely to be given no recognition of his own cognitive style or helped to learn and achieve through using his own strengths. This is then followed by the stress of having to try to change himself or his way of approaching the task at hand if he wants to succeed in the non-dyslexic world. The alternative is to encourage broader understanding among non-dyslexic people to ensure that the talents and strengths of dyslexic adults are recognised and valued.

It is worth noting, however, there are occasionally advantages even to the problems associated with being dyslexic. Helen tells the following story of a dyslexic soldier:

> He went on an interrogation, information and escape course. And they had to give him the information – the message. Then they got him out and he escaped. And then he had to be interrogated. And he never broke under interrogation because he forgot what the message was!

Chapter 2
Diagnosis, definitions and being 'dyslexic'

For the dyslexic adult, being diagnosed is at the heart of coming to terms with being dyslexic and can have a profound effect, making sense of years of confusion, frustration and failure. The fairly recent acknowledgement and willingness to address dyslexia in adults has largely been in response to an expressed need of large numbers of adults for diagnosis and help. Dyslexic adults who were not diagnosed at school are more and more frequently seeking an assessment in later life. The impetus may be a return to education, changes in employment, the diagnosis of their children or an awareness and curiosity stimulated by watching a TV programme about dyslexia.

Whereas the main function of diagnosis in childhood is for others to identify reasons why the child is not learning, the purposes in adulthood are very different. Adults may want to establish the condition for educational, employment or other reasons such as legal rights or eligibility for grants. However, they will also have significant personal reasons. The desire for a diagnosis may come from a deep inner need to know 'what is wrong with me' or 'why can't I do the simple things that others can do'; it is usually prompted by a search for an explanation that will replace painful labels acquired in childhood such as 'thick', 'lazy' and 'careless'. It is thus often the starting point of huge changes in self-perception, learning experiences, ambitions, motivation and even personal relations.

Diagnosis can mark the beginning of a process of 'reframing' early experiences, both in the family and at school. Gerber et al. (1992) stress the importance of 'reframing' the experience of having the learning disability in a more positive and constructive way as an internal process for gaining control. In their study of successful dyslexic adults, they identified gaining control as the 'key to success for adults with learning disabilities'. They found, in contrast, that many less or moderately successful adults with learning disabilities 'sought control mainly to cover up their weaknesses, rather than focusing on moving ahead'.

Gerber et al. identified four stages of the reframing process. The more successful adults progressed through all these stages to a greater extent than the less successful ones, who had problems accepting their difficulties and whose understanding was less complete. The four stages of 'reframing' are:

1. recognition of their difficulties and their difference from others;
2. acceptance that the differences are real, and include both positive and negative aspects;
3. understanding their strengths as well as their weaknesses, enabling them to build on their strengths;
4. the willingness to take conscious action towards their goals in spite of their difficulties.

Helen found that being diagnosed and arriving at the stage of understanding her strengths and weaknesses enabled her to take charge of her life. Through the teaching interaction with a specialist tutor, she was able to 'unpack' her dyslexia. She describes how things would 'go wrong' and her tutor would explain why:

> She'd say 'I think that's a motor problem – it's your hand not following through', or she'd say, 'That's a sound problem and that comes with not being able to put the symbol to the sound.' And I learned what happened and how the disability worked – and how being dyslexic affected me. Then I understood why I couldn't tell the time . . . and why I get lost and things. And I started to see how it worked independently of me and that was really something that gave me a lot of confidence. It was like taking apart something that had built up for years. Taking out all the emotions and getting right down to seeing what goes wrong.

Jean provides a good example of gaining courage to take action in spite of her difficulties and the embarrassment she might suffer:

> I suppose I put myself on the line when I go for an audition . . . Last Friday I went to a workshop – there were four or five words, three of which I didn't know and two I couldn't pronounce. And I thought, why do you do this? You're going to stand up here and people are going to say, 'She's stupid and she's

illiterate'... I just did it and of course I got it wrong... but I thought, well I did it – you've got to do it.

Issues in diagnosing adults

The significant impact that diagnosis can have on an adult's life raises important considerations with regard to access to diagnosis and diagnostic approaches used with adults.

A diagnosis of dyslexia opens doors to opportunities, grants, equipment, support and special examination provision. By shedding light on the reasons for past failure, it can also be personally enabling and affect self-esteem. However, financial constraints may deny access to a diagnosis, which is usually expensive and may be difficult to obtain. The fact that decisions are made about who is given the label and resultant entitlements raises serious equal opportunities issues. Even when a diagnosis is available, restriction by narrow definitions of dyslexia, or requirements for specific tests may result in exclusion from the 'label' for some dyslexic adults who may not fit a classic pattern or who have developed compensating strategies which confuse test results. The methodology used may empower the dyslexic adult or may undermine his confidence. It may illuminate or leave the dyslexic person no wiser.

Approaches to diagnosing adults are not commonly agreed. Beliefs about reliability and appropriateness of both standardized and informal tests vary among professionals. Moreover, many adults have learned to read and some to spell passably. They have often developed a variety of strategies to compensate for their difficulties, which may mask the obvious characteristics evident in children; consequently, the identifying features in adults may be difficult to tease out. As Beaton et al. (1997) point out, 'Definitions which had previously seemed to provide fairly clear guidelines for the identification of dyslexia in childhood soon become muddled when the researcher or clinician is confronted with a variety of adult cases exhibiting highly heterogeneous profiles.' They go on to note that many dyslexic adults 'show high degrees of compensation for their difficulties' which in turn may 'confound the assessment process'.

Others in the field (Rack, 1997; McLoughlin et al., 1994; Turner, 1997) have also commented on the difficulties in assessing adults; indeed, many have noted the problematic nature of diagnosing children. Pumfrey, in his review of the Dyslexia Screening Instrument (in Beech and Singleton, 1997) draws attention to this:

> Dyslexia is a complex and variable syndrome, rather than a discrete condition. In my view, there is neither an unequivocal conceptual consensus concerning its nature nor empirical consensus as to its identification. The diagnosis of children as having dyslexia is notoriously problematic . . . The discriminant analyses build on already identified groups. How confident are we that this initial classification has been done, even though guidelines exist? False positives and false negatives remain ever present threats to the validity of *any* assessment procedure [our italics].

These difficulties in diagnosing dyslexia are even more pertinent in assessing adults as very little research has been done on dyslexic adults, a fact noted by many writers in the field (Beaton et al., 1997; Reiff et al., 1997; Snowling et al.,1997). Moreover, most existing research has been based on populations of university students or successful dyslexic adults, leaving a large population untapped. People from working-class or ethnic minority backgrounds, those who speak English as an additional language, and adults involved in manual occupations, have traditionally been excluded.

When considering the diagnosis of adults, several factors need to be considered. We need to think about who 'owns' the diagnosis and to take into account the different reasons the dyslexic adult may have for wanting the diagnosis. The purpose of the diagnosis may influence aspects of the procedure (e.g. local authorities often insist upon specific tests before they will consider eligibility for grants) and/or the way in which the report is written.

The issue of methodology is particularly important in assessing adults, in terms of appropriateness, accuracy and fairness – and as importantly, how the diagnosis affects their lives. The desirable intention of diagnosis is to promote more effective learning and achievement. As many dyslexic adults were not diagnosed at school, reconsidering definitions and the consequent methodology of assessment is extremely important. Lack of consensus renders access to fair and accurate diagnosis and resulting benefits in regard to support and technology inconsistent, at best. As test scores and spelling and reading ages can have devastating effects on self-esteem, it is worth considering whether these give useful information, whether they are always necessary and whether there are other ways of establishing evidence of dyslexia.

When considering adults, we need to rethink the implications of some of the commonly accepted ways of determining dyslexia; for example, a discrepancy between reading age and chronological age and/or general cognitive ability. Do reading 'ages' for adults actually have any meaning? At university or college, what reading age is acceptable? However high the reading 'age', the student who is prone to misread or who reads very slowly will be disadvantaged in an examination and in keeping up with course work.

There are considerable problems with existing tests for adults. Beaton et al. (1997) point out that 'few reading and spelling tests are standardized for people beyond the ages of 16 or 17 years'. They argue that it is 'more important to be able to say that the reading of dyslexics is abnormal when compared to their peers. Unfortunately, given the paucity of data regarding 'normal' reading in the adult population, this . . . presents difficulties.'

There are other concerns about using standardized tests as a basis for diagnosing dyslexia. There is usually little information as to the population sample for research with reference to cultural or linguistic background (Cline and Reason, 1993). Geva, from the Ontario Institute for Studies in Education at the University of Toronto, has done extensive research on dyslexia and bilingualism in adults and children for many years. She observed that she had never yet seen a culture-free test (1999).

Those who speak English as an additional language and those from different cultural backgrounds may perform poorly on tests, many of which are culturally biased and are unlikely to have been normed for a multilingual or multicultural population. Cline and Reason (1993) studied all the research reports on specific learning difficulties (dyslexia) in the *British Journal of Educational Psychology* over a 15-year period from 1976 to 1991 to examine the social characteristics of the populations used. In the 27 reports studied, only nine gave the socio-economic status of the sample, only five noted bilingualism and only three specified ethnicity. They cite a similar study in North America by Sleeter and suggest that 'it is likely that many of the samples were in fact white, monolingual in English and fairly homogeneous in socioeconomic status'. They conclude that 'definitions which exclude environmental, cultural or economic factors provide no basis for formulating unbiased criteria' and emphasize the importance of minimizing cultural bias in assessment materials.

Other issues such as gender may affect the accuracy of procedures for researching and identifying dyslexia. Though traditionally
research has identified more boys than girls as dyslexic, there is a
suggestion from some studies that schools are over-identifying boys.
Shaywitz et al. (1990; cited by Cline and Reason, 1993) found in
their Connecticut longitudinal study that when schools themselves
were not directly involved identifying students with dyslexia, 'the
preponderance of boys was reduced'. Fink (1998) notes that recent
studies by Shaywitz and others suggest that dyslexia may in fact
affect both sexes equally. Zabell and Everatt (2000) further point to
'referral bias' and argue that 'the male/female ratio may be intimately linked to the method of diagnosis and our definition of
dyslexia'. They suggest that testing may reflect a male bias and that
'current diagnostic procedures will require modification . . . to
increase their sensitivity to the female dyslexic'.

Other established ways of diagnosing dyslexia are based on
discrepancies in performance on IQ subtests. The use of IQ tests is
particularly contentious as there are concerns about the value of
identifying discrepancies and also of using an average or above average IQ as one of the discriminants of dyslexia. The latter view has
been challenged by a number of researchers, most notably Stanovich
(1991, 1996) on the basis that if dyslexia is defined as a difficulty in
processing language, then there can be no correlation between such
a difficulty and IQ. In addition, although some psychologists accept
that a low IQ can yield a positive diagnosis of dyslexia as long as
there is a discrepancy between specific weaknesses and general
levels, this assumes that IQ tests give an accurate reflection of
general intelligence and that subtest results are valid.

Additionally, recent research by Siegel and Himel (1998) suggests
that definitions based on IQ discrepancies may discriminate against
both older children and those from a low socioeconomic status. Individuals from both these categories are more likely to be classified as
poor readers than as dyslexic when IQ scores are used. This is likely
to be even more true with adults.

In a study of reading and spelling impairment in dyslexic undergraduates, Hanley (1997) found that the majority of students in the
study had not been identified as dyslexic at school, and suggested
that this 'raises some fundamental and potentially controversial
issues regarding diagnosis'. Commenting particularly on the use of

intelligence tests, he points out that 'when one is assessing university students . . . it seems unreasonable to suggest that an individual's poor reading and spelling is a result of a general intellectual handicap'.

The same questions may apply to non-academic adults, many of whom have been falsely labelled 'slow learners' but who are able to master skills in work, business or running a family, thus clearly demonstrating that they are not lacking in general cognitive ability. Miles (1993) used the holding down of a skilled job along with a history of late reading or other literacy difficulties as criteria for inclusion in a study of dyslexic adults in the absence of figures for intelligence, reading or spelling.

Feuerstein challenged the value of IQ tests as a reflection of an individual's potential. His work is of particular value when considering those whose cultural background is not taken into account in existing tests. One of his basic tenets is that intelligence is an elastic, modifiable state. In his view, an IQ test only presents a snapshot of a moment in time. He argues that changes occur through the learning process and therefore learning is the major route to assess the individual:

> The assumption that intelligence is not a static product but a dynamic process, the very essence of which is change and not stability, requires that we take a fresh look at our current assessment practices.
>
> (Feuerstein et al., 1981)

Feuerstein points to the limitations of IQ tests and encourages a new approach to assessment, in which an assessor conducts a test of cognitive functioning, teaches the individual the weak skills and then retests to determine how well learning has taken place. This work presents a fundamental challenge to our current methods of assessment.

What sort of tests might be useful and reliable for adults? Snowling et al. (1997) note the lack of studies on dyslexia beyond the school years, but conclude from their own and other studies that 'from a practical perspective, the best tests for identifying dyslexic students [in higher education] are likely to be non-word reading and a test, like Spoonerisms, which taps phoneme [sound] awareness'.

However, as Beaton et al. among others (e.g. Reiff et al., 1997) point out, dyslexic adults are often highly compensated, so problems that might show up on tests with children are not necessarily manifested in adults, and test results may be misleading. We have seen many dyslexic adults who do not fit current criteria because they have learned to use alternative strategies to deal with certain tasks, so that their weaknesses are masked in testing. These individuals have consequently been excluded from the support they need. Frith (1999) quotes an example of a 17-year-old who scored well on a test of phonological skills by using his excellent visual memory to create a good visual image of the words, enabling him to 'bypass' his phonological difficulty.

There has also been a serious underestimation of the value and validity of what adults can tell us about their learning experiences, their difficulties and the strategies they may use to compensate for these; all of which can inform research as well as diagnosis. Fink (1998), however, reports that 'recent literature indicates that self-report of childhood reading difficulties by learning disabled adults is valid and reliable'. Beaton et al. (1997) also note that 'some people are impressed by the "clinical feel" of individual cases of dyslexia in adulthood'.

Our own experience has confirmed the view of one specialist dyslexia tutor that 'the longer I work with dyslexic adults, the more I value the diagnostic interview most for making an accurate diagnosis'. Among the several hundred adults with whom we have worked, nearly all say they knew there was 'something wrong' or 'something different' about them very early on at school. They all have a history of difficulties with reading and writing from an early age, though this was not always recognized by the school or even by the individual.

Sensitive, open-ended questioning from an experienced and trained assessor can also elicit detailed information that pinpoints the distinct nature of the individual's problems. Dyslexic adults often offer eloquent descriptions of their difficulties, ones which clearly suggest a diagnosis of dyslexia: 'I can't *hear* the sounds' (of course, it is important that any hearing loss is identified before making a diagnosis); 'when I try to write, my hand doesn't do what I want it to'; 'sometimes I spell a word right and a short while after I can't remember it'; 'when I see the word "the", for example, sometimes I don't know what it means – I know that I know the word, but I just don't know what that word is'.

The influence of definitions on diagnosis

Problems in diagnosing dyslexia are not limited to adults, since diagnosis is influenced by definitions. Methodology and criteria used in diagnosis are integrally linked to the way in which dyslexia is defined. Efforts to find agreement in defining dyslexia, or 'learning disabilities' (the more encompassing term used in the US) have been well documented (e.g. Hammill, 1990; Miles, 1993; Pumfrey and Reason, 1994). Many researchers and practitioners in the field have commented on the inherent problems in defining dyslexia, and it is as well to remember Humpty Dumpty's admonition in *Through the Looking Glass* – that definitions are a question of 'which is to be master'.

The question of definitions is not merely an academic issue, as definitions determine who receives the label that may act as a passport to accessing public money, appropriate support, and possibly a more sympathetic response from teachers, employers, supervisors and others. There is a tension between researchers' desires to classify difficulties clearly according to underlying causes and the political, social and economic implications of such categorizations.

Definitions are influenced by research and change in accordance with current agreed models of dyslexia. They may include or exclude individuals from the label. A language or perceptual processing deficit is usually cited as the determining feature of dyslexia, though other definitions have focused on discrepancies between reading performance and intelligence. 'Dyslexia' may be more simply understood as 'trouble with written language', though many have attempted to paint a broader picture to include memory, sequencing and organizational problems.

Currently, the most commonly accepted model of dyslexia among researchers is that of a basic phonological processing deficit, i.e. a problem processing the speech sounds that make up language, underlying other behavioural features (Frith, 1999; Snowling, 1987; Shaywitz, 1996). Indeed, Frith suggests that a phonological deficit is the defining characteristic of dyslexia. She also proposes, however, that it 'does not preclude the existence of non-dyslexic reading-disabled children who do not have phonological problems'. The question is, why should this population be labelled differently?

Should they not also be called dyslexic, i.e. a 'non-phonological' subgroup? They too have 'trouble with the lexicon'.

However, research into the brain and the 'hard wiring' of dyslexia is now proceeding at a rapid pace and is contributing to our knowledge; new technology allows direct study of both the microstructure of the brain and the areas involved in perceptual and motor processing. There is some evidence to suggest that the underlying perceptual system responsible for rapid processing of fast-changing visual or auditory stimuli may be sluggish in dyslexic individuals. Stein and Talcott (1999), for instance, conclude from their research: 'The visual magnocellular system together with its auditory and motor equivalents can all be abnormal in dyslexics . . . These impairments could cause dyslexics' visual instability, reduced phonological skills and their plethora of motor problems . . .' Research by Nicolson and Fawcett (1990) suggests that the cerebellum, the part of the brain that plays a significant role in motor functioning, may be involved in dyslexia. If this is so, it might help to explain the often ignored motor aspect in dyslexia, manifested in poor handwriting and organizational and planning difficulties common among many dyslexic adults and children.

There is also growing evidence from studies of adults that there are at least a small number of dyslexic adults who do not conform to the phonological impairment model. Hanley (1997), for instance, found examples of dyslexic students who showed no significant phonological difficulties and had problems that were more visual than phonological.

In a study of adolescents with reading disabilities, Boden and Brodener (1999) found that some of them had difficulties processing visual sequences, which compound their problems processing verbal information while reading. These deficits were 'not limited to the written word but were general to visual temporal processing.' Research in the US by Irlen (1991) and the UK by Wilkins (1995) supports the existence of visual stress as a contributing factor for some dyslexic people. Certainly, many of the 'classic' descriptions of reading difficulties offered by dyslexic adults in the literature (e.g. Susan Hampshire, 1981, Helen Arkell, 1977 and others), as well as among our students, include losing their place, having trouble moving from one line of print to another, experiencing print dancing, jumping or dropping off the page and many other descriptions of visual stress. One adult noted that her eyes simply 'did not want to move from left to right'.

Because of the historical emphasis on defining and identifying dyslexia in children, there has been little attempt to acknowledge real differences between children and adults. Reiff et al. (1997) comment that debate on definitions has largely disregarded adults. They attribute this in part to the lack of research and the relatively recent acknowledgment of the importance of recognizing learning disabilities in adults.

Rack (1997) carried out one of the few available studies of adults. He studied 28 adults (aged 17 or over) referred to him at the Dyslexia Institute over a period of 15 months. They were a mixture of self-referrals and referrals from other sources, including student support services, employers and other psychologists. Fourteen showed a classic pattern of memory and phonological processing difficulties, although four of those were complicated by other factors. In a further six out of the 28, he found that the most significant weakness was in visual-motor co-ordination. In two, he found no evidence of dyslexia. The remaining six showed a pattern that he felt was 'probably not attributable to a developmental learning difficulty' although most had literacy difficulties and 'many had an "uneven cognitive profile" indicating specific information processing difficulties'. The question is again, what are we to label these 'non-classic profiles' if not dyslexic? What explanation can we offer for their difficulties? What exactly are these 'information processing difficulties'? Rack suggests that their educational opportunities may have been restricted, but there is no reason that dyslexia cannot be coexistent with restricted educational opportunities. Restricted educational experience in itself may not be a sufficient explanation for failure to learn to read and write: indeed, there are many examples of individuals with poor educational backgrounds who do not continue to exhibit literacy or information processing difficulties as adults. Obviously, educational deprivation may be an explanation for low levels of literacy in some adults, but, as Rack points out, it is not necessarily the sole cause.

However, Rack does go on to conclude, most importantly, that 'there is a need to investigate further the possible subgroups of adult developmental dyslexics and, in particular, to establish the extent to which they differ from 'normal' comparison samples. *Until this is done, there is some merit in preserving a broader conceptualization of the dyslexic syndrome alongside the more narrow phonological pattern'* (Rack, 1997; our emphasis).

Other definitions of dyslexia are too narrow to encompass adequately the difficulties seen in adults since they are based on problems acquiring and developing reading skills. Although many adults continue to have reading problems, others have overcome earlier struggles with reading and may appear proficient on existing reading tests. In the National Development Project in Developing Learning Support for Students with Specific Learning Difficulties (Klein,1992), dyslexic students most commonly reported their main difficulty to be spelling, and we continue to find this is frequently, though not always, the case. Other persistent problems include planning and organizing, and written expression – aspects of dyslexia that are more difficult to measure. It is worth remembering that research is most prolific in areas that lend themselves easily to quantitative analysis.

A story from the middle East illustrates the point:

> A neighbour came upon Nasruddin on the ground searching for something. 'What have you lost, Mulla?' he asked.
> 'My key,' said Nasruddin. So the neighbour joined him in the search. After a while, the neighbour asked him where exactly he had dropped it.
> 'At home,' said Nasruddin.
> 'Then, why, for heaven's sake, are you looking for it here?'
> 'There is more light here.'
>
> (Shah, 1964)

The British Psychological Society (BPS, 1999) set up a working party to come up with a 'working definition' of dyslexia that does not rely on any particular causal definition, is not based on IQ discrepancies and is more 'culture-fair'. Their working definition is somewhat narrow and aimed at dyslexia in children, but nonetheless eliminates exclusionary criteria and reliance on any one theoretical explanation:

> Dyslexia is evident when accurate and fluent word reading and/or spelling develops very incompletely or with great difficulty. This focuses on literacy learning at the 'word level' and implies that the problem is severe and persistent despite appropriate learning opportunities. It provides the basis for a staged process of assessment through teaching.

Although the working party based their definition on dyslexia in children, their criticisms of current methodology and existing definitions apply equally to adults. For instance, they quote research on the

'ACID profile' of the Wechsler Intelligence Scale for Children (WISC), commonly used as an indicator of dyslexia, which concludes that 'the low incidence of this profile in clinical samples renders it clinically meaningless'. The 'ACID profile' refers to a common profile in dyslexic subjects whereby they show a discrepancy between the scores on four subtests (all of which are dependent on an efficient short-term memory) and those of the remaining subtests. The BPS working party's criticism is extremely important as some local authorities in Britain continue to specify the adult version of the profile as the determining factor in the diagnosis of dyslexia in adults. Individuals who do not conform to this profile have been denied access to special examination provision or higher education grants.

Definitions also create expectations and assumptions of numbers; how narrowly or widely a society or culture defines dyslexia may influence how many individuals are 'allowed' to be dyslexic. Narrow definitions permit the 4–10 per cent commonly quoted in Britain. In the USA, wider definitions lead to 10–20 per cent of the population being identified (Shaywitz, 1996). 'Definitions can be chosen or manipulated to increase or decrease the number of students likely to be identified' (Reiff et al., 1997). Again, it is tempting to agree with Humpty Dumpty.

It is also interesting to note that, although there is regular and alarming research into the number of adults in Britain with poor literacy and numeracy, with current estimates exceeding seven million (Moser, 1999), there is no research on the incidence of dyslexia within this population, or of those attending adult basic skills classes. Claims are often made about the causes of poor literacy, but the possibility of dyslexia as a factor has never been researched. In a two-year project developing learning support for dyslexic students (Klein, 1992), careful records in one inner-city adult education centre showed that in a range of literacy and 'return to learning' classes, 26 per cent of students were positively diagnosed dyslexic; this excluded those with backgrounds of English as an additional language. Anecdotal reports provided by adult basic education tutors with specialized training in dyslexia frequently estimate 30–40 per cent of their students to be dyslexic. Butterfield (1996) studied two basic education classes in an inner London college and found that 10 out of 14 'virtual non-readers' had a weakness in phonological processing exhibited through significantly poor awareness of rhyme. Three others had some difficulty recognizing rhyme;

one had none but did have problems with visual analysis. Though none of these figures constitutes hard evidence, they certainly indicate the need for further study.

It is important to keep a certain distance when evaluating research. Given the difficulties in designing and administering quantifiable research on the adult population, we welcome Rack's recommendation that definitions should remain flexible.

A model of diagnosis for adults

The questions of who should assess dyslexia in adults and what methods are acceptable inevitably raise concern about 'false negatives and false positives'. However, as Pumfrey argues (in Beech and Singleton, 1997), this is a concern in any assessment procedure. We must decide what our values are: one risk is that some people may be given the 'dyslexia' label without being (in certain views) 'truly dyslexic' and thereby also gain access to provision or money to which they may not be entitled. However, perhaps a greater danger is that some who are dyslexic will be denied access to the support they need to succeed and fulfil their potential.

Historically, since Hinshelwood first defined 'word-blindness' in 1917, the medical profession assumed primary responsibility for identifying dyslexia. In recent times, educational psychologists have been the main 'keepers' of the diagnostic process as the central focus has been on children. Since the 1990s, there has been a widening acceptance in Britain of diagnosis by specialist trained teachers for the purposes of special examination provision and additional learning support. A recognition of the problems inherent in diagnosing adults and an acceptance of the need to rely on the 'clinical (or professional) feel' of dyslexia supports the view that those working within adult education or training establishments/environments may be best placed to diagnose dyslexia in adults. Teachers and psychologists with primarily child-based experience may be less sensitive to the issues relating to adult diagnosis.

Accessibility to diagnosis for adults may be problematic. Colleges of further education in the UK offer a diagnosis by specialist trained tutors or psychologists, but this service is usually available only to full-time enrolled students. Some, but not all, higher education institutions have facilities for assessment. However, dyslexic adults are often outside the education system – or may even want to re-enter education, but need first to clarify for themselves their own ability to learn. Alternatively they may be facing difficulties in employment, need to change employment or produce more writing in their jobs. In some of these cases, diagnosis may be done through the employment service but, for many, the only option is a private, and expensive, assessment by a clinical, occupational or educational psychologist.

The choice of methodology and the way the diagnosis is conducted will depend largely on the training, beliefs and values of the assessor. What outcomes are important to the person conducting the diagnosis? What does she see as the purpose? For whom is the diagnosis being done – the individual, an educational establishment, a local authority or an employer? How does the assessor see the diagnostic relationship between herself and the adult being assessed? What are her views of the person being diagnosed?

Methodology needs to be appropriate for adults and not borrowed from models or definitions based on research with children. Relational aspects of the diagnostic situation also need to be considered: the fact that there are two adults present and the dyslexic adult has a personal history, maturity and competence in many areas of life – he may even be more skilled in some areas than the person diagnosing him. The dyslexic adult's purposes in getting the diagnosis should also inform the diagnostic process; the dyslexic person will need explanations of both the process and the result to help him understand and make sense of the experience. The assessment will be of little value to him if he is left baffled or demeaned by the experience.

Since the diagnosis of adults is relatively new ground, there is no uniformly accepted methodology. A successful diagnosis relies on responsible and sympathetic handling by the assessor of the issues that are significant to adults. A holistic approach ensures that the individual is not merely being subjected to 'testing', but is actively involved in the assessment process and respected for his contribution. Assessments may be conducted by specialist dyslexia teachers or by psychologists, but in either case the assessor should be specifically trained and experienced in working with adults rather than children.

Whether administered by a psychologist or teacher, it is important to consider that existing tests (many of which are not normed on adults) are not the only tool for diagnosis. There are several reasons why the diagnostic process we use and recommend for specialist trained teachers working with adults does not rely on standardized testing. First, as discussed, there is a lack of reliable standardization based on the adult population; second, compensating strategies developed by adults may affect scores; and third, test scores often fail to give clear practical indicators of the kinds of difficulties adults may experience in areas other than reading and spelling. For instance, many adults find their greatest difficulties may be with skills relating to planning and organizing, which are not measurable by standardized tests. The report of the National Working Party on Dyslexia in Higher Education (Singleton, 1999) corroborates our concern about the lack of appropriate tests: 'Unfortunately there are few standardized tests that are appropriate to this age and ability group that can be strongly recommended at the present time and there is an urgent need for research and test development in this area.'

As important, tests frequently have a detrimental effect on dyslexic adults, leading them to doubt themselves and their abilities when they see low scores. Though this can be ameliorated by careful preparation and sympathetic interpretation, low test scores tend to have a negative effect on individuals' self-esteem, particularly if they have had a poor school experience. We have met many students who have broken down and cried when relating a negative experience of assessment. Even sympathetic assessors often fail to recognize the devastating effect on an adult of receiving low results on spelling and reading tests. One student said she left her university course because she didn't believe it would be possible to succeed since she had a reading age of 15 and she was 32. She had not appreciated that the test she had been given had a ceiling of age 15 and the psychologist had neglected to explain this. Fortunately, some psychologists who assess adults acknowledge the limitations of reading and spelling tests that offer results in terms of 'ages'. However, there remain many educational psychologists whose child-based training does not easily transfer to work with adults.

It is disheartening to read or hear admonitions by some educational psychologists about the unreliability of first-person accounts. This is curious in view of the classic medical model of diagnosis, which relies heavily on the patient's reported symptoms. Indeed, there are many illnesses or conditions, such as migraine, which are identified *only* on the patient's reported symptoms.

Evidence may come in many forms and, given the paucity and inconclusiveness of research on adults, the disagreements over definitions, and the acknowledged problems with assessment tools, first-person reports may be extremely useful in helping to draw an accurate diagnostic picture. Although we are not arguing for 'self-assessment' by adults, we feel that open-ended questioning by a skilled assessor can generate considerable useful information to inform the diagnosis. The use of adult reporting can contribute a significant piece of the larger picture.

Criteria for a diagnosis of adult dyslexia usually include some or all of the following:

- a history of persistent difficulties in acquiring reading, writing, spelling and often fluent handwriting in spite of extra help or 'normal' schooling. Sometimes these problems are unrecognized due to lack of awareness, low expectations or a student's avoidance or 'cover-up' strategies. There may also be a history of glue ear, speech or language problems or sometimes lack of a reference eye.
- a pattern of difficulties that may include problems with quick and accurate processing of written and sometimes oral language, word retrieval, sequencing, direction, short-term or 'working' memory and memorizing tasks, organization, estimating and managing time and a lack of automaticity or motor integration, often showing itself in difficulty with handwriting and motor co-ordination tasks
- a pattern of errors in reading and spelling that indicates difficulty with phonological processing, visual recognition and/or visual memory for words. Such a pattern of errors is more useful than a reading score or age as it reveals errors that are usually non-developmental in type; that is they are not the sort of errors that children make as developing readers and writers, and often include inconsistent spellings and difficulties in 'seeing' inconsistencies.
- a range of discrepancies, for instance, between oral and written language, between conceptual understanding and written expression or reading ability, between understanding spoken information and accessing information from a text, between non-verbal and verbal tasks, and between written work performed under time constraints compared to that done in the student's own time

- a particular learning style characterized by being 'quick forgetters' of factual information, spellings and rules, along with a good
  long-term memory and a poor short-term memory, often showing the development of complex compensating strategies for
  remembering information, frequently learning 'differently' and
  failing to respond to remedial strategies.

A distinctive though individual pattern will nearly always emerge
unless complicated by other educational, cultural or psychological
factors, or by other coexistent learning difficulties. When more
general learning difficulties are suspected, additional testing may be
necessary. In these situations, it is worth remembering Feuerstein's
(1981) 'test, teach, test' paradigm to arrive at a realistic assessment of
the individual's abilities to undertake, for example, further or higher
education courses.

An in-depth interview is the foundation of the diagnosis, enabling
the person diagnosing not only to obtain background information
demonstrating persistence of problems and detailed descriptions
of difficulties, cognitive style and compensating strategies, but
also to observe the person's language and listening skills. Of equal
importance, the interview allows the dyslexic adult to participate
fully in the exploration and to uncover strengths as well as weaknesses. Discrepancies can frequently be established through the
interview. For example, an interview with a 53-year-old man, who
until being made redundant had worked in a flour mill where
he needed few written skills, revealed that he had had difficulties
learning to read and was held back at school. He always received
poor marks in English compared to his other subjects. He was taken
to school by his sister because he always got lost. He was sent to
a special school at age 12 because of his poor reading and spelling.
He reported problems telling the time, concentrating while listening,
recognizing words out of context, remembering instructions
and discriminating sounds. He still has difficulties with the alphabet
and needs a ruler for staying on the line. He can remember the
compass only by using a mnemonic ('**n**ever **e**at **s**hredded **w**heat')
which he worked out because he likes sailing. He reads books on
carpentry, photography and sailing and also likes to read poetry,
especially Dylan Thomas, whom he spoke about eloquently. Even

before any 'testing', many indicators of dyslexia were established.

The interview is also extremely important when diagnosing those who speak English as an additional language. Their previous education and difficulties in other languages need to be identified. Their problems with English sounds, for example, need to be explored in relation to the sounds in their other languages.

Additional evidence and confirmation of sequencing, phonological processing and short-term memory problems can be obtained from a range of tasks integrated into the interview. For example, the individual might be asked to pronounce multisyllabic words, recount the alphabet, multiplication tables and months backwards, undergo tasks involving digit span and create spoonerisms or perform other phonological processing tasks. These can be introduced informally, do not take long, and their purpose and results can easily be explained in a non-threatening way. Explaining the relation of such tasks to dyslexia can assist the dyslexic person to gain greater insights into the complex nature of dyslexia and to understand the particular profile of strengths and weaknesses that are personal to him.

An analysis of reading, spelling and free writing follows the interview. These need to reveal the types of errors individuals make at the level necessary for them to function. The person should be given a selected text of appropriate difficulty and length to identify reading problems in decoding, word recognition and comprehension. This is supplemented by single word and non-word tests. In spelling, a diagnostic dictation will often clearly reveal the most prevalent type of difficulty. We find that many adults with primarily auditory processing difficulties omit, confuse or mis-sequence significant sounds or syllables and can frequently recognize where a spelling is wrong, though they may be unable to correct their error. Those who experience weaknesses in visual-motor processing spell phonetically, omit or mis-sequence significant visual elements and may have great difficulties recognizing when a spelling 'looks' wrong or may be unable to 'see' that they have spelled the same word several different ways. (For full details of the diagnostic process and useful materials, see Klein, 1993, and Sunderland et al., 1997.)

The ideal result of the diagnosis is when, as Jean put it, it helps 'to put a lot of things together and make sense of the things I found so difficult'.

Diagnosis as a starting point

The diagnostic process itself can serve as an explanation for many of the struggles that a dyslexic adult has experienced in his life. However, to ensure that this opportunity is illuminating rather than damaging, the assessor needs to explain clearly the purpose and process of the diagnosis and to listen to the dyslexic person. Many adults state that it is the first time they have felt anyone has really listened to them and understood what they are saying.

The process must include a feedback session with an opportunity to clarify questions, talk about the implications and deal with emotional issues. The diagnostic report is of the utmost importance in helping the dyslexic person to use the diagnostic experience in a positive and constructive way. It needs to be reviewed carefully with the individual to 'unpack' the terminology. Keeping in mind that it is often difficult for a newly diagnosed adult to process so much new information at one time, a subsequent visit to the assessor should be arranged. This could address questions that arise after the person has had the chance to 'digest' the contents and implications of the report. The report should then 'belong' to the person, to be used as they like in the future. It is, as one said, 'proof that I'm not stupid'.

The most common experience of adults upon being told they are dyslexic is relief – relief that they are not to blame and that they are not stupid. There is also relief that they are 'not the only one' and that 'there is a name for it'.

The diagnosis can be very empowering and may mark the beginning of a process of significant change. Most dyslexic adults find the label gives them a new confidence as a result of gaining insights into their own learning. It is important for professionals to recognize the importance of the diagnosis and labelling process, as many dyslexic people have grown up with a confusion about themselves which can be resolved through diagnosis. Jean expressed her bewilderment about her difficulties:

> One day I was sent to a special unit, and she asked me something like, 'What would you do if there was a fire? Would you call the fire department, post a letter or – I don't remember?' And I thought, she's stupid . . .
>
> But nothing ever came from that, and then when I went to secondary school, I was excited – I remember we were in the hall and we were allocated our classrooms, and they put me in the bottom class. And I was so offended and disgusted, and I thought, oh gosh, you know, it really hit home. From then onwards, I really strived to better myself but I couldn't – I couldn't spell. And I

kept thinking, one day I'm going to wake up and I'm going to be able to spell. I thought it was just something, you know, I haven't grown up yet, my mind hasn't worked yet.

Jean describes the effects of her diagnosis:

I remember I was in the kitchen one day and I'd just been diagnosed and I thought, I'm going to make a cake. And I got out the cake pan and I made a cake and I thought, that's because I'm getting confidence . . . And I made this cake and I thought, yeah, great. Because when I was at school I was so used to them saying like 'You'll never achieve anything, you're no good.' They didn't actually say that but it was just taken for granted. And then I began to really believe that.

Janet explains how being diagnosed gave her confidence:

I knew there was something wrong . . . and then you're diagnosed, and it opens another world for you . . . because you think maybe I am capable. I mean, I took O levels once I found out. I wanted to prove to myself and to other people that I was intelligent, that I was capable of doing other things . . . I was just doing a menial job . . . I think it pushes you on and it helps having the label and knowing. Once you know exactly what's going on, then you can cope with it far more easily.

Graham explains how the diagnosis lent credibility to his own feelings:

I wasn't surprised because, basically, I assumed that I was [dyslexic], even though nobody would take it seriously. But I was very frustrated and really annoyed at my past educators and also at the education authority. But also it was comforting in a way to know that it was verified. It wasn't just like – everybody always said that I was lazy or just wasn't paying attention or just didn't do the work – all those kinds of things.

A diagnosis can also change behaviour towards others. Probation officers and others working with the Dyspel Project in London, which provides diagnosis and tuition for dyslexic offenders, have remarked on sometimes dramatic changes in offenders, once they are diagnosed. A receptionist at a probation centre participating in the project commented with wonder, 'I don't know what she [the Dyspel tutor] does with them in there – they come in all hostile and surly, avoiding eye contact – and then the next week they come in smiling and saying "Good morning".'

Diagnosis may bring about an increased need to talk about one's experience. It may also intensify feelings of isolation. Janet spoke of how she felt cheated out of her education and her need to share her new understanding:

> When I was diagnosed, they didn't understand the way I was feeling. I wanted to talk to somebody about it. I took out several books and read up on it but I desperately wanted to talk to somebody else who was dyslexic – because you tend to think you're the only one in the world who's dyslexic and where are all these other people?

She tried to talk to her husband,

> but he didn't believe in dyslexia and is still very sceptical about it.

Initial reactions of adults may also include feelings of resentment towards a system that has let them down by not identifying their difficulties at school. There may also be considerable anger toward teachers, parents or other family members for failure to provide help and support. Sometimes, reactions include a mixture of feelings and it may take some time to sift through the complex emotional responses. Patrick summed up the complicated emotions he felt when he was first diagnosed at age 22:

> I felt very sad, very bitter, very relieved, very happy – I felt everything. When I look back on it now – I'll never forget the day – it was amazing. I walked out, with tears in my eyes. It was an enormous amount of feelings.
>
> I felt very angry against the people who'd put me through school and not picked it up . . . I was put in a class for slow people and . . . I should never have been put in there because even my school reports said 'Bright lad, he just doesn't apply himself.' I think what made me sad was the fact that I think, even in 1995, at that same school, they still wouldn't have had the facilities to pick someone like me up and assess them as having a problem.

Jean describes her response to diagnosis:

> I was diagnosed as being dyslexic and it was a relief. I thought, great; I knew I wasn't stupid. I thought, so that's what it is, it's not my fault. And then I was so angry at the school for letting me just rot there.

When Jackie was eventually diagnosed at age 22, the psychologist's report argued that her school records provided convincing evidence to suggest that an assessment should have been undertaken when

Jackie was a child. Jackie's anger at the school system led her to take legal proceedings against her education authority for their negligence in failing to provide her with schooling appropriate to her needs. Jackie describes her reasons for pursuing legal action:

> When I found out I was dyslexic, I just wanted to see whether there was any negligence against my school, whether my junior and infants and senior school should have picked it up and I went to see a solicitor to see whether they were negligent. And he said it was a very hard case, because there was only one case that he knew of and they're very difficult cases to prove and then he said about the money. And I said, it's not really about money; it's about someone giving me a letter, a hand-written letter that's been written personally by some big, head person, to say, 'Yes, we failed you. You're not stupid, you're not thick, we made a mistake, sorry . . . '
>
> *You want an apology?*
>
> Yeah, and that's what it's down to, whether there was negligence on their part and that's what I was looking for, a letter of apology, but then they said you'd get compensation money if you won the case. Because when I talked to the barrister, I said, at the end of the day, I just want someone to say, 'Sorry.' He said, 'If it was that simple, we could go and ask them and they'd write it for you now. It's not like that. You're entitled to some sort of compensation.' But all I want is someone to say sorry; I'm not really interested in the money. The money won't improve anything, the money won't turn the clock back, the money won't give me my education, my childhood that I missed. But an apology will make things – it will be some way to know that it wasn't me. It's something beyond my control; I'm not thick, I'm not stupid, I'm not mental. There was a problem, but it was out of my control. The fault lies with them. The system failed me. I'm one of that small minority that it failed. Failed big time.

In Britain, it is extremely difficult to prove negligence on the part of a school authority and, consequently, the number of lawsuits similar to Jackie's is relatively few. However, many mature adults who have benefited from diagnosis only upon their return to education share her anger and feelings of having been failed by the educational system. The long-term damage in terms of self-esteem and emotional toll should not be underestimated.

The label is important also for access to appropriate support and to ensure that previous experience of failure is not repeated. However, the label alone is not enough; it must be 'unpacked' through the diagnostic process and the written report. The diagnostic report, if written in a helpful way, which explains the results of the diagnosis in terms of both the dyslexic person's strengths and his weaknesses, can be a basis for planning learning, identifying support needs in work or study, exploring effective strategies for dealing with difficulties and helping the person build self-esteem.

Although dyslexic adults are frequently angry when they are diagnosed, the anger can be seen as positive, releasing energy for change. They are also hopeful that things may be different. If they are going back into learning it is important that they are given appropriate and effective support: a repeated experience of 'more of the same' can undo many of the positive benefits of the diagnosis.

Dyslexia is not just an educational issue: it also affects employment and personal life. Consequently, whether dyslexic adults are employed, intend to seek employment or have other personal goals, they will need to deal with the effects of dyslexia on their lives. However successful they are in coming to terms with their diagnosis, there will always be new situations and challenges that are affected by their dyslexia. It is in these situations that the impact of dyslexia as a 'hidden disability' may be felt, where the person may be the target of negative responses from relatives, employers or colleagues. An explicit understanding of dyslexia and how it affects individuals in different contexts can make a profound difference in the experiences of the dyslexic adult.

Explaining dyslexia to others

One of the issues for dyslexic adults that arises from the diagnosis is the need to explain dyslexia to others. They frequently assume that, if they reveal they are dyslexic, people will understand. Some responses to the question, 'How would you explain your dyslexia to others?' include the following:

> **Graham**: Gosh, I don't really think I do define it to anybody, to be honest. I normally just tell people that I'm dyslexic and expect them to understand. I don't really go around defining dyslexia. It's me. Don't really think I need to [define it] – it's this thing about attaching words to something. Being dyslexic, I don't really want to do it. It's about me as a person; it's about the fact that I can't spell; it's about the problems I had before; it's about coping with those problems and how I internalized those problems.

> **Anne**: . . . a lot of people perceive dyslexia as just not being able to spell. In my case that is true, but it's such a common view that the general public have and it's so wrong because they don't realize the emotional side to it as well.

Isobel: I would say it's an academic disability . . . it can be very tiring because you have to work that little bit harder the whole time.

Michaela: . . . when I look at a text book, I can't just read the book. I have to concentrate a lot, to read the words, to break down every single word into sounds, or to recognize the words. I have to improve my memory to recognize the words that I know. I find that sometimes the words move up and down. I think my emotional state, my mental state, everything, the ambience, every-where I am, who I'm with, what I'm trying to read, all relates to my dyslexia. It affects me when I'm travelling as well. And time – I never used to be able to read the time, like the twenty-four hour clock? I never used to be able to read that. When people ask me, how does it affect you, I just say I'm not very good at spelling, reading, writing. I'm not very good at anything; I can just talk.

Veronica: Actually, the way I try to explain it is that it's like trying to get infor-mation from a filing system; my brain takes time to get to the information; it just takes a bit longer.

Rob: Illiterate. No, maybe not, it holds you back. If someone asked me, I would be like, I just find it a lot harder. That part of your brain, the reading and writ-ing side of your brain just doesn't work as well. You can train it to work as well, but it doesn't, but then, it does hold you back. I'm sure it does, not being able to flow through the books.

Linda: I equate it to walking through treacle; it's always so hard.

Clearly, the definitions and explanations offered by these adults reflect a range of interpretations of what it means to be dyslexic. Although public awareness of dyslexia has increased in the past 20 years, considerable ignorance and misconceptions remain. From the dyslexic person's view, the greatest difficulty about being dyslexic is the responses of the non-dyslexic world. Helen conveys this movingly:

Other people don't allow you to make mistakes . . . they have to get the red pen out. And being dyslexic, you make so many mistakes (like your tongue slips and you say the wrong word) and people are always jumping on you, putting it right . . . Other people come down hard on you for making those little mistakes and you don't need that . . .

PART II
Living in the
Non-dyslexic World

Chapter 3
Formative influences, self-esteem and patterns of behaviour

It is impossible to determine the extent to which the fact of being dyslexic influences personality and behaviour. However, many adults, when reflecting on their past, place considerable emphasis on the impact of dyslexia on their general self-esteem and personality development. There are several external factors which undoubtedly influence the individual's perception of the significance of dyslexia on his or her life. Perhaps the most important variables are the stage at which dyslexia was first diagnosed and the type of support, both emotional and academic, that was received. Saunders (1995) attributes the degree of family stress created by a dyslexic family member to three factors: 'the age of the person (child or adult) when first discovered, the facilities for educational treatment, and the "excess emotional baggage" which the various members of the family have endured before the awareness of dyslexia as an added "burden".'

Another crucial factor is the degree of severity of the individual's dyslexia. There are many mildly dyslexic people whose difficulties do not significantly impede their success. Yet these individuals, while not inhibited by reading and writing difficulties, may nonetheless experience hesitancy and uncertainty resulting from other aspects of their dyslexia. They might be reticent to voice opinions or answer questions in class as a result of previous embarrassment caused by misunderstanding or misinterpreting questions or discussions. They may also suffer from low self-esteem resulting from such difficulties as being unable to remember simple instructions, confusing factual information, or mispronouncing words.

The issue of diagnosis for these individuals may not, however, be as crucial as it is for those whose dyslexia has posed greater problems. Adults who suffered from delayed or limited development in literacy skills resulting from lack of recognition or appropriate intervention in their education may carry deep scars resulting from feelings of inadequacy, frustration, anger and resentment. These feelings may have been exacerbated by having been mislabelled as 'stupid', 'lazy' or 'careless'. Some adults report having borne the label of 'slow learners' or 'retarded', causing immeasurable damage to their self-esteem. Karl's parents were told he was not motivated and was acting the 'class clown' at school. He was assessed by an educational psychologist when he was studying for his A Levels and told he was 'borderline mentally retarded' and that it was 'a fluke' that he was in grammar school. It wasn't until he was at university that he was diagnosed dyslexic and was told he had an IQ of 147, which was 'borderline genius'. But even years later, he would sometimes break down and cry and feel he was stupid.

One dyslexic woman remembers attending a remedial class at school. She and others in the class were teased on the playground and got into a fight. The teacher called the remedial group in and told them:

> What those children did in the playground was wrong, but what you must understand is that you are not very bright and this kind of treatment is something you will have to get used to.

She describes absorbing the teacher's words 'like water into a sponge' and never questioning them until she was much older.

Early education and self-esteem

Brinckerhoff et al. (1993) identify the lack of a positive self-concept as being the one consistent counselling issue that presents itself in people with learning disabilities. In our experience, reported perceptions of self-esteem are likely to be lower among recently diagnosed adults than those adults who had the benefit of diagnosis from childhood. However, even those diagnosed as children and supported by school and family may suffer from low self-esteem in response to the inherent frustrations of not being able to perform academically as well as their peers.

Mark, who was diagnosed at age 22, gave a candid description about his low self-esteem resulting from the failure to identify and address his dyslexia when he was a child:

> There is a memory that's very, vivid to me to do with having very low self-esteem at school. I remember these war comics – they were really racist war comics when I was a kid – of the Japanese and the Germans. I must have been about 9 or 10. I used to read them like all the other kids and I remember thinking, which was a strange comforting thought at the time, and really did reflect my low self-esteem, that if the Germans invaded Britain, they wouldn't waste a bullet on me. I felt invisible. You know, I was on the margins of the class, I was considered to be really stupid and when I think of my expectations, I remember thinking, 'I can't wait to leave school' and I used to have all these fantasies just to get these people off my back. My expectations became incredibly low.

Jackie's diagnosis at age 29 came as an enormous relief, as it provided an explanation for the frustration and anger that had characterized her childhood. She still feels bitterness at the total lack of support she received from family, school and peers and openly discussed the ways in which her difficulties with learning affected her behaviour, personality and self-esteem:

> When I was at school I used to pick up chairs, or whatever, and just throw them at people. I was so aggressive, but at the same time I was provoked because the other kids in my class used to know that I would do it if they provoked me. They used to call me names, call me thick, stupid, just hit me and stuff like that.
>
> I was bullied big time. The last four years in my school, I was bullied verbally, physically, and it just affected me emotionally. I used to get bullied by the teachers. They used to tell me I was mental . . . Yeah, yeah they used to say that I was mental and men in white coats were going to come and take me away. [Jackie went on to explain that her grandfather suffered from senile dementia and she occasionally visited him in a mental hospital.]
>
> So when the teachers were saying that to me, I knew exactly what it was like to be in a mental institution and when I reacted, I was in the wrong. They were always in the right; I was in the wrong. So, they would provoke me, the other students would provoke me and I got into so much trouble that my mum was always at the school, and of course my mum would take their side. I was always wrong, so she'd come home and she'd beat me and this was going on for the last four years of my [secondary] school.

Jackie sees the correlation between her frustration and her resultant behaviour:

> I had loads of behavioural problems at school because the teachers only see what they want to see and I was just classed as a problem child. When I was coming up to the end of my fourth year, so I'd just turned 15, they sent me to see a psychiatrist because they kept saying I was mental. Anyway, it came out of the blue. My mum came home one day and she said, 'You're going to see a psychologist tomorrow.' I said, 'I ain't; I ain't going to see no-one.' And she goes, 'You are, because if you don't go and see him, I'm going to beat you when I get home.' Anyway, I had to go and see him and some woman, I didn't know who she was, she come and picked me up from school and then she picked my mum up and she took us to see a psychologist and, he just sat and talked to me and then he turned around to me mum and said I was immature, but . . . it still didn't stop the problems. And, even at that stage, they still could have assessed me then. Even though I was coming up to the end of my education, they still could have assessed me and seen what the problem was, but no one ever did. Obviously, I was always wrong, the teachers were always right, so I was the one who got the beatings.

Jackie's bitterness about her childhood experiences is not unusual.

Dyslexia and the peer group

Responses from the peer group can be a powerful influence on the individual's perception of self. Children who attend special schools for dyslexic pupils may be able to overcome feelings of isolation and the sense of being 'different'. Most dyslexic children (and adults) can be happily integrated into mainstream classes if the appropriate support is available. However, adults who were not diagnosed during their school years report a range of responses, including feelings of difference and inferiority.

Jenny describes her sense of loneliness at school:

> I found school particularly difficult, basically because I didn't understand what the teachers were saying . . .
>
> And then, when I was at school, I didn't have any friends. I didn't have friends like other people could have friends. I don't know why . . . That really went back to infant school. I never had friends at infant school. Or junior school. I had a couple in the senior school but not really friends that I'd call friends. Because they always seemed better than me – and perhaps that was my problem. I think they thought I was a bit of a featherhead. I think I did try – but then you sort of revert into yourself because I think you can try so many times and then – it just wasn't working.
>
> I think a lot of it was because I didn't always understand what people said – even now as an adult, I sometimes won't understand the words that people say . . . It was a difficult time. Really sad as well.

Jackie also comments on her sense of loneliness. The impact of her desperately unhappy childhood was that she became a loner. She describes how her experiences as a child influenced her as an adult:

> I've always been a bit of a loner, I think. I tend to prefer my own company. I think I took so much . . . I just shut myself away from everybody. I used to have a small group of friends, but they were always better than me at things, were in higher groups than me, so it was just hard to communicate with them.
>
> I tend to keep myself to myself. I'm a home student; I just go home, and I'm at my home; I'm not in any halls or I'm not in digs with people. My home is my home; it's where I lived before I came here and it's where I'll live when I finish. I tend to keep myself to myself.

Such an awareness reflects the ability of dyslexic people to make comparisons with peers and to recognize intuitively their undefined and unacknowledged learning differences. Many dyslexic adults report that they felt different from their peers from an early age. At age 5, Rob told his parents he wanted a new brain like the Tin Man in *The Wizard of Oz*. He said that his brain didn't work in the same way as the brains of the other children in his class, all of whom were beginning to read and write.

Mark, too, commented on his sense of being different from his peers. He describes his transition from primary to secondary school:

> I started to feel that I was different. I felt I was acknowledged by my peers as being quite witty and quite good at sport and quite artistic but I was basically told by everybody that I was thick and slow; I did feel socially excluded. I remember very vividly a summer day on one of the last days at my primary school; one of my peer group who had been selected for the grammar school came up to me and said, 'I'm going to [the grammar school]; you're not, are you?' I'd always detested this guy and I said, 'No, I'm going to [the secondary modern school].' And he said, 'That's because you're really thick.' I remember looking at this guy, he was very bright and he'd done very well throughout. It's funny how your memory works. This guy had one of these cotton shirts and you could see right through to his vest underneath it. I remember because I couldn't look at his face because I would have hit him if I'd looked at his face and I was biting my lip. I said, 'People are good at different things.' I said, 'I'm better at drawing than you are and I'm a better footballer than you are.' I remember, it bit so deeply. It was a very powerful experience.

The sense of loneliness and isolation is typical of many dyslexic people. Tur-Kaspa et al. (1998) conducted a study of 70 eighth-grade boys in a special school in Tel Aviv. Their findings revealed that the students with learning disabilities had significantly higher levels of loneliness than their non-dyslexic peers and that they had 'high expectations of feeling lonely – in the future, in general, and in new social situations in particular'.

In attempting to understand the myriad of factors that contribute to the impact of dyslexia on personality formation, one crucial point must be kept in mind. Although dyslexia is often referred to as a hidden disability, dyslexic children can't conceal their inability to read and write from their teachers, parents and friends. The responses they receive to their difficulties, which frequently include negative and confusing labelling, will have a significant impact on their self-esteem and emerging self-concept.

Race, class and ethnicity

Dyslexia is not an issue just for white middle-class people; it transcends race and social class. However, the question of how ethnicity and social or cultural factors affect those with dyslexia has not been explored in the literature. Indeed, Cline and Reason (1993) question the accuracy of existing research on dyslexia because of the limited inclusion of issues of diversity.

Our own experience has included working with many non-white as well as white working-class adults. We have found very few non-white, working-class or bilingual speakers from non-European countries who were diagnosed at school. It was often the case that black and Asian individuals were not identified as dyslexic at school in Britain because teachers had low expectations for non-white children. Barbara, now a social worker, was put in a special needs class where she didn't learn to read and write and describes her school experience as 'very hostile'. She left school at 16 and learned to read then. She tells of her white foster mother going into the school:

> Basically they were saying that I would never go to college and I would only be able to do a factory job and her response was, 'That's all you've got for all the black kids in the school anyway, worse if they've got other problems.' And they weren't prepared to give her any support so she just took me out of school.

Similar low expectations for working-class children have also been described by dyslexic people. Janet speaks scathingly of expectations by the school that they would all work in a factory. Similarly, Mark recalls:

> I remember at school . . . I'd just been introduced to a word which really resonated with me, and that word was 'factory fodder'. And I thought . . . I was destined to just work in a factory for the rest of my life; that's what I was being prepared for.

Many have also told of their parents being treated condescendingly when trying to get their children's difficulties properly diagnosed and to secure appropriate help. Some, such as Michael, recall his mother being 'intimidated' by teachers and psychologists who made her feel inferior in the face of professional opinion, which she found hard to counter. But all these adults felt it was their learning problems rather than class or race that were most significant in setting them apart.

Adults from other countries tell much the same story of their childhood experiences. Halima describes her schooling in Somalia (Sunderland, 1998):

> It wasn't easy for me from the first time, that's why they say OK maybe she's stupid, or she's lazy – she doesn't want to learn . . . No one would understand me, even my family or even the teacher . . .
>
> I did want to learn but after that when I saw I'm just – every time I'm behind other children . . . then I just say maybe it's just the way I am . . . My heart is broken and I never learn.

Working-class culture can also affect experiences at school. Michael wrote in an essay on dyslexia:

> I had a certain cockiness that a lot of working-class boys have that got me through most things at school and afterwards through work. A blind belief that what they don't know is not worth bothering about. It is a very good philosophy as long as you don't meet things or people from outside these narrow working-class boundaries which it confined you to. Then the thin, rigid skin would burst.

However, he notes that:

> The hierarchical structure of pupils comes into play here. In this structure, I was in the middle ground. I was not a good fighter, but could hold my own. More importantly, I was in a group . . . Here education skills do not matter. It is the socializing in and out of school that is important, your attitude and behaviour which mark you as normal.

Cultural expectations sometimes affected adults' responses to being diagnosed, particularly with regard to their family. This is partly because of the increase in dyslexia awareness in recent years in Britain and also because 'culturally, it is not always appropriate to admit there is a problem'. Extreme sensitivity is needed 'to ensure that words like "disability" are not used' (Sunderland et al., 1997). One young Pakistani man, for example, was particularly upset by reference to his mother's difficulties in his diagnostic report as he felt this was a slur on his mother, suggesting his problems were her fault. Others, like Ying, had great difficulty accepting her dyslexia and even greater difficulty explaining it to her family. They attached great shame to having a learning problem, however well it was explained, and simply would not accept it, increasing Ying's sense of isolation.

Children who are diagnosed as dyslexic may find that their families consider this label a stigma, creating a rift between their family and their teachers. Veronica, who came to England from Angola at the age of 11, is distressed because her family is ashamed of her dyslexia. She herself found the diagnosis to be a welcome explanation for her unrelenting struggle to master literacy skills:

> At first they took it all right, but basically, were a bit shocked. Now they say that I'm not dyslexic. [They think] it could be because I didn't start school until late. That's what they think it is and I'll just develop, I'll progress. I just feel that is awful because I feel relieved that I know that I am dyslexic and I'm trying to help myself to get better and they're telling me that I'm not dyslexic. It's awful. They think I'm being given false ideas; I'm just being told something and I shouldn't believe it because I'm not dyslexic, they tell me. I actually brought them booklets explaining what it was and they've watched programmes but they think the psychologists are talking nonsense, basically. I feel happier being dyslexic instead of not knowing. I feel happy this way because I'm working at it.

It may be that Veronica's situation is aggravated by the fact that she is the only one in the family who appears to have any difficulties with learning. It is easy for her family to blame her persistent literacy problems on her poor educational background. It is natural for them to take into consideration the fact that she is an immigrant who had attended only one year of school prior to arriving in England. However, after eight years of schooling in England, during which time Veronica was a committed and hard-working student, her difficulties persist. Despite fluency in spoken English, Portuguese, French and her mother tongue, Lingala, she cannot read or write fluently in any language. Her diagnosis clarified for her why her struggle to attain literacy skills differed from the experiences of other immigrant children:

> I felt relieved [by my diagnosis] . . . that it was going to help me to find out why I was different, why I couldn't learn like everybody else. I felt different. Other students who came from different countries didn't seem to be struggling like me. I could speak English, but when it came to reading and writing, I just found it hard.

It is important to recognize the positive contribution of cultural backgrounds. Benjamin Zephaniah (1999), a dyslexic poet, believes the oral tradition of Caribbean and Islamic cultures not only helped him compensate for his reading and memory difficulties, but was an enormously positive factor in his creative development:

> When I was permanently excluded from school, I was called a failure. I was only 13 and illiterate, but I had memorized the Bible, The Philosophy and Opinions of Marcus Garvey, the teaching of Malcolm X and much of the Koran. I could recite hundreds of traditional Jamaican songs and poems (as well as my own) and could convince any policeman that my name was Robert Marley, a self-employed rude boy from Handsworth.
>
> Although I was unable to read, my exposure to the oral tradition seemed to expand my ability to memorize information.

Importance of support from others: 'someone to believe in me'

A common thread running through the experiences of many dyslexic adults is the significance of having someone who believed in their abilities. Once again, age of diagnosis, severity of difficulty and nature of any support received clearly influence the impact dyslexia has on the individual's self-esteem. The experiences of Rob, who was diagnosed as a child, illustrate the benefits of early diagnosis and a supportive family:

> I always had certain people believe in me. Always . . . all the friends and family, Mum, everybody . . . they were always there. Support makes you strong and 'cos I've got this learning disability, it makes me even more strong.

Although Rob finds it 'horrible' to be dyslexic, and has clearly struggled throughout his life as a result of his severe reading and writing difficulties, at the age of 21 he embarked on a successful career as a chef and sees his future in a positive light. He openly states that he would prefer not to be dyslexic, but he has clearly adapted well and chosen a path that offers him personal satisfaction.

Some adults are not as lucky as Rob, and never received the necessary encouragement and support to help them pursue a successful career. It is difficult to isolate the decisive factors that determine the path an individual pursues. Perhaps it is most realistic and reasonable to consider the synergistic influences of social class, educational opportunity, family situation and individual personality when assessing the impact of dyslexia on a person's life. However, it is significant to note that recent research (Alm and Andersson, 1995; Antonoff, 1995; Kirk and Reid, 2000; W. Morgan,1996) has identified a disproportionately high percentage of dyslexic adults and young people among the population of offenders. Studies from England, the USA and Sweden all suggest that between 30 and 52 per cent of the prison population in all three countries may be dyslexic, depending on how narrowly dyslexia is defined. These figures are a shocking contrast to the accepted estimates of the general population who are believed to be dyslexic (in England, four to ten per cent as reported by the British Dyslexia Association and in the USA, 15 per cent according to the International Dyslexia Association). They also raise the question of why such a large number of dyslexic individuals choose the socially unacceptable route of crime while others operate within expected social mores. The answers to this question may at least partially revolve around the 'someone to believe in me' factor.

Mark had a near miss with a spell in prison. He described how, growing up in a New Town in Britain in the 1970s, he was influenced by the 'tough, working-class male peer group' into which he was placed, largely due to his struggle to perform at school. As a result of his literacy difficulties in primary school, he was sent to a secondary modern school, where he was placed in the lowest stream, with students who were unmotivated and non-academic.

Despite his love of books and ideas, Mark needed to demonstrate his prowess to gain acceptance with his peers:

> I remember when I was about 14 or 15, I used to get beaten up quite a lot and it was almost run-of-the-mill sort of stuff that was accepted by a lot of people of my age. I remember going out for my first drink when I was about 15 and I was just walking out of the pub . . . and then I got attacked by a gang; they were quite a famous gang and I remember getting beaten up. Then I turned – that happened to me for about a year and a half and I remember I was with a peer group who started to get that bit older and bigger and I remember I suddenly lost it. Someone started on me, and I was a sensitive child; it was very unusual. I was hauled into this very tough culture which wasn't really me and I remember I just started fighting back.

Perhaps inevitably, Mark eventually got into trouble with the police:

> I ended up getting involved once in a big gang fight with guys from a neighbouring town where I was not doing anything, but I got arrested and charged with threatening behaviour and I was advised to plead guilty. They gave me a conditional discharge. It was very strange because I was totally aware of everything that was going on and I was being drawn into a culture I despised. I'd been drawn into a criminal culture here and I was starting to mix with people who . . . a lot of my peer group did end up in prison.

Mark attributes his behaviour during his teenage years to the frustration he experienced as a child due to his unacknowledged dyslexia:

> I found that I had a tremendous anger that I'd never expressed as a child, never in school. I always held it in . . . in my teenage years, I found that I was one of the most volatile, and I was openly acknowledged as one of the most volatile.

Mark's analysis of his behaviour highlights the influence of both social class and teacher expectations. His inability to perform at the expected academic standard resulted in being placed in the bottom stream at school, where he felt he never 'belonged'. Dyslexia-related problems had relegated him to this status. His negative behaviour appears to have been determined partly by his need to be accepted into the peer group and partly by his previously unacknowledged anger created by the frustration of not being taught according to his needs. His life could easily have taken him on a road to crime, but he was one of the lucky ones who escaped going to prison. Ultimately, at the age of 22, Mark met a tutor who identified the root problem for him. The diagnosis of dyslexia marked a change in the direction of his life.

Others were not so fortunate. Bob Turney (1997), former alcoholic and drug addict who received jail sentences totalling 18 years, ascribes his substance abuse and consequent criminal behaviour to the lack of support he received growing up in a dysfunctional family and to his undiagnosed dyslexia. He left school at the age of 15 virtually illiterate.

> If someone is told often enough that they are foolish or plain idle they will start to believe it – and that is what happened to me. I assumed that the things my parents said about my abilities were true. After all, there was nothing to say that they were wrong and even the teachers said that I was slow. My self-esteem plummeted until it was almost non-existent.

It was not until years later that his dyslexia was picked up by a teacher in prison. Bob's ultimate success (he attended university and became a probation officer) is certainly partly attributable to the eventual diagnosis of dyslexia and the insights that that afforded him. Tragically, many of those languishing in prison today have not had the benefit of such a diagnosis.

The Dyspel Pilot Project (Klein, 1998), which provided diagnosis and specialist tuition to dyslexic offenders in London, found that fewer than five per cent of those diagnosed during the project had had their dyslexia identified at school. Many were serious truants or left school as early as 11 or 12; others had been excluded or sent to special schools for behaviour problems – without their specific learning difficulties being addressed. Most told of very distressing memories of school including frequent public humiliation in front of their peers, and they described violent outbursts in response to frustration at not learning and being mocked, humiliated or called stupid. They had often given up any hope of being able to succeed at something they might want to do. Frequently, they were also intimidated by the thought of going back into education and none knew of the support available to them in further education. Several spoke of standing outside colleges, too frightened to go in, certain they would be told they were too stupid to get on a course.

The seeds of offending behaviour were often sown in childhood experiences. Nick described the background which led him into offending. His father beat him when reports from school said he was lazy and not trying to learn. To avoid beatings, he used bullying tactics to get the smartest boy in the class to do his homework. In class, whenever he was called on, he would make a scene, throwing furniture around and stomping out of the room to avoid being humiliated in front of his peers.

Nick realized quite early that his literacy problems would preclude him from getting a job that could earn him the kind of money he desired. As a consequence, he became involved in illegal activities. After his diagnosis as an adult, he wanted to impress upon the probation officers the importance of his discovery that he was dyslexic – this knowledge meant that he wasn't stupid. He said that he wished he had known earlier because his life might have been different. He might have gone to college and had other choices. Although he said he would like to 'go straight' now, he didn't know if he would be able to. He recently turned down a job offer because it involved handling money and he feared making a mistake with the money and being accused of stealing. In his words, 'There was no way I could take that job. I knew I would fail.'

There are other dyslexic adults whose behaviour may not result in involvement with the criminal justice system, but who nonetheless have responded to their frustrations with violent behaviour. Both lack of understanding at school and home and bullying by teachers and peers can lead to violent reactions. In response to her desperation, one woman, now employed as a tutor for other dyslexic adults, actually stabbed a teacher's hand with the sharp end of a compass because 'she called me stupid once too often'.

Helen, now a practising solicitor, ended up fighting at school with other children who picked on her and called her 'duncey' and 'stupid':

> But also I was very frustrated because I didn't know what was happening to me or why it was happening . . . I was just constantly told I was lazy and wasn't working hard enough, but I *knew* I was working hard enough.

Even at home, frustration can cause violent reactions. Michaela recalls her mother trying to help her learn to read:

> When I was young, she'd sit down and read with me and I would just scream and tear up the book and throw the book and just, like, punch her out of the way. Anything to do with reading or writing, I was really violent . . . I don't think she understood what dyslexia was. She tried to deny it, in fact. 'My

daughter's not stupid. She's not dyslexic.' Because they didn't understand what dyslexia was.

On the other hand, some people find that having someone who understands them may offer constructive options. Barbara recalls how her art teacher helped her avoid trouble:

> She was very good because she could see I had other skills and talents. So, where maybe I would have got into a fight, I didn't bother – I went to the art room. I could go there anytime I wanted to and create what I wanted to create.

McLoughlin et al. (1994) corroborate our view that age of diagnosis can impact significantly on individual self-esteem. Many dyslexic people 'have experienced problems with confidence and self-esteem because their difficulties were not identified until well into adulthood. The earlier the problems are identified the less likely it is that confidence and self-esteem will be affected and that other secondary symptoms will develop.' Reiff et al. (1997) found that early assessment, diagnosis and identification are the beginning of a road to self-actualization.

However, children who are identified as dyslexic but not given the appropriate learning intervention can still develop feelings of failure and low self-esteem. While the importance of parental support is recognized in the study by Reiff et al., it is not considered sufficient to 'ensure a childhood development unruffled by learning problems'. As Michael described:

> I had an edge on my fellow victims in the remedial class. My mother had brought me up to think that I was clever; rightly or wrongly I believed that . . . I could take part in most school activities like normal children. Only when reading and spelling reared their ugly heads would my self-confidence open up at the seams . . . This abrasiveness or protective armour I had in school would experience a meltdown whenever I needed to spell or read in public. I would always shamble through, feeling utterly humiliated at my weaknesses being shown up in public.

The 'not knowing' phenomenon takes its toll on the individual's perception of self. As Michael said:

> These shortcomings pointed to me being thick. I had not admitted this to myself and it caused a dislocation of my self-image.

Michaela was first diagnosed at age 15. Now, six years later, she reflects on her behavioural problems as a child:

> ... until I was 15, I had no idea why I was the 'problem child' – why I caused so much trouble. I thought I was just like everyone else's kids, so I thought maybe I was dumb, because that's what they [teachers] kept on thinking. So, I think if it had got recognized much earlier on, in primary school, my GCSE results would be much better. I would have done different things in my life; I would have been more confident in myself. I think maybe because it happened that way, not knowing that I had dyslexia until I was 15, it made me angry and made me have more determination to achieve in my life.

Impact of dyslexia on everyday life

Considerable emphasis is placed on the effect dyslexia has on literacy skills. In children, the most obvious manifestation of the difficulties is usually the delayed development of reading, spelling and writing. For many people, these problems persist into adulthood and can be the cause of great stress in their lives. Jean arrived in class in tears one day because she had lost her purse. It wasn't the loss of the purse or even the money in the purse that upset her, but the fact that she was unable to put a notice up to say that she'd lost the purse because she couldn't spell 'purple' and she couldn't spell 'purse'.

However, many adults, particularly those who have benefited from early diagnosis and appropriate teaching, have overcome their weaknesses in literacy. They may remain slow readers and have residual spelling problems, but nonetheless have reached a stage where these difficulties no longer impede their ability to conduct their daily lives. This is not to say that they are no longer dyslexic. 'Their dyslexia has not disappeared: they have not "grown out of it" but have overcome many of the more obvious symptoms' (McLoughlin et al., 1994).

It is often the other aspects of dyslexia that intrude into everyday life. Even those adults who have only minor dyslexic difficulties report that their dyslexia affects their daily life, particularly in placing them under extra stress through the enormous effort and control needed to perform ordinary tasks, from reading a page to taking in what people are saying. Jenny describes the extra effort she must put into simple things:

I find everything really difficult – really, really tiring – the stress of trying to keep your feet straight so you don't fall over, the stress of trying to remember to open a door so I know I've got to open the door to walk through it and I don't walk straight into the door. In my own head, I'm on the other side of the door, so why am I opening it? . . . In my own mind I've done it . . . Also, I really do have difficulties with the alphabet. Even today I was trying to find the time of trains to come here and I couldn't find them on the board.

When I'm with someone, I really have to make a point of looking at them because all the other noises are interrupting me all the time. So I find that difficult. I have to be very focused.

I find when I'm really stressed everything goes – my co-ordination, can't think – I have no coping strategies.

Some years ago she had a breakdown and described how her dyslexia 'took over':

I felt – it seemed as if my dyslexia was exaggerated. My co-ordination, my balance – everything was extreme. I've always had difficulties with my coordination, but it seemed very extreme . . . My speech was badly affected and I couldn't remember things. I had no strategies left to retrieve information. I didn't have any coping strategies left – I had nothing.

It wasn't until I was better that I actually thought about the way I was – and it seemed to me the way I am now is the way I was then, but very, very exaggerated. And that was quite frightening. It was as if my dyslexia was all of me, had taken on the whole of me. It wasn't just dyslexia affecting bits.

Dyslexic people may also find that the reactions to past experiences recur when faced with stress-producing situations. Jenny recalls an experience that reawakened her childhood memories. Despite her general confidence in telling colleagues about her dyslexia, she reports the following episode:

It was when I was Head of School and the director called us into a meeting and we were given lots of papers and we were told to put them in alphabetical order. I couldn't do it because I couldn't get past 'A'. And I couldn't understand where they all came. And I panicked and I just wanted to leave the meeting because I felt I had just been appointed to be Head of School and they were all new and some of the people didn't know me and perhaps some of them didn't know I was dyslexic. Some people didn't think I should have got the job because I didn't have the academic qualifications. It was sheer panic and I actually said to the person next to me, 'I'm just going to leave,' and she put them in order for me – she knew I was dyslexic. Otherwise, I would have left the room.

It's okay if I've told people I'm dyslexic but it's not okay if they find out things about me and they don't know I'm dyslexic . . . But a simple thing like knowing the alphabet and the more you can't see it, the more you think they're going to think you're stupid and I suppose that's the fear in that meeting – that people would perceive me as stupid because I couldn't organize the papers. And I can't face that fear again.

There is substantial evidence (Hales, 1995; McLoughlin et al., 1994; Miles, 1993; Saunders, 1995) that dyslexic difficulties are exacerbated by stress. The status of adulthood incorporates multi-faceted roles, each involving a multitude of responsibilities, the demands of which tend to increase stress for the dyslexic person.

Success in juggling several roles requires good time management skills and the ability to prioritize and break down required tasks to manageable constituent parts. These are the very skills that dyslexic people find problematic because they place an unrealistic load on short-term memory. In addition, there are also language processing, directional, sequencing and organizational problems. There may also be a poor sense of time, orientation and motor co-ordination difficulties, aspects that are often neglected when considering the ongoing nature of dyslexia-related problems, even among compensated adults.

A day in the life . . .

Consider the following scenario:

Elizabeth has a demanding job as a graphic artist for an advertising firm. She is married with two children, aged 6 and 8. Her husband's work involves a great deal of travel, leaving Elizabeth largely responsible for managing household affairs, including paying bills, organizing social activities, making holiday arrangements and overseeing the children's needs.

A typical day for Elizabeth involves getting up at 6.30 a.m., preparing packed lunches for the children, cooking breakfast and getting the children ready for school. When her husband is home, he takes the children to school, leaving Elizabeth some freedom to get ready for work. She leaves the house at 8.15 and drives to work. Her job finishes at 4.30, allowing her enough time to collect the children from the after-school activities that she has arranged. She then returns home to cook the evening meal, help the children with their schoolwork, tidy the house and do the laundry. Elizabeth and her husband are jazz buffs and try to attend concerts at least once a month. Elizabeth purchases the tickets and arranges babysitters. She also assumes primary responsibility for stocking the house with food and household supplies. She organizes doctor and dentist appointments for the children as well as planning their social life and after-school activities. Although her husband helps with many of these tasks, his variable work schedule results in most of the responsibility being placed on Elizabeth.

In many ways, the above description is typical of large numbers of women who manage family responsibilities and full-time jobs. Most of the activities highlighted in Elizabeth's day may be taken for granted by people whose lives are similarly demanding. However, Elizabeth is dyslexic and therefore the need for multi-tasking places a heavy load on her in situations where she needs to retain a lot of details, to organize and manage time, to process auditory information and engage in rapid responses to written material. Remembering everything she has to do takes its toll on Elizabeth; although she keeps a diary and makes lists, she finds it hard to 'hold' in her mind the sequence of things she may need to do after work. The resulting increase in stress levels affects her efficiency as well as her confidence and sense of well-being. In a typical day, she might experience difficulty with any of the following activities:

- **Collecting the children from a friend's home**

Elizabeth has a poor sense of direction and finds it difficult to interpret a map. She relies on writing down the directions, but it is difficult for her to read what she has written while she is driving. She sometimes miscopies the information or misspells the street names. She also sometimes misreads street signs because of the difficulty of concentrating on reading while driving. Passing the driving test was a major accomplishment; she had to take the test three times because she constantly confused left and right and therefore had difficulty following the examiner's instructions. She passed only by using her wedding ring to distinguish right from left. She also found it necessary to take many more lessons than her friends because her difficulties with motor integration result in poor hand-eye co-ordination. This made it challenging to master driving a car with a manual gearbox, which requires the ability to co-ordinate several different actions.

- **Household management**

There are many aspects of running a smooth household that Elizabeth finds daunting. She tends to be poorly organized and often forgets items that should be included on the weekly shopping list. She has tried writing lists, but misplaces the list and winds up beginning a new one, omitting items that were on the original. Even if she remembers the list, she often misses one or two items that she doesn't 'see'. Elizabeth is very slow at reading and finds instructions in user manuals confusing. She relies on her 8-year-old daughter to set the video.

Elizabeth has always found mental arithmetic difficult; she cannot hold information in her head long enough to manipulate the figures. Consequently, she never checks her change and has a drawer full of small change because she always pays in notes. She often makes mistakes when writing cheques, so puts everything on her credit card if possible, in order to have only one cheque a month to write.

There is a plethora of paperwork that characterizes contemporary life. Elizabeth feels inundated by the piles of bills and forms requiring written responses. As an equal breadwinner in the family, she resents leaving all financial management issues to her husband, but when she tries to get involved, she becomes increasingly anxious.

Even simple daily activities regularly create difficulties for Elizabeth. Sometimes she gets confused by language. For example, today she is buying some pens that her daughter wants; she knows she wants the kind that are not permanent, but she can't remember whether those are 'water-soluble' or 'water-proof' and ends up getting the wrong ones as she is too embarrassed to ask the salesperson.

Elizabeth likes to cook, but it is a family joke that some of her dishes are inedible due to her missing out an ingredient or putting in a tablespoon of chilli powder instead of a teaspoon because she misreads the recipe.

Her difficulties also impinge on her social life. Even though she keeps a diary, she still sometimes double-books events. She gets flustered when she needs to take information down from the telephone because she frequently miscopies telephone numbers or misinterprets dates and times, resulting in her being late or even turning up on the wrong day. This can cause others to be inconvenienced, which affects her social relationships. She also has trouble remembering names and, sometimes, what people have just said, creating anxiety and acute embarrassment. She tries to make a joke of it, to let herself 'off the hook', but is aware that this is not always successful.

• **Parenting responsibilities**

Elizabeth places great importance on her role as a mother. However, she finds that the myriad responsibilities involved in looking after young children cause her considerable strain. Her poor judgement about how long it will take to get to places means she is often late and she worries that she appears negligent if she misses an appointment with the dentist or arrives late for her daughter's music lesson. When her husband is home, he will often accompany her on a 'trial run' to a new place so she is less likely to get lost. Sometimes she has been reduced to tears, trying to get to somewhere she has never been before. Frequently, she will take a taxi, although it is expensive, to ensure she arrives on time. Today, she is collecting her daughter at a friend's house but, although she has been there several times before, she is still worried about getting lost. She is also anxious that she will forget the name of the friend's mother. She has already had one disaster today: as the result of misreading a letter from the school, she failed to send in money on schedule for her child's school trip; her daughter felt embarrassed and Elizabeth was put in the uncomfortable position of trying to explain her apparent lack of responsibility.

Although Elizabeth feels confident that her reading, albeit slow, is appropriate for her own needs, she is still embarrassed when she has to read aloud. The school expects her to do paired reading with her 6-year-old son, who is a beginner reader. Elizabeth finds this stressful as she occasionally stumbles even on simple words and she does not want her children to witness this weakness. She also feels frustrated and inadequate when her daughter needs her to check her homework as she often can't identify errors.

By the end of the day, Elizabeth feels exhausted by the extra effort she has had to put into everything and by all the mistakes and mishaps she has had to rectify. Although her husband is supportive, he occasionally gets impatient with her mistakes. While grateful for his support, the fact that she needs so much of it sometimes undermines her confidence.

Dealing with dyslexia in daily life

There are countless examples of how dyslexia affects the day-to-day life of adults. For instance, many dyslexic adults who had difficulties learning to tell the time as children may continue to have problems reading an analogue clock. The digital watch was a major benefit for them. However, the 24-hour clock still mystifies many dyslexic people because of the mental arithmetic involved in 'translating' the time. Gary, a young architecture student, was very excited about his planned trip to visit his father in Nepal for Christmas. He was determined to arrive at the airport with enough spare time to purchase some duty-free gifts. Gary was extremely proud of himself for managing to organize his activities to get to the airport two and a half hours prior to departure. Unfortunately, he had miscalculated the departure time of the plane; 20.00 hours was not 10.00 p.m. as he had thought. Therefore, when he arrived at 7.30 p.m. he was shattered to be told that he was too late to check in. Not only did he miss the flight, but he also had to forfeit the ticket, which was not exchangeable. His costly error left him devastated.

Difficulties reading instructions can be more than an inconvenience. David, a theatre arts student, wanted to dye his hair black for a leading role in the drama society play. Lacking confidence in his ability to read the instructions on the bottle, he relied on the sales assistant to recommend a product and give oral advice on how to use it. The result was that he purchased a permanent dye rather than a temporary hair colour. David blamed the sales assistant for the fact that he had to spend considerable effort trying to bleach his newly acquired jet-black hair and eyebrows to restore his normal colour. It was not clear whether his disastrous results were attributable to his incorrect processing or his poor recall of the information he received, but had he been more comfortable with reading the manufacturer's information, he would most likely have avoided this predicament.

Patrick finds his difficulty in reading maps a source of great frustration:

> I can drive a car, but can I read a map? I cannot read a city of London map; I just cannot do it. I've got a company car, but I do not use the car in central London. I know my main roads; I will not venture off. I cannot get around London. It's a handicap.

Steve found that by officially registering as disabled, he was able to get a special sign to put in his car permitting him to park in areas designated for people with disabilities. When his tutor queried this, suggesting that perhaps it might be stretching the entitlements of his disability, he explained that he was unable to remember where his car was parked unless it was immediately outside the door!

Linda is so conscious of her problems in finding her way around the underground system, that she often organizes a practice run of a planned journey. However, even this strategy does not always solve the problem:

> I spent days getting ready for a really important conference. I knew where I was going and then I got off at the wrong station because there was one small difference in the name and I misread it. It totally threw me; I didn't know how to get back. I was so convinced I was at my destination. I felt so stupid.

Mark's difficulties with numbers resulted in his need to disguise his prowess at darts:

> I was about 15 or 16 when I first started going to pubs; darts and table tennis were the standard things that people would get into. I used to enjoy darts, but it was quite humiliating playing 301 because of the mental arithmetic involved. I used to always try to get people to play what they would consider very puerile games which is like 'going round the clock', you know, the darts game on doubles. I used to always think of tactful ways, especially in mixed company, where girls were involved, of not playing darts. I actually stopped playing darts because it was so embarrassing to reveal my poor mental arithmetic.

Ben described how his marriage came under threat when he agreed to join his wife in ballroom dancing classes. She was furious and he was mortified every time he misconstrued an instruction to put his left or right foot forward and wound up stepping on her toes. Her intolerance was somewhat ameliorated after his diagnosis of dyslexia, when he was at least able to explain that there was a reason for his lack of success as a dancer.

Jean describes how dyslexia has impinged on her life as an actress:

> I am always going stage left instead of stage right . . . And sometimes I can't control my mouth . . . The wrong word comes out . . . Or you know, I can't read a word and it comes out completely different.

Janet's difficulties with interpreting language affect her confidence socially:

> Social situations can be really difficult. I tend to take things that people say literally, but I know that sometimes I get it wrong. But I'm never sure how to take things so I often feel uncomfortable in social situations.

Many dyslexic people defer to shopkeepers because they cannot work out how much change they should receive. Mark adopted a conscious strategy to try to address this hazard:

> I have my own techniques. I still can't work it out, but I've got rough ideas of getting the right change. If someone's fiddling me, I really wouldn't know, but I give them a studied look and sometimes I say, even if I'm not sure, 'Is that right? Could you please check it?' It's like a game of double bluff.

To illustrate the frustration caused by his dyslexia, one adult related the following anecdote to Gates (1996). Having dropped out of school due to his reading problems, Harry joined the Navy where some fellow black colleagues introduced him to the work of W.E.B. Du Bois. He struggled to decipher the words on the page, but his motivation was great and he persevered:

> I discovered that at the end of some sentences there was a number, and if you looked at the foot of the page the reference was to what it was all about – what source Du Bois gleaned this information from. So when I was on leave . . . I went to a library with a long list of books. The librarian said, 'That's too many, young man. You're going to have to cut it down.' I said, 'I can make it very easy. Just give me everything you got by Ibid.' She said, 'There's no such writer.' I called her a racist. I said, 'Are you trying to keep me in darkness?' And I walked out of there angry.

Despite his eventual success, Harry Belafonte still bears the scars from his earlier experiences. His story is but one of many where the denial of access to print results in misconceptions and anger.

Newly diagnosed adults often experience relief when they realize that dyslexia can impact on areas of their lives other than school and college. It can be reassuring to understand that their difficulties with numbers, direction, time and organization may be connected to their dyslexic profile. The act of making this connection may mark the beginning of a conscious effort to develop strategies to address the problems.

Many adults have, either consciously or unconsciously, evolved helpful coping strategies that enable them to overcome many of their difficulties. Many dyslexic people learn to use their charm and good verbal skills to 'talk their way out of trouble'. Rob feels he has tapped into his dyslexic strengths to enhance his social status with women:

> I think I'm quite a good flirt and I think that comes through being dyslexic as well, for some silly reason. Because you can't write letters and things like that so

you need to make it special when they actually see you. Really, you have to make up that little bit that they're going to miss out because you're not going to write letters or if you do, they'll be small letters, nothing special.

Some people use humour to soften the effects of forgetting to perform a promised task. Many dyslexic adults assumed the role of the 'class clown' at school as a way of making people laugh to distract attention from their struggle with reading and writing. Adults may continue to use humour as a way to deal with the embarrassment caused by mispronouncing words or making a glaring spelling mistake. However, there is generally a limit to how far charm and humour can be used; it is more effective and results in less anxiety to use existing strengths to develop strategies for dealing with the difficulties.

Technology can play a part in helping the dyslexic adult manage time more efficiently. It is a curious fact that many poor time-managers fail to wear a watch, which may explain their poor sense of time. However, the decision not to wear a watch might be the response to problems in telling the time. It may be that the person never had a watch or never got into the habit of wearing a watch as a result of the childhood delay in learning how to tell the time. This was the case for Peter, who was habitually late for all appointments. When queried about how he managed his time, he replied that he relied on his partner to get him up and out of the house in time to meet his commitments. At the age of 38 he had still not taken responsibility for his own timekeeping! His coping strategy was to find a partner who was willing to assume this role for him, but it was not always successful. His partner might have been more helpful if she had given him a watch and encouraged him to assume responsibility for himself.

Other poor timekeepers may simply have difficulty conceptualizing time and are therefore unable to estimate how much time to allow. The supervisor of a trainee social worker was incredulous to find Marion sitting at her desk ten minutes before she was scheduled to meet a client on the other side of the city, easily a 30-minute train journey. Assuming that Marion had forgotten about her appointment, her supervisor angrily reminded her. The supervisor was amazed to discover that Marion was fully aware of the appointment; she simply had no idea how much time she needed to allow for travelling.

A dyslexic probation officer explained his poor sense of time:

> I know I have to leave at 8.30 to be at work on time, and from 7 a.m. when I get up to 8.30 there is 'enough' time. I have no concept of 'how much' time there is left.

Some adults find electronic personal organizers the solution to their time management problems; the added facility of having an auditory 'beep' as a reminder of important appointments can solve many problems. However, the electronic solution works only for those who remember to enter all their engagements and to check the organizer each day. For less technologically minded people, the paper diary can be the answer. Once again, it is necessary to develop the habit of regular checking, since a written entry will be helpful only if it is read. Diaries or Filofaxes are essential for most busy people; for the dyslexic person, they may be even more crucial. However, they carry the inherent danger of being lost or forgotten. Moreover, the total reliance on the entered data may create its own problems. Sometimes encouraging a duplicate entry system may overcome this risk, although this has obvious disadvantages. Tutors working with dyslexic offenders on the Dyspel Project find that many of their clients are unable to use a diary as they do not understand the 'conventions' of a diary. When shown how to use a diary that displays a full week over two pages, they can 'see' the week as a whole, which results in noticeable improvements in keeping appointments on the right day and time.

Frequently, dyslexic people overcompensate for organizational difficulties. For example, Jackie describes how colour helps her as an organizing tool and aide-mémoire:

> I am an organized person, because if I don't organize things, it will become a mess. So I organize everything. When I was on my access course, they used to laugh at me because I had subject dividers and I used to colour code everything. So, if I had a subject with a certain colour, say yellow, if I wanted to highlight something, I'd use a yellow pen. And they used to laugh at me because of my colour coding. But I said, look, at the end of the day, I'm organized, so I know what I'm doing, I know what goes where and what goes with what. I'm like that

at home as well. Everything's got a place and it stays in its place. If I take it out of its place, once I'm through with it, it goes back in its place because I can't stand untidiness. It's just the way I am.

Many of the strategies described are used by non-dyslexic people, who view them as a normal modus operandi and don't consider them unusual. However, unlike their dyslexic peers, the self-esteem of non-dyslexic adults is not at stake in performing simple, everyday tasks. The dyslexic adult always risks embarrassment if dyslexia-related problems 'get in the way'. Many successful dyslexic adults have told us, for instance, how they continue to hide their writing from others' eyes.

The problems with self-esteem and behaviour and the struggles dyslexic people undergo in their daily lives are largely in response to the expectations of the non-dyslexic world. Jenny sums up:

I just want people to remember that we're human and we have feelings and that we're not stupid and to give us an opportunity to show what we're capable of, perhaps in an unconventional way, in the way that best suits us.

Chapter 4
Dyslexia in the family

Inheritance factors

Recent research has confirmed the long-held belief that dyslexia runs in families. Many dyslexic adults can easily point to other family members, either in the immediate nuclear family, or the extended family, who share problems similar to their own. Adults with whom we have worked have often commented on their ability to spot dyslexia in other people, including members of their families. Graham described how his own diagnosis shed light on his mother's difficulties:

> When I got diagnosed at 30, I phoned my mother because I know my mother's dyslexic, I can spot it, even though, obviously, she's never had it diagnosed. And she said, 'Well, we all know that, don't we?' Even though it was one of those hidden taboo subjects that the family never spoke about. I spoke to her about [my diagnosis] and she told me that she had lots of the same problems at school. Her father basically bullied her because she couldn't spell; she couldn't write very well.

In some cases, several siblings in the same family may be affected, with the degree of severity varying from mild difficulties to quite severe problems. Although dyslexia is not an illness, and there is no 'cure', the scientific evidence pointing to a genetic causality may have major implications for the future. A recent study in Norway (Fagerheim et al., 1999) examined 36 members of an 80-member family and established the existence of a 'dyslexia gene' located on chromosome 2. The authors suggest that 'a molecular test . . . for dyslexia . . . would allow earlier diagnosis of children at high risk for dyslexia. This in turn would permit institution of therapy while the language areas were at an earlier, more plastic stage of development.' The genetic links established by this research suggest that it may in future be possible to develop a totally objective way to identify dyslexia. This would help to overcome the considerable controversies that exist in relation to the criteria for a diagnosis of dyslexia.

Familial incidence is frequently mentioned when adults are asked about other family members with similar patterns of difficulty. The lack of awareness and understanding about dyslexia, coupled with the non-academic nature of qualifications required for many vocational jobs, may explain why these problems rarely came to light in the past. However, people who are diagnosed in adulthood are usually more likely to pick up the signs in their own children or other extended family members. This can have a significant impact on helping the next generation gain access to resources and support. Sometimes it is through the diagnosis of a child that the adult learns about his own dyslexia. Paul, for example, followed his father into the plumbing and building trade and developed a highly successful business. However, when his son was diagnosed, Paul recognized many of his own problems and went for an assessment himself. He now realizes that his father was also dyslexic.

There are, of course, cases in which the familial links are not obvious. In these instances, there may be a recessive gene or it may just be that the individual's knowledge of the extended family tree is limited. However, being the 'only one' can result in lack of understanding and a tendency to substitute other labels to explain the problems. Jackie expressed her bitterness about being the only one in her family who seemed to have dyslexic difficulties:

> They say it's inherited, but no one in my family has got it. Everyone in my family is, like intelligent . . . I was classed as unintelligent; my father was intelligent; he did O levels, my brother did O levels, my uncle went to grammar school. My brother was told that if they were still doing the 11+, he'd be doing it, so everyone in my family was intelligent. I've got no cousins. That was just it, where did it come from? But my mum said it had to start somewhere and obviously, it started with me.

Impact of dyslexia on family life

For many dyslexic adults, the demands and responsibilities of family life are enormously taxing. Some adults who have gone through life without knowing the cause of their difficulties have nonetheless developed effective coping strategies and may have managed to hide their literacy-based problems from their partners. Clever ploys are often devised to get their partners to complete forms, write cheques and deal with 'official' matters. However, parenthood frequently becomes a catalyst for unveiling difficulties, when the embarrassment of not being able to respond to children, either through reading aloud to them, or helping them with school work forces the adult to acknowledge his or her own problems. This exposure often serves to motivate adults to return to education to address the weak skills that they can no longer easily conceal.

Reiff et al. (1997) found that one of the factors influencing success of the dyslexic adults in their study was getting support. This is confirmed in our experience by successful dyslexic adults who often have a partner, parent or friend who will check spelling, read and answer letters and even help with time management.

When an adult has been successful in hiding his or her problems, the partner's response when weaknesses are revealed can be a major test of love and loyalty. Louise's partner began to suspect a problem when she repeatedly made excuses for not having time to read newspaper articles that he wanted to discuss. She would rely on her strong auditory skills to gain information through listening to the radio and television in order to contribute to discussions about current affairs. However, when her husband asked her to read a specific article, she was unable to bluff her way out of it, and admitted to him that she was barely literate. He encouraged her to attend adult literacy classes and helped at home by labelling items in the house, reinforcing her learning from classes and generally encouraging her to persevere. Louise was highly motivated because she had two children and was struggling to help them develop their own reading skills. The need to stay 'one step ahead' of her children coupled with the positive reinforcement of a supportive husband formed the basis of a new start in education, ultimately resulting in a university degree.

Sometimes it may be through watching children develop that adults begin to identify problems that they experienced during childhood. Often the projection of their own experience acts as an incentive for parents to seek assessment and appropriate intervention for both parent and child. The poignant experience of reliving one's childhood struggles through the battles of one's child may crystallize the need for assessment and clarification of the problem. Many adults whose own dyslexia was not diagnosed until adulthood are determined that their children should have a different experience from their own. As one woman put it:

> When I saw Len struggling with his spelling and having trouble learning his times tables, I knew that I didn't want him to go through the same school nightmare that I had. I badgered the teacher until the school finally got him diagnosed. I realized then that he was just like me.

An intergenerational study

Isobel, at 28, is in the final year of training to be a primary school teacher. She is married with two children, Lee, aged 10, and Jake, aged 7. Isobel and her younger sister Bridget were raised in London. Her parents came to England from Ireland and the family regard themselves as a close-knit, working-class family. Isobel and Bridget were raised on a housing estate in London and both attended Catholic schools. Isobel will be the first member of her family to gain a university degree.

Interviews were conducted with Isobel, Lee and Isobel's mother, Catherine, to explore the similarities and differences between the childhood experiences of Isobel as an undiagnosed dyslexic child and those of her son, who was diagnosed at the age of 6. Catherine provided the perspective of both mother and grandmother whose views evolved through her emerging understanding of dyslexia.

Both Isobel and her mother shared the experience of early motherhood; each gave birth to her first child at the age of 17 and to her second child three years later. In both families, the first child is dyslexic and the second child is not; a major difference is that Catherine herself is not dyslexic.

Lee: I'm only dyslexic at school

Insights into what dyslexia is and how it affects both personal and academic life influence both the individual's self-image and self-esteem. Lee exuded self-confidence and a positive self-image when he talked about his many strengths and his future ambitions. His view of dyslexia is largely confined to his academic problems, but he also sees some positive advantages to being dyslexic. When asked about his understanding of dyslexia, Lee replied:

Well, it just means that I'm slow at writing and not so fast at reading. I still can read and write, but it just takes me longer than you . . . dyslexia – that's just like saying that you're English or you're something like that.

He went on to say:

Really, I like being dyslexic. It makes me feel that I'm special in a way that nobody else is.

Lee was quick to offer a list of things that he considers himself to be 'really good at', with football heading the list, but including tennis, swimming, basketball and acting. He sees himself as a good talker and as having additional talents in working with animals and babies. He also feels he excels at outdoor activities, such as camping. Throughout his discussions, he minimized the significance of being slow at reading and writing and stressed the importance of having good social skills:

Sometimes, with dyslexia, you are good with reading and writing, but you're not good at catching balls, and I'm just glad that it's reading and writing for me, because I know that I can get over that. I'm glad I play football, because at the end of the day, I'm going to play football [with my friends]; I'm not going over to read and write, am I? If I can't play that, I wouldn't be much use, so I'm just glad that, really, it's only in school that you notice it, but you don't really notice it that much.

Lee is overwhelmingly positive about his school experience and feels the help he receives makes a big difference. He openly states that he likes school and is pleased with the individual and small group help that he receives from a Special Needs teacher. Lee expresses no concerns about being withdrawn from the mainstream class; indeed, he appreciates the fact that:

. . . they don't make it too noticeable that I'm always going out of the class and they don't make me do anything different. It's actually the same, but you're out of the class just doing the same thing, really.

His teachers have instilled in him a sense of confidence in his abilities and he appears to have a realistic assessment of the extent of his difficulties. Several of his comments attest to the fact that he has internalized the high expectations the teachers have of him. He mentioned a retired teacher who continues to come into school to work with him;

her openly expressed belief in Lee's ability has clearly had a positive influence on his self-perception. When asked whether he considered himself to be intelligent, he commented:

> Yeah, Miss H. said I was. She said, 'That's why I'm going through all this, just because I know you are and I know you can do it.'

And, in response to the question, 'What do you think being intelligent means?', Lee stated:

> . . . say, if you never played football in your life, and then you became the best footballer in the world, I think that's a bit like me. Like I'm not good at reading and writing, but when I came to my new school, I really became quite good at it. Like, now I love writing stories. I write really long stories.

Lee appeared to have mixed feelings about the fact that he is dyslexic and his brother, Jake, isn't:

> It really kind of gets on my nerves because he's really good at maths and . . . I was never that good at maths, but I just think, some things that I'm good at, he isn't. I think that when you're dyslexic, you've got other things that other people haven't got.

His contradictory feelings about Jake not being dyslexic were also apparent:

> I'm glad that he isn't dyslexic, but I'm not that upset that I am dyslexic either.

Although there was evidence of some expected degree of sibling rivalry, Lee's overall views of Jake were exceptionally positive:

> . . . he's one of the cleverest people in his class. I think he is *the* cleverest and I thought, cor, I had to have a brother who's the cleverest person in the class, didn't I . . . he's got a good imagination. He loves football as well, and I like training him. And when we play the computer games – I've noticed that nobody else in his class can play the computer, so I'm just glad that he can play computer games; it gives me a challenge. 'Cos other people in his class, I couldn't have them as my brother. They just are so annoying and stuff like that. But he's nice; yeah, I like him.

Lee's views of the differences between his experience of dyslexia and that of his mother indicate his general insightfulness and understanding of the issues:

This is a hard question. You know your mum is dyslexic and I'm sure she told you that when she was your age, she didn't know, right? How do you think your life is different from hers in terms of dyslexia?

Well everybody thought she was just thick. Nobody ever . . . they just thought that she was dumb, she couldn't do anything. But my mum just like, done it. Nobody really listened to her, because they thought, oh, you can't do anything, but she just found it really hard, but she kept on going. She said that I'm really lucky that people know that I've got dyslexia and I'm getting extra help; she got none of that.

Do you think you're lucky?
Yeah.

Isobel: the child and the mother

Many of the positive views expressed by Lee can be directly attributed to Isobel's efforts to ensure that his experiences are different from her own. A major contrast is the fact that Lee was diagnosed at such a young age, and this has obviously influenced his understanding of his struggles. Moreover, the early identification has enabled Isobel to advocate for special help for Lee at school. Her own insights into dyslexia combined with her current training in teaching have made it possible for her to be a positive role model and to encourage Lee's understanding of his individual strengths and weaknesses.

In contrast to Lee, Isobel's experiences at school were marked by frustration created by a lack of understanding of the cause of her difficulties, by herself, her parents and her teachers. When she left school, she joined a Youth Training Scheme where she was placed in an architect's office to work in a clerical job. After Isobel made a terrible mess of the filing system, the architect showed some concern and ascertained that she was also having difficulties with reading. He was the father of a dyslexic child and, as such, recognized the symptoms; it was he who first suggested that Isobel might be dyslexic. This was the first time she had heard the term, but no further investigation was made at that time because Isobel became pregnant and left the job.

Isobel's first child was born when she was 17; she and her husband became publicans when she was 18 and she helped serve at the bar. At 19, when she was pregnant with her second son, she began an A level course in sociology. She comments about her determination to continue with her education:

> . . . it really surprises me because my educational experience would detract and deter anybody from going back into education, but there was something else that told me I wasn't stupid. Something . . . it was like an inner voice that would say to me, 'You're not stupid'.

Unfortunately, her lack of academic skills caused her to drop the course because she 'couldn't cope with failing again'. However, she went on to do a PPA Diploma in childcare and an RSA Diploma in counselling.

> . . . all of these things had no emphasis on spelling or grammar – it was on understanding; they were practical certificates – so I could succeed in them and that was going to give me an appetite, a bigger appetite.

She moved on to take a GCSE in maths and English and, at the age of 24, began an access to university course at a college of further education. It was during this course that Isobel was formally diagnosed. The psychologist suggested that she should think seriously about her decision to pursue the teacher-training course she had chosen. In view of this, it is not surprising that Isobel's reaction to her diagnosis was mixed:

> . . . for me it was the best label I could have had because all of a sudden, people had to recognize that I wasn't thick, I wasn't stupid, that I had a specific difficulty. But, on the other hand, she had taken it away from me, by undermining my ability . . . my self-esteem was extremely low.

However, after a few weeks, Isobel's determination returned:

> Again, this inner strength came to me and I said, no, why should I let them put me off doing what I'd set out to do.

Isobel successfully completed the access course and gained a place on a three-year teacher-training course, which she is currently completing. While on the access course, she received two hours per week of specialist learning support. This provided her with significant insights into her learning strengths, thus enabling her to develop strategies to overcome her areas of weakness.

In describing her childhood and young adulthood, Isobel distinguishes between her self-esteem in academic and social spheres. Like her son, she sees herself as having had strong social skills as a child:

I think as I grew up on a [local housing authority] estate and we were all very assertive young people – we had to be – we went to inner city schools, we went to school in King's Cross [a deprived area of inner London], we used to walk past prostitutes, and we had to be very streetwise. I think that I compensated in many ways – I could skip and ride a bike because we were out on the estate from morning to night, so I had these other skills that I had learnt through being on an estate, from where I lived and they helped me in school. Whereas other children had the mickey taken out of them, say for not being able to skip, not being able to catch a ball, not being able to do certain things, I could do those things and it put less emphasis then on my academic ability because I was in with the 'in' crowd.

In contrast to Lee, her lack of academic success impacted greatly on her self-esteem. The failure to understand why she struggled at school and the absence of any positive reinforcement for her attempts at producing schoolwork left Isobel feeling deflated and angry:

. . . in secondary school . . . I started to misbehave. When it came to academic ability, my self-esteem was on the floor.

Isobel's school reports reflect the disparity between her social confidence and her academic achievement. The following extracts illustrate the progressive nature of teachers' changing perceptions of this [unacknowledged] dyslexic child:

Marks on a Scale of Abilities from A to G:
A – Excellent
B – Above Average
C – Good Average
D – Average
E – Poor Average
F – Below Average
G – Poor

(N.B. marks are indicated only when they appeared on reports – Year 2 and 3 reports did not contain marks.)

Year 1: (July 1977 – age 5 years, 8 months)
Language: Reading and Written Expression: E – Isobel is very confident when talking with her peers and adults and always has plenty to say. However, she holds very little interest for reading and writing . . . she can do it if she tries.
Mathematics: E – Once again, Isobel holds very little interest in the subject. She tends to still get some of her numbers back to front . . . She is very lazy in all her 3R work.

Year 2 (July 1978 – age 6 years, 8 months)
Language: Isobel has made slow but sure progress with her reading. She does however need much help and encouragement because she lacks confidence in her own ability.
Mathematics: . . . more effort could be made.
General Abilities: Isobel lacks confidence in her abilities. This is a pity because she has an industrious nature . . . she has a tendency to lose her temper and to become very stubborn . . .

Year 3 (July 1979 – age 7 years, 8 months)
Language: Isobel's reading is still not up to standard. She has a poor visual memory finding words difficult to remember and she is still writing some letters and figures back-to-front. Her handwriting is mostly untidy and not yet well formed.
Mathematics: . . . Her number work is a lot better than her other work.

Year 4 (July 1980 – age 8 years, 8 months)
Reading Age: 7.09; Reading exp. Age: 6.03
Language:
  Reading: (E) Isobel is progressing steadily. She is fairly fluent and will attempt words she's not sure of. She doesn't always understand too well what she has read.
  Written Expression: (E) She tries hard but has difficulty with sentence construction and her spelling and punctuation are poor. Her handwriting tends to be untidy and she is still reversing 'd's and 'b's.
Mathematics: (D) Isobel is making satisfactory progress . . . she reverses some of her figures.
General: Isobel enjoys PE and games. In dance lessons, she is well co-ordinated and inventive in her movements. Isobel is a sensible and reliable pupil. Her behaviour in the classroom is very good.

The comments from her teachers in Year 3 and Year 4 strongly suggest a child who should have been investigated for a specific learning difficulty. These reports contain salient pointers to dyslexia, including observations about weak visual memory, poor reading, spelling, sentence construction, reversal of 'b's and 'd's and poor handwriting. Yet no assessment was undertaken; Isobel had to wait 16 years before receiving an explanation for her difficulties.

In reflecting on the differences between primary and secondary school, Isobel recalls that her behaviour went from being 'helpful and well-mannered' (as described in her Year 2 and Year 3 reports) to being disruptive and difficult. She explains the change by referring to the higher expectations that were held in secondary school and the fact that she was unable to fulfil them:

> My behaviour became bad; I misbehaved at school. I didn't have the help I
> needed . . . a lot of it was going over my head anyway so I became bored and
> disruptive . . . the expectations rose, so you needed to know more and to have to
> think more and I started to misbehave and at home, I was moody.

Throughout the interview, Isobel interjects her memory of renewed determination that was always hampered by lack of positive reinforcement. She recalls starting each academic year with a resolve to apply herself. Unfortunately, her good intentions were always thwarted:

> . . . I'd spend a lot of time on homework and it would come back covered in red
> pen. And I'd think, what's the point?

The lack of encouragement was also inherent in the system of setting:

> I was in the bottom sets – it was Form 1 to 6, the sets, 1 being the top. I was in 5
> and 6 for most of them and you just knew you were a loss; you weren't going to
> get on. Because you don't get put into those sets unless you're a dead loss. I
> remember distinctly feeling, oh, I'm in 5 or 6, what's the point?

Being placed with a peer group of non-achievers in the bottom sets reinforced the lack of incentive to work hard. Isobel did not feel she belonged there and this added to her mounting frustration:

> I looked around, and there were people that were really struggling and people
> who were, you know, I don't like to say it, but thick, and I just didn't feel I was.
> There were some there that were, truly, I don't know, slow learners or some-
> thing, but there weren't specific problems there. I mean, just because I couldn't
> write it down, my intelligence was there.

Again, in contrast to Lee's experience, Isobel was made to feel that she was unable to achieve and was punished for her poor behaviour, rather than encouraged to excel in her areas of strength. One of her most bitter memories is being denied the chance to pursue a course in art, because she had been excluded from the class for misbehaving. This was an area in which she felt she could have succeeded.

Isobel describes her behaviour at home as being moody and challenging. She feels that her parents valued her directness and her stubbornness, while finding her a difficult child to handle. In retrospect, Isobel doesn't blame her parents for their lack of recognition of her problems. However, she does feel that they didn't acknowledge her abilities:

> ... [my mum] didn't say I was thick, but she didn't sort of positively say to me, 'Oh, you can do these exams.' She just assumed that there were people in our family that couldn't read or write and I was just going to be like them. So she didn't actually say 'thick', but she did just think that I was a lost cause in the education system ... I don't resent it, but I just wish somebody had helped me ... anybody.

Isobel has fought hard to achieve her personal goals. As an adult, her self-confidence has grown, but she acknowledges that, despite developing many compensatory strategies, her dyslexia still affects her:

> For me it means that when I'm reading, words will be read wrong. I'll have to work a little bit harder at reading than most people to gain meaning. It'll mean that spelling is the most frustrating thing I ever have to do, because if I get it wrong, I can't look it up in the dictionary because it's so wrong. It'll mean that I'll want to kick myself when I spell some words wrong that I should know how to spell or when I have a mental block. It means that maths and phone numbers are a nightmare because I've got no memory of procedures or methods for maths. For phone numbers, I just mix them up, get them the wrong way round. On the whole, it can be very tiring because you have to work that little bit harder the whole time.

However, Isobel is also aware of her many strengths. She feels her oral communication skills are her major strength, but also describes her compassion with others, which she feels stems from her own difficulties:

> I think, in a way, I'm a better person for being dyslexic, that I understand more about other people's special needs and other people's disabilities [and about] people who go through racism and sexism. I really feel that I empathize because I am not the 'norm' either and it's given me a better understanding of the world.

Interestingly, Isobel believes that an advantage in being dyslexic is that she has more understanding of the problems of her own son and has greater insights into ways to help him: 'That's an advantage – to be a dyslexic mother of a dyslexic child.'

Catherine: the mother and grandmother

Both Isobel and her mother, Catherine, agree that it was extremely difficult for Catherine to help Isobel as a child because of complete lack of understanding of the underlying cause for Isobel's difficulties at school. Like Isobel, Catherine was a young mum and had little experience or knowledge of children who have difficulties with learning. Catherine's main aim for her two children was for them to be happy, and if success at school was not easily attainable, she didn't feel that pushing them would be the answer. She tried to help Isobel, but her attempts met with little success:

> I'd teach her to spell 'would' and 'could' and two weeks later, she'd leave out 'u's; and she'd mix up 'b's and 'd's; I never could understand why she couldn't learn. But my main aim for my children in life was to have them happy. I tried and when she couldn't, I thought, well I'll leave it because a lot of my husband's family are not very bright and one side of my family are not very bright; some can't read or write. Because of that I felt that it must be the genes that Isobel has picked up from them, so why push her and make her unhappy.

However, Catherine did not see Isobel as 'thick'. On the contrary, her view of her dyslexic daughter was consistent with what Sally Smith (1991) defines as 'street smarts – a shrewd awareness of what's going on and how it affects one's own survival':

> No, she was very bright and she had lots of common sense; I found her not being able to learn difficult to understand.

Despite Isobel's academic problems, Catherine was convinced she would succeed in life. She identified with Isobel in terms of strong character and strong personality and felt that Isobel's determination would enable her to accomplish whatever goals she set for herself. Catherine sees Isobel's stubbornness as a positive attribute. This position is supported by Smith's comment that 'maybe we need to look at stubbornness in a more positive light and see it as the grit that contributed to later success.'

In contrast to Isobel's views of her children, Catherine was more concerned about her non-dyslexic younger daughter, who exhibited a 'school phobia' and, despite having no obvious difficulties in learning, never enjoyed school and left without any qualifications. Catherine openly states her anxiety about her younger daughter:

> I was disappointed there; the one that could [learn] and the one that didn't have a problem learning, didn't.

Catherine's responses to the differences between her two daughters seem to be related more to her perceptions of their personalities than to their academic abilities. She readily acknowledged that she had very specific expectations for the girls, wanting Isobel to be a nurse and Bridget to be a teacher 'because she was bright'. She saw Isobel as being:

> good with people and . . . a strong character and [someone who would] be able to take the death, the sickness; she'd be able to cope well. If somebody had told me when Isobel was 14 or 15 that she would go to university and do a teacher's degree, I wouldn't have believed it, but I think it's excellent that she is. I'm really proud of her, very, very proud.

The overarching principle that Catherine feels is paramount in raising children relates to their happiness. Although she recognizes the importance of diagnosis in terms of accessing appropriate interventions, she voiced a concern about the impact on Lee of knowing that he is dyslexic:

> I think that sometimes it's made Lee very unhappy and he'll get upset. He said to Isobel once, he'd rather be dead than be at school, because he'd had a real bad day where he couldn't pick up stuff. She didn't say that, so she went through without knowing and I didn't know, but I feel he's got the benefit in another way because she's able to help him. So, it's difficult, I look at it in two ways.

Discussion

This case study illustrates the complex ways in which dyslexia can affect family life. Even within three generations of a closely-knit family, there are huge variations in perceptions about how to deal with a dyslexic child. Attitudes, behaviour and parental expectations can impact significantly on self-esteem and academic success. It is always difficult to establish the degree to which dyslexia influences personality attributes, but it is nonetheless important to be cognizant of the way in which school failure (or success) affects a child's self-perception.

The awareness by dyslexic parents of their own strengths and weaknesses and a sensitivity to the way in which their own dyslexic profile affected their school careers can be a major factor in determining how they deal with the educational system to help their children. Parents who are themselves dyslexic often become powerful advocates for their children because they are determined that the education of their dyslexic children does not mirror their own negative school experiences. Acting as a role model and fighting for their children's rights to have their difficulties identified and addressed affords such parents the opportunity to redress the balance of their own unhappy past. Unfortunately, parents may encounter a hostile reception from the school authorities. Helen is one example of a parent who was told that the problems she highlighted with her daughter were 'emotional'. The school's 'solution' was to organize family therapy sessions. After much effort, Helen managed to get her child assessed, only to be told that her reading was at an acceptable standard and her poor spelling and writing were not as bad as that of other children in the class and therefore no extra help could be arranged. The school's view was 'her spelling will come when she is ready'. Such an experience can be doubly distressing for a parent who has her own history of painful memories of education and whose spelling has never 'come'.

When she expressed concern about the lack of progress of her 6-year-old son, the response Claudia received from the school was similar to Helen's experience. It seems that teachers are quick to suggest emotional problems as the cause, rather than the result, of poor academic progress. Undeterred, Claudia joined a local parents' support group for advice about how to get an assessment for her child, whom she was convinced was as severely dyslexic as she. The other members of the parents group came from affluent backgrounds and their solution to dealing with uncooperative schools was to pay for private assessments. This was not a viable option for Claudia, who was struggling to make ends meet while studying social work at university. However, she managed to put her social work training to good use and wrote letters (with help from her support tutor) arguing that, under the Children Act (1989), her child had a legal right to be assessed. Her case was based on the grounds that the welfare of the child is paramount and that he was entitled to have his educational needs met. She was successful in her battle and her son was diagnosed, given a statement of educational needs and provided with the support he needed.

Perhaps an even bigger challenge faces non-dyslexic parents of dyslexic children, for they must first understand their children's struggles before they can advocate for the most effective interventions. Certainly, Catherine indicated that she would have responded differently to Isobel had she been more knowledgeable about dyslexia.

Riddick (1996) conducted structured interviews with 22 dyslexic children aged 8–14 and their mothers to examine the social and emotional consequences of living with dyslexia. Her study found no difference in parental involvement between dyslexic and non-dyslexic fathers or mothers in terms of the support they offered their (diagnosed) dyslexic children. It is likely that the degree of awareness and knowledge that the parents had regarding dyslexia is correlated with the amount of support they offered their children, though this was not explored in Riddick's study. In our intergenerational study, Catherine showed as much concern for her (undiagnosed) dyslexic child as Isobel did for her dyslexic son. However, Isobel (and therefore Lee) benefited from the knowledge she had about dyslexia and this enabled her to act as an advocate to ensure he received appropriate support at school.

Dyslexia and sibling relationships

In families where only one sibling is dyslexic, the success of other siblings may impact on the self-image of the dyslexic child. Often, dyslexic children perceive themselves as less intelligent than their non-dyslexic siblings. Jackie's response to questioning about siblings was typical:

> I had an older brother, but my brother was very intelligent. My brother did O levels; he was always intelligent, he was always with his nose stuck in a book, you know. So, he did really well at school, and there was me, just like lagging, but then again my brother used to call me stupid.
> *Did you think you were intelligent?*
> I don't know. You don't think, do you? Because I heard it from every direction; I heard it from the teachers, from the kids, at home, so like, you just start believing what they say, you know.

Michaela's views echoed those of Jackie:

> My mum and dad just thought that, I'm not the very bright one and that my brother was the bright one in the family and that he'll do well and I won't do well. And I was very work-orientated. They didn't really believe that I would go to college. In fact now, they're still amazed and they always say, 'If you can't handle it, just leave. It doesn't matter.'

Many adults who were not diagnosed as children report that their parents assumed that their dyslexic child was just 'not very bright' and expectations were related to this perception. Catherine's expectations for Isobel differed from those she had for her other daughter, whom she perceived as the 'bright' one. Graham sensed that his parents had a different set of expectations for him from those they had of his brother. The contrast in parental response created a sense of difference in Graham:

> I was never pressured to do well at any point during school. My brother was a straight 'A' student and he was pressured when he got grades that weren't as good as they should have been. I realized I wasn't being pushed, so there was obviously something strange or different about me.

In cases where the child was diagnosed, there may have been jealousy and resentment on the part of siblings who felt that the dyslexic child received additional attention from the parents or was excused from certain tasks and responsibilities that were expected of the non-dyslexic siblings. Saunders (1995) highlights this situation by suggesting that both parents and grandparents may feel it necessary to devote more energy to the dyslexic child, thus fuelling the resentment of the non-dyslexic siblings. Problems associated with sibling rivalry are compounded by the presence of a dyslexic child and jealousies and resentments occur in both directions. Smith (1991) points out that siblings may resent the extra attention that the dyslexic child receives from parents and suggests that this can be the root cause of considerable rivalry. On the other hand, the dyslexic child may envy the accomplishments of his non-dyslexic sibling(s).

Rob is quite open about expressing his jealousy towards his sister:

> Yeah, Annie is the 'perfect sister'; it happens to everybody and you need to get over it, but I'm going to do a lot better than her in the long run, I know, but there was a lot of problems there. I hated that. Annie always was top dog; 9 GCSEs; all As; 3 A levels, all Bs, getting into Manchester then coming down to London. She does really well.
>
> *Do you still find that a problem?*
>
> No, I'm happy for her. I've got my own goals now and I can see myself doing very well and if I don't, I'll find new goals and do well in that. But as a kid, it was a real problem; I was very jealous of my sister.

Family dynamics

Sibling relations and family functioning can be influenced by the response of parents to the needs of the dyslexic child. Once again, this may be determined by the extent to which there is an awareness of dyslexia. In a study exploring issues of parental stress, family functioning and sibling self-concept, Dyson (1996) reports that there was no difference between family functioning and self-concept of siblings in families with a learning-disabled child and in families of non-disabled children. However, parents of learning-disabled children experienced more stress. Moreover, although relationships between learning-disabled children and their siblings tended to be positive, parents expressed feelings of guilt for investing more time in the learning-disabled child than on the siblings.

In the Dyson study, there was further parental concern about high-achieving younger siblings and the resulting embarrassment that this could cause the learning-disabled child. Smith, on the other hand, highlights the embarrassment felt by siblings about the behaviour and problems demonstrated by their dyslexic sister or brother.

The findings of the Dyson study were partially supported in the intergenerational study conducted with Isobel's family. One of Isobel's main concerns was to protect Lee from feeling overtaken by his brother, who is three years younger. She seemed worried that Jake's facility with numbers would overshadow Lee and undermine his confidence. On the other hand, Isobel's mother, Catherine, appeared to be more protective of her younger, non-dyslexic daughter, since she felt that Isobel's strong character would see her through life. One possible explanation for the apparent contradiction in these maternal responses is the difference in perspective from which each woman is viewing the situation. Isobel, being dyslexic herself, may be more able to empathize with her dyslexic child whereas Catherine, who is non-dyslexic, viewed her daughters in terms of their personalities only and was unaware that Isobel's difficulties were due to dyslexia. She expressed more concern for the future of her non-dyslexic, younger daughter whom she feels has less determination and direction than Isobel. Moreover, she sees Isobel's 'stubbornness' as being her key to success.

Interestingly, persistence was one of the factors identified by Reiff et al. (1997) in their study of successful dyslexic adults. Jackie also referred to stubbornness as an asset. When asked about her strengths, Jackie stated:

> My strengths? Um, maybe my stubbornness is one of my biggest strengths. I've learnt to be stubborn. I've learnt to be stubborn and I've learnt to be persistent because I've had to be to get to where I've got today, I think.
>
> *Do you see that as a dyslexic strength?*
>
> Yeah, I do, because I think where I grew up, I've been knocked back and knocked back and every time, I've just picked myself up, dusted myself down and just gone forward. And now, if I can't do anything, I just see it as an obstacle. OK, I suffer from dyslexia, my dyslexia is stopping me from doing this, so I can't take the direct route, so I'm going to work around it. So now I work around things if I can't do it, and it's just made me, I think it's made me more determined in doing things.

There are obviously many factors that affect the responses of grandparents, parents and siblings of a dyslexic child. Family functioning may be affected by such variables as the age of diagnosis, the availability of external support from school and specialist teachers, the degree of difficulty of the child concerned, the number of other family members who are also dyslexic, and the child's position in the family.

Only through ongoing awareness and consciousness-raising among teachers and the general public will a new generation of dyslexic children be in a more favourable position than their parents' generation. If parents don't know that their children are dyslexic, they may become exasperated by what they interpret as laziness or unwillingness of the child to apply himself to school tasks. Parents and teachers must look beyond the surface and question why a child is not learning. The mother of one young man accepted the view of his teachers that he was lazy, in spite of the fact that she knew he struggled for two hours in his room to produce one page of writing and then crumpled the paper up because it was 'not good enough'.

Individual responses to dyslexia vary enormously and are affected by many different influences. Those who are most likely to emerge into adulthood with their egos intact are usually the ones who have received diagnosis, understanding and appropriate support, both academically and emotionally. In making this possible, the family is of great significance.

Chapter 5
Choosing a job or career

Dyslexic individuals are employed in careers as varied as those of their non-dyslexic peers. There are successful dyslexic people in jobs across the spectrum, in fields that rely mostly on right-hemispheric functioning, such as design, architecture, music, drama, painting and other creative arts, as well as in more conventional 'left-brained' fields such as medicine, law, teaching and accountancy. Many dyslexic people choose careers that place limited demands on language skills as a conscious strategy to avoid jobs with heavy requirements for reading and writing. We have known several dyslexic people who opted for careers in sciences or mathematics, openly admitting that their choice of study was determined by the desire to avoid writing essays. However, many talented actors and actresses such as Tom Cruise, Whoopi Goldberg, Cher and Susan Hampshire are dyslexic: some of their talent may be attributable to a sensitivity to mood, tone and connotation, all aspects of language that are processed in the right hemisphere. Some dyslexic people, such as the poet Benjamin Zephaniah, may apply their highly developed imaginations, combined with a flair for spoken language, to develop skills as creative writers.

Making choices

Undiagnosed dyslexic adults may have left formal education at the age of 15 or 16 and entered the world of work and/or family commitments. Lack of formal qualifications often meant that job opportunities were limited to unskilled work. In Tony's case, the choice was made for him:

> I can bang a nail into a piece of wood. My eye co-ordination, hand co-ordination are very good – all those skills are there and in fact that's what I kind of like excelled at, at school and that kind of helped me go through and get work. I mean I ended up coming out of school and going into something to work with my hands, just as a kind of, just on a treadmill. I didn't have another choice. I didn't have another route to take. It had to be, you know, selling what physical skills I had.

The childhood experiences of being labelled 'thick', the public humiliation caused by failing often resulted in choices which reinforced low self-esteem and led dyslexic individuals to avoid areas requiring reading and writing. The pain of these memories has a long-lasting effect and can influence future career decisions. Rick, a café manager and cook, says:

> I really think it [dyslexia] did influence me. There was no question of going into any of those fields [which needed reading and writing], no question whatsoever. I went for something more working with my hands, which was cooking and pottery. And now I think back, it's quite odd – the number of people I met with the same sort of problems as me. Maybe we're all doing it, we're all avoiding one side.

Many dyslexic adults tread a labyrinthine path to their career destinations, sometimes because of poor guidance; in other cases through attempts to avoid having to read and especially to write. Reiff et al. (1993) comment: 'In almost all cases, learning disabilities necessitate alternative approaches to achieve vocational success.' Often their success depends on how lucky they are in having employers, managers and work colleagues who recognize their abilities.

Jenny, who eventually became a head of department in a further education college, was advised at school that, being non-academic, she could either do office work or hairdressing. She took up hairdressing as it was practical, something she felt she could do. The salon she was working in encouraged her, even though she was slow in acquiring the skills, and sent her to college to gain a qualification. This, she says, was fine until she had to study theory. As far as exams went,

> I couldn't get what was in my head on to the paper and I couldn't understand what they wanted me to write.

However, she got through the exams, and then did other courses related to hairdressing. In response to encouragement by one of the managers, she started to teach hairdressing at the local college. Shortly after, she began to teach young women with emotional and behavioural problems:

> These young girls were bussed in one day a week to learn hairdressing. No one wanted to teach them so I said I would. I recognized myself in them.
> *Do you think they were dyslexic?*
> Oh definitely several of them were. They had other problems too, like family problems, but yes definitely. I wanted to teach them because I wanted to find out more about myself. I suppose I was still doing that years later when I went on your course on dyslexia.
> Then the teacher left and they wanted me to take over teaching those with special needs. And I wanted to do it. But I wanted to be trained. I knew that if I wanted to work with these students I needed a qualification . . . [On my first course] I had to write a 3000 word essay. I had paragraphs in the wrong place, but the teacher could see I had all the ideas. I passed all my courses because they came and saw me in the classroom – they saw me in operation. And for the first time I got a distinction.

Another dyslexic person who followed a roundabout path to his career was George. After beginning his working life as a road sweeper, he got a job as a van driver. It was during this time that he began to feel he wanted to get to grips with his education and decided to pursue a career in art, something he had enjoyed at school. He managed to pass the exams to allow him into art school, and after a foundation course, eventually got his degree. But, he says:

> I found the criticism extremely difficult. I had quite a lack of confidence in my own work. I got my degree, but having left college – I actually did photography – I decided that I never wanted to touch a camera again and went back basically to doing manual work, and I began doing painting and decorating. But gradually I began to realize that I was doing very well. I was getting jobs from architectural firms . . . They knew I had a good colour sense and very often I was consulted by the architects about the colour schemes and various jobs I worked on. I got a great deal of satisfaction that people trusted my abilities.

In many cases, dyslexic individuals strike out on their own and become successfully self-employed in various businesses. Paul used his entrepreneurial and practical skills to set up a highly successful central heating business; Marion's job as a hair stylist eventually led her to open her own beauty salon. Francesca, at 23, set up a catering business and sold her intricately decorated cakes through a major store. For such people, school experiences did not augur well.

Saunders (1995) describes the situation of a ' . . . bright, creative, personable, likeable employee who is advancing up the "company ladder" [who] may be frightened that the next step up is a "desk job", which places great emphasis on reading and writing'. He recommends appropriate accommodations, such as a good secretary to help overcome potential obstacles to advancement. Helen agrees:

> I think a solicitor is a perfect job for a dyslexic person. You can dictate every-thing into a tape machine and you have a secretary to type and correct things and keep your appointments for you.

For Paul, Marion and Francesca, the eventual success of their busi-nesses relied on employing a bookkeeper and accountant to deal with the day-to-day financial management and detailed record keep-ing required.

For those people who are not self-employed, experiences of frus-tration at work may result in being locked into a dead-end position on a career ladder. Opportunities for promotion or career develop-ment may be turned down for fear that there will be increased demands made on reading and writing skills.

Michaela believes her father is dyslexic and that this has stood in the way of his promotion. She comments on her father's lack of career progression:

> My dad is not very good at spelling and reading, but he's never had a test. He says there's no need for him to have a test to realize if he is or not. He doesn't find reading and writing very easy. He's a prison officer, so when there's been talk of promotion, he never really wanted to do it because he hates paperwork, so he's just kept off it.

For others, although promotion is a logical development on the career ladder, it may create obstacles to success. Will, a telephone engineer, had his difficulties exposed when he was promoted and his new supervisor complained about his reports. This served as the impetus for his company to sponsor him to attend classes to improve his writing skills.

Poor reading and writing can create barriers to getting any job, even those that seem to demand minimal reading and writing, but nonetheless contain unanticipated problems. Jed faced a miserable struggle in his attempts to gain 'the Knowledge', a necessary prerequisite to become a London taxi driver. To be successful, Jed had to learn the names of all the streets, and the locations of all hospitals, hotels, restaurants and police stations within a six-mile radius of Charing Cross in central London, as well as more general information regarding outer London. He continually confused street signs and had problems memorizing the names of all the streets and other locations. Jed's ultimate success in passing his examinations attests to his ability to develop the necessary visual map, despite his dyslexia-related difficulties in recalling correct street names. Interestingly, recent research suggests that the hippocampus (the part of the brain associated with spatial memory) of London taxi drivers was millimetres larger than a control group of non-taxi drivers (Radford and Woodward, 2000).

Tom drove a delivery van and, because he had a good 'inner map' of London, found that he could handle the deliveries. The problem he faced was being unable to leave a note saying he had called to deliver a parcel when no one was in to receive it. He would sometimes have to make several trips until he found someone at home. It was this frustration that finally led him to seek help in adult basic education classes.

Lack of literacy skills has caused many young dyslexic adults to set aside ambition and has condemned them to a work life characterized by boredom, lack of fulfilment and low wages. Others have a dream or ambition which they have abandoned as being unrealistic, but will admit to with coaxing and encouragement. One manually-employed adult attending an adult education class had always wanted to be an actor, but believed he couldn't as he could never read plays. Encouraged by his tutor, he applied to a prestigious drama school which had many more applicants than they could accept. For his audition, he recited a passage from a Shakespearean play which he memorized from listening to a tape and, despite never having read any Shakespeare, he performed well enough to win a place.

Susan, a 26-year-old factory worker, had such low self-esteem that she was unable to acknowledge any ambitions. During her assessment, she claimed she was quite happy working in a factory. After being diagnosed as severely dyslexic she was encouraged to consider enrolling on a college course where she could also receive support with her reading and writing. However, she still insisted that there was nothing she wanted to do. It was only after an inspired mention of someone with problems just like hers who had done a catering course and now had her own business, that Susan 'came alive', declaring 'That's what I've always wanted to do!' She went to the local college the next day to enrol on a catering course.

Many young offenders on the Dyspel Project who take and drive away cars believe they will never be able to pass the theory test to get a driving licence. This sense of hopelessness contributes to their offending behaviour. When they discover that they can get special provision to take the test using an audio tape, hope re-enters their lives. More than one has got his car licence and then gone on to study for a heavy goods vehicle licence.

Sometimes, even those in successful careers have felt their career choices were as much influenced by the denial of opportunities as by their talents or abilities. Later in life they find the confidence to leave successful careers to pursue further or higher education. When Graham left school he embarked on a successful career in the music industry. He was a talented musician who had won a national competition for his flute playing. However, he had not been allowed to take certain subjects in secondary school and feels that his career choices were limited and determined by the decisions of the school authorities. He wanted to go into business when he first left school and is at last, at 33, completing a degree in business studies. Despite his success in the music industry, he feels bitter at the way in which decisions were forced upon him. He recalls his experience with career guidance after leaving school:

> I remember I did an aptitude test with the careers department and it basically came out that I was very interested in business, commerce, banking . . . as well as all the artistic things I was doing at the time, which are the dyslexic strengths, obviously. But I wasn't allowed to do it [study business]. It was just a case of, no you'll never go and do this. You haven't got the right qualifications. I went into music because I really didn't have any other option and I would have liked the option to choose. I was pushed.

For many dyslexic people, getting a job means finding ways around the initial hurdles so they can show their abilities. Often this involves help from others. Mac described how he managed:

I got a job as a hospital gardener and did that for about two years. The money was poor and an advert came in the paper; probably someone told me because I didn't read the papers, hardly ever read the papers – headlines maybe, but that would be it. I loved listening to the news – listening to it. There was an ad for a van driver for a firm of delis and I got my pal to apply for me – I signed the letter and I got it.

. . . [Then] there was a better job. This pal said, 'Apply for that – the wages are there, 12 pound a week, and you're on a fiver. You know, you'd be guaranteed twelve plus commission, plus probably a car and food allowance.' And I said, 'You know, I don't know how to apply,' and he said, 'Do this,' – and he wrote it down and this got me the job. He put the conditions that they wanted: preferably a married man, a driver, living in the Merseyside area and he wrote it and I copied it out: 'I comply with all the conditions you require as sales rep in the Liverpool area. Please interview me and I will convince you of my ability to be a good servant.' I got the interview . . . I got the job. I could sell, there was no doubt about that, I could sell.

Many, like Jenny and George, have certainly taken circuitous routes to find their niche. Yet others, like Rob, have benefited from good guidance, support and positive experiences at school. His decision to become a chef was influenced by his home economics teacher:

She was terrific. She gets you up to your elbows in grease and gets you making pastry and chocolate cakes, sausage rolls and everything else you could think of every week. It was great. I used to go in there and spend a good two hours cooking. I enjoyed it more than anything. She showed me lots of little tips. It's more of an art.

Course and career guidance

There are many aspects to consider in choosing careers. For the dyslexic person, it is essential to have a clear picture of strengths and weaknesses. This is important in considering not only a career, but particular jobs within vocational and professional frameworks, and also selecting the education or training route that is the best match to the person's learning style, and which will maximize success.

Unfortunately, those giving guidance and advice are often ill-informed about dyslexia and its implications for career choices. This results in well-intentioned but misguided advice. For example, young women who have not performed well academically are frequently advised to pursue 'office work', one of the least suitable options for dyslexic people. Poor literacy skills are too often equated with lack of cognitive skills or ability to learn. Lack of knowledge by those involved in initial advice, assessment and course placement can lead to failure, drop-out or wasted time and resources.

Forty-four-year-old Marilyn was educated in a comprehensive school, where, she says:

> They decided in their great wisdom that I was going to be a secretary, which I did actually find very difficult. I couldn't type properly. I type words backwards and miss whole chunks out of sentences.

She took many jobs such as telephone operator, shop assistant and waitress:

> Occasionally I did try to be a secretary and that was just absolutely hopeless. It was extremely traumatic. I spent a lot of time with Tipp-Ex and rubbers and rubbish bins full of paper because I just wasn't able to make any sense of anything. Or I thought there was a sense, but unfortunately the boss couldn't read it.

Her solution was to avoid jobs that required reading and writing:

> I'm happily out of all that nonsense of paper and words in one respect. I give Shiatzu massage and I'm a martial artist and that seems to me okay. I enjoy a physical existence.
>
> Where I do feel the lack of words is creatively . . . It happens from time to time that I start to write, but I don't really feel I'm good enough. I do it. I sit and write. But I don't show it to anyone else.

It is still unfortunately true that many dyslexic young people and adults are given advice on career routes and job opportunities based on their written language skills. Though these can be improved considerably with appropriate support, in most cases they will never be commensurate with their other abilities. Indeed, such discrepancies are common indicators of dyslexia. Dyslexic students have frequently become frustrated and demoralized by being told to improve their 'basic skills' before being allowed on a course in their chosen vocational or academic area. As many will never reach the required literacy level, they are condemned to underachievement; whereas with knowledgeable support and special examination provision, they may do well, some achieving success at a high level in a field where they have talent and are motivated.

Helen, who has severe reading, writing and spelling problems, achieved her aim of becoming a solicitor only because someone recognized her difficulties as dyslexic. She went to a local university to enrol on an access to law course to realize her long-held ambition. After taking an entrance test, she was advised to attend a basic education course to improve her literacy skills before she could be allowed on the pre-law course. Being both persistent and highly motivated, she refused, making it known that there was no way she was going to a literacy class. As she was about to storm out, a tutor came up to her and suggested that she might be dyslexic. From there, she was diagnosed and consequently offered the support to enable her to take the access to law course, the first step on the ladder to the career she wanted.

Another commonly held assumption is that success at school is necessary for success in the workplace. This fallacy ignores the importance of understanding cognitive styles. Indeed, many dyslexic people perform better in a concrete, 'real' situation than in the abstract environment of the classroom. College tutors have commented on the number of dyslexic students who do poorly in the classroom but who shine once they are in a work placement. One young person, labelled a slow learner at school, upon leaving school at 16 got a routine job in a local factory which made electrical components for cars. Within a very short time he had rewired one of the components in such a way that it was more efficient and used less wire, saving the company large sums of money (Klein and Sunderland, 1998).

Many dyslexic people quite appropriately choose careers that utilize their strengths, but may be discouraged when they realize that the demands of some aspects of the job or the training may be difficult for them. For example, professional training schemes in architecture and interior design attract many able dyslexic students, who produce excellent design work but who founder when asked to submit academic essays. Similarly, many occupations which, on the surface, do not appear to require reading and writing skills, turn out to have unforeseen expectations such as report-writing, message-taking, filing and record-keeping, all of which may create obstacles for the dyslexic person.

One student at a further education college commented that he chose a vocational qualification because 'I thought I'd be able to *do* more, but we spend all our time writing, writing, writing.' Sometimes, other options such as modern apprenticeship schemes may be viable alternatives, although selection for such schemes often relies on written tests.

Students themselves do not always know enough about courses on offer or their own learning needs to select the best course, type of qualification or progression route. Jack had wanted to study performing arts but was afraid he wouldn't be able to remember lines; Bill wanted to study music but thought he wouldn't be allowed because he couldn't read music. Both students ended up on media studies courses but had difficulties with the written work and, after discussion with the dyslexia support tutor, decided to change to the courses they really wanted. They could have avoided wasting a year had they received appropriate advice.

The first concern of those providing guidance is to help individuals determine whether their career choice is realistic in terms of their own perception of their strengths and weaknesses. It is important that those involved in placement and guidance have some knowledge of dyslexia, as they are bound to be advising many whose dyslexia has never been identified. Referral for a diagnosis could be crucial in creating the best opportunities for such people.

Perhaps even more importantly, however, those responsible for guidance and careers advice need to be aware of the powerful role of motivation. Dyslexic individuals should be encouraged to pursue avenues that take advantage of their strengths, but which also represent an area of interest – to focus on their 'dreams'. Motivation is a critical factor in job satisfaction and job success. It is not sufficient simply to have the requisite skills for a job; there must also be an attraction to the aims and goals of the work. Moreover, an inner need or deep desire on the part of the individual is often essential for success. Dyslexic people commonly refer to the crucial role motivation has played in making career decisions, particularly as the efforts involved are so great that it is only their own motivation that gets them through the difficulties.

Marilyn noted that, in spite of her negative feelings about writing,

> I'm open to learning anything if I'm motivated and I know if I'm motivated I can learn to do anything.

In Jenny's case, from the very first, it was motivation to find out about herself that determined all her choices:

I left school at 15 – no examinations or anything – and I thought I'd do hair-dressing. I enjoyed it. Perhaps I found for the first time I was good at something. *But you said you had to work really hard at it to get the eye-hand co-ordination?* Yes. Cried every day going home, but I really wanted to do it. But I cried every day because I couldn't do the tasks they set me to do, the way they'd explained it.

Even with examinations, motivation was key:

If I knew there were exams, I did it – but only if I really wanted to do it. And then I could do it.

She kept taking courses:

It was really to prove to myself that I wasn't stupid. The more I did, the more I wanted to do – to learn about me.

Advisers also need to be aware that dyslexic difficulties may create obstacles in even the initial stages of getting a job. In the first instance, dyslexic applicants face the problems of finding out about and then applying for the job. The adviser needs to be sensitive to these aspects as well as those in choosing a career or vocational path-way. When presenting someone with leaflets and application forms, it is useful to highlight important information. Hales (1995) describes the daunting prospect for a dyslexic person of completing an appli-cation form. He points out that this task makes demands on the person's organizational and sequencing skills and can take a dyslexic individual a long time to complete.

There are the dual problems of having to read the form and having to complete the information with correct spelling. Rob described the panic he felt when put under pressure:

At the brasserie, I walked in and filled out an application form. When you go in to fill it out, they're usually standing over you. Very hard. Rob breaks out in a sweat, you know? OK, I can do this, starts panicking, gets through it. I got through it alright, but there was a few spelling mistakes and that could lose you a job.

Mark, despite his maturity, still finds it humiliating to be asked to complete an application form 'on the spot'. He recently wanted to apply for a job in a social work agency where he had completed a student placement. He described his way of coping when he went to collect the application:

> ... they gave me an application form and they said to me, 'You can do it now, in the next hour,' and I said, 'I'm sorry, this would leave me at a tremendous disadvantage.' I said, 'I'm dyslexic; it would be full of spelling mistakes, I haven't got my references with me, there's no way ...' I think they were setting me up to fail.

Moreover, employers may inadvertently discriminate against dyslexic people if they are unaware – or even if they are aware – that a messy application form or a missed appointment is a function of dyslexia. Careers advisers can help by checking application forms for accuracy and spelling.

Showing examples of good CVs, personal statements and letters of enquiry can also help. Such 'models' can save applicants considerable time and anguish and encourage independence in the future. Suggesting the use of a duplicate form as a practice paper can reduce stress caused by trying to produce a neat final copy. Rob's strategy when applying for jobs was:

> I have everything written on a card you pull out. I had my CV when I went to one restaurant and that helped a lot; I just copied from it.

Depending on available time, an adviser might offer to scribe information for personal statements and then discuss how best to structure the data. A successful advice session might end with providing the student with a written 'to do' list and checking to make sure that there is no confusion about information discussed with the adviser. Although time may be limited, it is worth allocating extra time to spend with a dyslexic applicant since a rushed session is probably worse than no session at all and the outcome, whether it be an application form or the selection of a course, may affect the dyslexic person's entire future.

The rights of dyslexic employees

Many dyslexic employees can fulfil the requirements of jobs that demand reading and writing skills, but may need specific accommodations to help them overcome certain weaknesses. These arrangements may include adaptations that are legally incumbent upon the employer to provide.

In the United States, the Americans with Disabilities Act (ADA) of 1990 made it unlawful for employers to discriminate against employees on the grounds of disability. Employers must provide 'reasonable accommodations' to address the disability-related needs of the employee, unless to do so would cause 'undue hardship' to the employer. With regard to dyslexic employees (or those who are diagnosed as 'learning disabled' in the USA), reasonable accommodations might include appropriate technology, such as a computer with voice recognition software, or secretarial support. It might also consist of a reduced workload to accommodate for slow processing speed. This legislation has revolutionized the approach to employing individuals with disabilities, and has raised disability issues to a level of public consciousness, thus helping to improve awareness of the need to integrate people with disabilities into mainstream employment.

In Britain, the Disability Discrimination Act (DDA), passed in 1995 has had a similar, albeit not quite as wide reaching, impact to the ADA. The Employment Service has Disability Service Teams whose role is to provide a coherent employment advice and assessment service for both employers and people with disabilities. The teams consist of Disability Employment Advisers (DEAs) who act as intermediaries between employers and employees with disabilities. Their brief includes introducing suitable employees with disabilities to prospective employers as well as providing advice and guidance on the type of support available through the Employment Service. If employers need to make reasonable accommodations available for a dyslexic employee, they can apply for a grant through the Access to Work Scheme to cover approved extra costs (e.g. for computer equipment) that are deemed necessary to accommodate the employee's disability. One caveat of this scheme is that the assistance provided must not constitute more than 20 per cent of the job. This raises interesting dilemmas for dyslexic individuals who may be perfectly capable of performing the tasks associated with a particular job, but whose speed of processing may be too slow to accomplish the work within the required time. In such a case, an accommodation might involve reducing the amount of work required, but this job adaptation may appear unfair to non-dyslexic colleagues who might consequently have to shoulder greater responsibility.

However, despite this legal underpinning of the employment rights of people with disabilities, Reid and Kirk (2000) point out in a report for the Employment Service that 'it may even be suggested that dyslexia is the best known but least understood of the disabilities referred to in the legislation'.

The Access to Work Scheme provides a service to help assess and evaluate the difficulties of people with disabilities in relation to their career goals. Occupational psychologists will help individuals analyse their goals in light of the requirements of a particular job. They will conduct an assessment as a basis for offering advice, based on their clients' strengths and weaknesses profiles, to help them determine how realistic their goals are.

For those not diagnosed, there may be the possibility of a diagnostic assessment by an occupational psychologist. However, there is no legal 'right' to an assessment for dyslexia and no clear mechanism for getting one. As diagnoses are expensive, many adults who suspect they are dyslexic are unable to gain confirmation. Currently, DEAs can carry out an assessment to identify special training needs and give guidance on work-based support, but this does not constitute a diagnostic assessment. Reid and Kirk recommend that 'in view of the potential numbers of unemployed and undiagnosed dyslexic people, information on what constitutes dyslexia and how it can affect employment [should] be disseminated in a user friendly manner to each job centre'. They further recommend that 'Disability Employment Advisors should have a compulsory element in their induction training on dyslexia' and that they should also have opportunities to develop expertise in dyslexia. Furthermore, they stress that 'at least one Occupational Psychologist in each region [should be] trained to an advanced level in the area of dyslexia in relation to assessment and recommending and evaluating appropriate support'.

Dyslexia and the professions

There are important issues to consider for dyslexic people who choose to pursue professional careers. We have chosen to examine teaching and social work in some detail to illuminate these issues and their implications for both dyslexic individuals and non-dyslexic employers and policy makers.

Teaching

Among the dyslexic people with whom we have worked, the vast majority of those not diagnosed until adulthood have openly expressed painful memories of their time at school. Not surprisingly, many adults who gain insights into the teaching and learning process believe they could contribute much to the educational system as teachers. As a minimum, they consider that their own negative experiences make them more sensitive to the needs of children who are not learning through conventional teaching methods. It is therefore not unusual for dyslexic adults to consider a career in teaching, and we have known many who have gone on to become excellent teachers. Unfortunately, there is an inherent prejudice against people who have their own difficulties with reading and writing; a commonly held view is that if a teacher can't demonstrate proficiency in spelling, reading, writing and mental arithmetic, then she will not be able to impart these skills to young children. Can this apparent paradox be resolved?

In our view, the answer lies in offering guidance based upon careful evaluation of the student's goals and skills combined with help in gaining a realistic understanding of the job expectations. The student has to be encouraged to arrive at an honest assessment of her own strengths and weaknesses and how these mesh with the job requirements. It is certainly not sufficient to approach a career in teaching simply with the idea that if the teacher is kind and understanding, the children will learn. Mark is one case of someone who re-evaluated his desire to become a teacher with a realistic appraisal of his own abilities:

> I wanted to work with dyslexic children . . . I thought, if I get O level maths, I can go and do basic primary school teaching, and then I could go on to specialize in dyslexia teaching. But I could just not do that O level maths . . . It brought back all these painful memories and I didn't seem to be getting anywhere . . . and I thought, scrap this, because of the price this is going to extract from me. I think I could have done some really good work with dyslexic children, but . . . I just couldn't cope. And I realized also when I spent a week in my old secondary school as a trainee teacher just how important . . . to be a teacher, you have to have basic literacy and basic maths too . . . I realized in our competitive society . . . the parents are razor sharp and if they saw a teacher marking a kid's work with the spellings wrong, I think they'd hit the roof and you'd have a really tough time.

Mark's views are echoed by many dyslexic adults who have considered a career in teaching, but recognize the fact that their own limitations in certain basic skills would make it difficult for them to develop adequate coping strategies. Recent government policies have resulted in increased pressures on teachers in response to low levels of literacy in schoolchildren. The pros and cons of the changing emphasis in primary education are not appropriate to debate here; however, it is essential to appreciate these changes in terms of the requirements of the job. For prospective teachers to succeed, they must have confidence in their own skills or in their ability to employ strategies to overcome their areas of weakness.

There are, in fact, many arguments in favour of training dyslexic student teachers. Perhaps the most salient factor is their empathy with the needs of less successful learners. This is usually accompanied by considerable patience and understanding. As a result of their own difficulties, dyslexic student teachers are used to devoting extra time to producing their work and transfer this willingness to their classroom preparation. Their 'right-brained' talents and creativity can be exploited to produce exciting multisensory approaches to teaching. The personal educational backgrounds of dyslexic teachers may help them to spot children with special needs. They are less likely to label these children as 'thick, lazy or stupid' – the labels with which they themselves were branded as children. On the contrary, in accordance with the government's Code of Practice (DfE, 1994), they are more apt to push for early identification and diagnosis of children with special needs than their non-dyslexic colleagues, who might misinterpret the signs and focus on behavioural issues rather than on learning problems. Many instinctively use teaching strategies they themselves have developed which are particularly effective for those who respond least well to conventional methods. Often they are secretive about these methods, thinking themselves 'cheating' because they are not doing it the 'right way'. But in our experience of training teachers, some of the best teachers of a skill such as spelling may themselves be dyslexic. Because they have had to discover their own way to learn spelling, they are able to teach children who do not acquire spelling easily. Those who have themselves received support and have developed good insights into their own strengths

and how they best learn show considerable skill in adapting strategies to help all the children they teach.

The major arguments against training dyslexic adults to become
teachers seem to be steeped in unsubstantiated prejudice. The
primary contention is that teachers who themselves have difficulties
with reading, writing, spelling or arithmetic are impeded in their
ability to teach these to children. There is, however, no evidence to
support this position. All teachers vary in their talents in art, music,
drama and physical education; yet they are all considered 'trainable'
in these subjects. Dyslexic teachers often have greater abilities in
these areas than their non-dyslexic colleagues. In any case, it is not
necessary to be expert in a field in order to teach its requisite skills.
Dyslexic teachers, perhaps even more than others, recognize the
importance of helping children to develop good literacy and numeracy skills. It may be that the different abilities of many dyslexic
people can be tapped into as a resource to develop alternative and
innovative approaches to teaching children.

Another argument against training dyslexic student teachers is
that the additional support demands they require place a strain on
limited institutional resources. However, governmental legislation
makes it incumbent upon academic institutions to provide necessary
and reasonable support to students with disabilities. The goal of this
support should be to ensure that dyslexic students (as well as those
with other disabilities) are able to achieve parity with their non-
disabled peers. The specialist dyslexia support provided for dyslexic
student teachers could easily be seen as part of their teacher training.
By raising their level of awareness about how they learn and how to
develop strategies to overcome their weaknesses, prospective teachers are developing transferable professional skills that will enable
them to become better teachers.

As with non-dyslexic people, individual strengths and weaknesses
may determine the degree to which someone is suited to a career in
teaching. A dyslexic student enrolled on a teaching training course
had profound difficulties with her organizational skills, struggled
with general literacy levels and had extremely poor handwriting and
spelling. As part of the feedback given to her post-diagnosis, she was
counselled to assess the expectations of the course in relation to her
areas of difficulty. She was helped to see that, even with support, her
problems would make it extremely difficult for her to fulfil the

demands of the course or, subsequently, of the job. She was referred to a career counsellor who encouraged her to pursue an NNEB. Although she was not happy with this suggestion because of her perception of the lower status and accordingly low rate of pay of nursery nurses, she nonetheless accepted the guidance and completed the NNEB training.

In contrast, Isobel has a good awareness of how her dyslexia will affect what she can offer to children she teaches:

> I will appreciate that there are children that find certain things harder than other children and there are weaknesses and strengths in every child. Until now I only focused on my weaknesses. I never focused on my strengths because I didn't know what they were . . . but because of the learning support, I now know what my strengths are. The main area I'll work on with all children . . . is that they will have high self-esteem. If they come out [of school] with confidence, then they can gain those skills, but if they come out with low self-esteem, they are not even going to attempt them. So that would be my focus – not only to teach them how to read and write, but to teach them different strategies – to teach them to look at their strengths and not focus on their weaknesses.

In a small-scale study comparing dyslexic student teachers to their non-dyslexic peers, Morgan and Rooney (1997) found that the sample of dyslexic student teachers whom they interviewed had developed enough coping strategies to enable them to overcome their areas of weakness. None of those interviewed felt that they were unable to fulfil the expectations of the job, although they acknowledged that it was necessary for them to spend much more time on preparation than their non-dyslexic colleagues. Significantly, the dyslexic student teachers felt that their insights into themselves as learners contributed towards their development as teachers. Moreover, they recognized that their strengths could be a distinct advantage in making them good teachers. Several commented on their heightened sensitivity to children with special needs and felt their own experiences might enable them to encourage and motivate the less confident children in their classrooms.

In a survey of higher education institutions in the United Kingdom, the National Working Party on Dyslexia in Higher Education (Singleton, 1999) found that a total of 12 institutions indicated that they did not admit dyslexic students to all courses; of these, seven revealed that they did not accept dyslexic candidates for teacher training and three stated that they would not offer places to dyslexic candidates in medically-related courses. The Working Party concluded that it is necessary for professional bodies to address the complex issues that may lead to conflict among the three aims of providing equal opportunities, widening access for people with disabilities and maintaining professional standards.

As long as there is overt discrimination in training courses, potential students who are dyslexic will be unwilling to disclose their dyslexia on application and will risk being denied the support they need for success in their training. Preston (1996) describes how one teacher-training college in England responded to this dilemma:

> Students must be encouraged to disclose their dyslexia at the time of application, so that it can be discussed fairly and openly at the time of interview. The Chichester Institute is piloting a scheme whereby dyslexic students are accepted into Initial Teacher Training with the proviso that their progress will be reviewed after the first two years, and a joint decision will be made as to whether it is appropriate for them to continue with teacher training or to revert back to a degree course in their main subject.

On a practical level, this sort of sifting probably takes place at many other teacher-training colleges, although it may not be stated so overtly. Indeed, there may be many undiagnosed dyslexic student teachers who are encouraged to transfer to straight academic degrees simply because they are not performing to the standard required in teacher-training courses. It is more than likely that, were these students to be diagnosed and given appropriate support, they would be able to fulfil their original goal.

Social Work

Another 'helping profession' that attracts many dyslexic individuals is social work. It may be that the unhappy personal and academic backgrounds of many dyslexic adults compels them to choose a career that offers emotional and other support to clients.

In common with dyslexic student teachers, dyslexic adults who choose to follow training in social work bring with them a host of strengths, many of which may be attributed to their background experiences as well as to their dyslexic learning style. One of the most important characteristics of a good social worker is good listening skills. This is an area of proficiency for many dyslexic people, simply because they may rely on taking information in through auditory channels to avoid having to read or write. They may also possess such 'right-brained' attributes as empathy, creativity, innovative problem-solving approaches and lateral thinking, along with qualities such as patience and tenacity born of their own experience.

There are many ways in which supervisors can support dyslexic social workers to help them meet the job expectations. Asking them to identify their perceived strengths can be a good starting point. The acknowledgement and recognition of the positive attributes that the person brings to the job establish a relationship based on encouragement and respect, from which it is possible to explore weaknesses with a view to determining reasonable means of support.

Each dyslexic social worker will bring to the job his or her unique profile of strengths and weaknesses. There is, however, a range of possible areas of difficulty about which a supervisor should be aware. Poor organizational and timekeeping skills can have disastrous effects for the social worker, who must be able to prioritize tasks and ensure appointments are kept, and necessary written work is produced according to required schedules. A supportive supervisor can help the dyslexic worker to develop and follow a timetable.

Ongoing weaknesses with reading may impact on several aspects of work. If the person has poor comprehension, she may have difficulty absorbing the significant points in case records. This might be overcome by extending supervision time to discuss cases to ensure the worker has understood the important points and to reinforce the details. Another problem area for many dyslexic people is the slow speed with which they read; this makes it difficult for them to absorb information quickly for meetings and case conferences. The supervisor can obviate this problem by making necessary reading material available in advance. Another strategy that might help is the use of a tape recorder; if the dyslexic person reads the information aloud on tape, she can then absorb the content through listening, rather than relying simply on print. However, once again, this requires extra time and private, quiet space. If confidential materials cannot be removed from the office, a quiet room with the use of a tape recorder could be made available.

Persistent difficulties with writing might include poor spelling, which can impact on the social worker's efficiency in recording names correctly and taking messages. Other writing problems, such as poor sentence structure or organization of written work may affect report-writing, letter-writing and such tasks as taking minutes at meetings. One solution to these difficulties is the provision of sympathetic secretarial help. Reports and letters could be dictated for subsequent audio-typing or the social worker could be given access to a computer, possibly with voice recognition software. The provision of 'model' reports, minutes and letters can help to establish a type of template that can be adapted according to circumstances. Someone with particularly poor note-taking skills should be excused from taking minutes, since this not only exposes the individual's weaknesses to the other members of the team, but also results in inadequate minuting of meetings.

One common characteristic of many dyslexic adults is the inefficiency of the short-term memory. This can affect several aspects of the social worker's responsibilities, but strategies can usually be found to minimize the impact. For example, supplementary written back-up may overcome any difficulty with remembering verbal instructions. The use of a tape recorder can help with problems of taking notes during interviews, offering the social worker the reassurance that no vital information has been 'lost' because of problems getting information down in writing.

Mark's experience during a social work placement made him wary about sharing his support needs with future supervisors. His supervisor had received some training about dyslexia but, according to Mark, this resulted in a situation in which a little knowledge became a dangerous thing. He was particularly upset by the fact that she included her negative analysis of him in her placement report:

> . . . my supervisor felt that she had done courses on dyslexia and she knew what it was and, unbeknown to me, she was taking it upon herself to assess me. She was looking at my handwriting and making her own judgements, even though I'd had a proper, professional psychological report . . . having dyslexia made me very weak. There was a problem with my short-term memory. She was quite right about that. I was expected to hold at least eight or nine cases and I was assessed on six cases. It was a problem for me, but I think, with proper supervision, and if it was addressed in a proper, empathetic professional way . . . it wouldn't have been as big a problem as it became. With the right sort of support, I could have done a lot better. But I felt devastated, having it put on paper.

Any training about dyslexia should emphasize the importance of listening to dyslexic individuals to find out what their perceived needs are. Supervisors should be warned against presuming that all dyslexic social workers have the same difficulties. They must be aware of the need to express expectations explicitly and not to make assumptions about the dyslexic person's understanding.

Several of the above points are illustrated by the experiences of Joanne, a dyslexic social worker who was first diagnosed when she was in the second year of her social work training. Although she found the diagnosis a great relief, she nonetheless felt considerable embarrassment about her problems, and was reluctant to share them with her colleagues:

> I was ashamed of the word dyslexia. A lot of my colleagues had never heard of the word or what it really meant to be dyslexic. I kept it as a secret . . . private . . . only letting very close friends know, who would not use it against me.

When Joanne went on her placement, she informed her practice teacher that she was dyslexic. Joanne had good insights into her learning style and felt confident enough to confide her needs to her supervisor. Unfortunately, she did not receive the type of support that she had hoped for and was left feeling bitter and vulnerable:

> My needs were ignored . . . they were not taken into account. I had never worked in a noisy open-planned office before. I found it very difficult to concentrate.
>
> I brought in a tape recorder to tape my supervision. [My supervisor] insisted that it be switched off at certain points during the supervision; for me this meant missing out on what I considered to be vital information.
>
> As I was a very articulate student, it was very hard for my practice tutor to recognize what I was experiencing. I was not stupid, but she always spoke to me in a very patronizing way.
>
> I needed things reinforced in a different way. For example, she gave me written information and expected me to understand the text straight away. Now if the information was on tape and written down, I would have been able to grasp the text much easier. Or, if the text had been given to me overnight to study, it would have been more appropriate.

Three years after graduating, Joanne reflected on her training and subsequent work. Her bad experience on her placement had lasting effects:

> I got through my degree with a great struggle; I am not the same person I was when I entered university. Studying changes a person; it enlightens you. I am

really grateful to the dyslexia department for helping me to achieve my goals in life.

In some ways I am grateful for the label dyslexia because it made me feel like a whole person. However, I must admit that I have not informed my current manager that I am dyslexic.

Chapter 6
Experiences and creative solutions in the workplace

Many dyslexic people never get career advice, and find themselves from an early age looking for jobs. Many echo Sue when she says:

> There was nothing for me at school. I just intended to leave and get a job as soon as possible.

It is often in the workplace that they discover the true effects of their difficulties, and also how to get around them. It is there, too, that they may uncover their real talents and begin to thrive.

Disclosure

At the forefront of issues for dyslexic employees is the complex and often anxiety-producing question of disclosure. The Americans with Disabilities Act (ADA) and the Disability Discrimination Act (DDA) have been briefly outlined in Chapter 5. While the significance of these acts must be recognized, it should also be noted that their existence has not removed the fact of discrimination in the workplace. The onus often falls on an individual with a disability to raise issues relating to discriminatory practice and many people are reluctant to undertake lengthy legal battles or to create or intensify already stressful situations in order to obtain fair treatment. Moreover, many individuals are unaware of their legal rights. Although employees are entitled to request reasonable accommodation, the law does not require employers to ask individuals if they have a disability or need reasonable accommodation. The issue of disclosure therefore remains a decision which the individual must make after carefully weighing up all factors.

In the case of dyslexia, as with other disabilities, the most signifi-cant question to bear in mind is the degree to which the condition is apt to be a barrier to successful execution of the job. Therefore, care-ful analysis of the individual's strengths and weaknesses measured against the specific job requirements should provide a reasonable formula for making a decision regarding disclosure. A prospective dyslexic employee should be aware that failure to disclose the diffi-culty on application may result in a weakened case for requesting accommodations subsequently.

Aside from the 'barrier' issue, it is difficult to offer advice on whether or not to disclose one's dyslexia on an application form. The applicant must take several factors into consideration, including severity of the difficulties and strategies for overcoming them. If, for example, someone has a mild spelling difficulty which is easily over-come with the use of a computer and using a computer is part of the job specification, it is probably not necessary to disclose the dyslexia on an application or interview. Someone who feels less confident may respond quite differently. For example, one dyslexic undergradu-ate when asked about disclosure said:

> How could I not tell? I feel that just answering my e-mail is an achievement. Any bit of writing is a big thing for me. If an employer asked me to do any writ-ing, I would have a heart attack.

However, the decision to disclose or not is more often taken on the basis of the dyslexic person's feelings rather than on a rational weigh-ing up of pros and cons. Many people are reluctant to discuss their dyslexia for fear of prejudice or negative responses. Lorraine says:

> I would take the risk of declaring my dyslexia if I believed that the employer was not prejudiced.

Others rightly fear that this will increase discrimination and call unwelcome attention to themselves. In a US study of occupational and social status of 49 adults with learning disabilities (Greenbaum, et al., 1996), only 20 per cent of the participants had disclosed their learning disability. Their reasons included '(a) that they were not ashamed and had learned to compensate and (b) that their disability would have an impact on their performance of the job in question'.

For the remaining respondents, the predominant reason for lack of disclosure was concern about discrimination. One interesting finding of this study was the ignorance by employees of their rights under the ADA or their unwillingness to execute them. Legislation alone is not sufficient to change attitudes; employees must be fully informed of their rights and employers must make it clear that they will not discriminate in hiring practices.

It is up to the individual to make a fair assessment of his ability to perform the required tasks; if he does not consider dyslexia an impediment to success, then there is no need to mention it. If, on the other hand, an individual feels capable of performing most aspects of the job, but requires some accommodations to fulfil certain components, he is probably well advised to disclose the dyslexia.

Many application forms have direct questions relating to disability; consequently, omitting to mention dyslexia constitutes dishonesty. However, some people weigh the situation differently. Brendan observes:

> When you write a CV or a job application, there are rules about only writing good things and not saying anything bad. For an employer, dyslexia is probably something negative because they don't understand. So I wouldn't declare it.

Michaela, who worked as a fruit and beverage senior supervisor for a large hotel group, admitted:

> I didn't tell them until much later on, until about three months within the role, when they said that personnel thought I may be dyslexic, but because they saw my performance in the very practical base . . . they see their clients were happy, the staff were happy, so that means I kept the job . . . I didn't want them to know because people's perception is, 'She can't read, she can't do the job.'

The issue of disclosure can be particularly delicate in the case of people entering professional areas, such as teaching. Wertheim, et al., (1998) acknowledge the dilemma surrounding disclosure faced by prospective teachers:

> These questions have no easy resolution. Teacher educators must work closely with students to address these and other issues, on an individual basis, during the clinical experience. We recommend that teacher educators discuss such questions in a manner that communicates both respect for the student with LD and concern for the children in the classroom.

With increasing awareness on the part of employers and pressure on the part of government, however, there are many companies that actively seek to hire disabled employees as an act of positive discrimination. It is worth researching employers' attitudes and policies with regard to disability as many large companies and public sector employers have equal opportunities policies and disability policies. This can also help the dyslexic person in choosing a potentially 'dyslexia-friendly' employer. This view was reflected by the following comment from a student:

> I guess it would depend on what type of job it is, and if you consider that the organization or even your immediate boss would be understanding enough. One consideration could be, if you have a job with time constraints, if they know you are dyslexic they could be considerate. Some employers, especially large organizations and local authorities, have a positive attitude towards dyslexia and are not allowed to discriminate.

The issue of competence

The question of what is needed to fulfil the requirements of jobs or professions can quickly muddy the waters of the rights of the dyslexic person. Unfortunately, many aspects of dyslexia can easily be mistaken for carelessness or an inability to do the job. Some of these issues were discussed in the last chapter in relation to career choices, but they also arise once the dyslexic person is in the workplace.

One trainee social worker was devastated when she was advised that she would not pass her placement due to incompetence. She had been taking her turn at dealing with emergency calls and had omitted some important information on the forms. Her supervisor had interpreted this as negligence. When it was explained that it was not a case of incompetence but of dyslexia, the supervisor was able to work with her to devise a checklist for information which solved the problem. More importantly, it enabled the supervisor to see that the trainee was responsible and competent.

Janet, whose university employers knew she was dyslexic, found her competence being seriously challenged and her confidence severely undermined when her job changed from a clerical one to one that had more secretarial aspects. Her employers provided her with a word processor, assuming it would solve any and all problems she might have. Her difficulties with spelling and typing accurately were the least of her problems, however, for Janet found it impossible to prioritize the work she was given. Questions of her ability to do the job, her intelligence (in spite of the fact that she was doing an Open University degree) and also of her attitude were raised. There were threats on their side and tears on hers. It seemed that however much her managers were willing to accept the concept of dyslexia, its reality was baffling and seemed far more like ineptness. Janet tried to explain:

> I couldn't do what they wanted – I just couldn't understand why one thing would have to be done before another. They all seemed interconnected and they all had to be done, but I just couldn't get them in any order that made sense.

It is possible that Janet might have been able to prioritize tasks had she been given an overview so that the tasks made sense within a context.

Deciding what is an issue of competence may be very complex. In spite of many years successfully employed as a state enrolled nurse, Eileen suddenly found her competence called into question because of concern that she would misread drug labels or dosages because of her dyslexia. Eileen had always been particularly conscientious and got someone else to do drug rounds with her, as well as double- and triple-checking everything. Would this be 'reasonable accommodation'? Might it even be good practice generally? Might it even be more likely for non-dyslexic nurses to be careless, given that Eileen was aware of her difficulties and made extra efforts to ensure accuracy?

However, the issue of competence can also arise from definitions about what the jobholder or professional should be able to do. In 1994, an applicant for the New York bar, claiming that he was denied extra time on his legal exams to accommodate his learning disability, lost his case. The judge ruled that it was 'reasonable to expect a bar applicant, whether learning-disabled or not, [to] have a reading capacity of the ordinary person' (Coyle, 1996). Another dyslexic lawyer criticized this ruling. While acknowledging that his employer invoices clients for only half the time he spends on reading and writing, he argues, 'that is not all I am doing. I am reasoning and constructing arguments and explanations, and I do that as fast as anyone else.'

This court case raises issues for all occupations in considering what constitutes competence. While many employers identify literacy and numeracy as underlying competences, the reality is that, for many occupations, creativity and problem-solving are equally essential, if not more so. With effective compensating strategies and accommodation, the dyslexic person may be able to surmount the difficulties to perform adequately or even excel.

Coping strategies

Dyslexia is often referred to as a 'hidden' disability, largely because there are no obvious physical manifestations. Many dyslexic people adopt strategies to hide their weaknesses. For example, poor handwriting may actually be developed as a means of disguising spelling errors. However, there are many situations in which it is extremely difficult to hide the weaknesses that result from being dyslexic, particularly when the dyslexic person is required to write or read quickly, or do tasks such as filing.

There are countless instances in the workplace where the dyslexic employee may be at risk of having weaknesses exposed. Some of these may be predictable, but others are unanticipated. To what extent can dyslexic difficulties be covered up? If employees do not disclose their dyslexia, they run the risk of being 'found out' or, perhaps worse, of being criticized for dyslexia-related errors. This may lead to admitting to the problems to avoid future embarrassment. In some cases, such as that described by Lorraine, it might even have positive side-effects in assuring that certain tasks are undertaken by other staff:

> I found that my own problem came in useful for tasks that I hated doing, like filling in the appointment book or filing cards. After many generalized complaints from colleagues (that the filing cabinet was in a mess and because people were not writing neatly in the appointment book) I stuck my hand up and volunteered that they should take me off filing and reception work as I may have been the cause of the problem and I did not want to make it worse. They did so and eventually made a rule on the staff notice board that anyone who thinks they may be dyslexic should not file cards. I know that I was not the only dyslexic, but I was the only one that owned up.

Some people use humour as a means of handling embarrassing situations. Isobel describes the difference in her coping strategies before and after she discovered her dyslexia. She found working behind the bar at her husband's pub quite demanding:

> I'd say, 'What did you ask for?' or 'How much did you give me?' when they handed me a note, and it never occurred to me that these were problems. Or giving change to the wrong person, and I still do it. I make a joke of it now, but all these things were happening but I had no understanding of why they were happening . . . Ten years down the road, I've learnt how to cope with just going back and saying, 'oh, what did you ask me – like playing stupid, to cover it up. Joking and playing – you know, 'It's Friday evening – oh, I'm so tired.'

Although self-mockery can take the edge off embarrassing errors, it is not always possible to cover up when weaknesses are exposed under pressure. Mark describes his memory of his first job when he worked in the greengrocery department of a supermarket:

> I remember panicking . . . My first two or three customers were an absolute disaster – I was getting 'a pound of potatoes, a pound of this' and I was getting it mixed up, getting the change mixed up and my colleagues were starting to look at me and thinking, 'There's something wrong with this guy.' I was going bright red with embarrassment and I was sweating profusely. I could feel the sweat pulsating through me and I wished the ground would swallow me up. And then I saw my next-door neighbour walking toward the fruit and veg and I realized this would go around my whole street and I'd shame my whole family. I just ducked down behind the counter and I sort of slithered out and made my way to the toilet and stayed there until the end of the shift. I was just, immobilized, really. I felt great confusion, great shame. They were looking for me. I said, 'I'm no good at maths,' so I was demoted to being a trolley boy. Luckily it was the same wage.

Others just cope as well as they can, hoping for the best. Rob describes his difficulties remembering an order in the restaurant where he works:

> I just try. I'm not very good at it.
> *Do you ever get it mixed up?*
> Yeah – I need to get boxes to tick. [In response to a suggestion for using a whiteboard, he continues] But people would take the mickey out of you. They won't even let you use a timer, you just have to remember . . . these boys are hard core. The way it is, you manage, and I do, and just leave it at that. In these big kitchens it's absolutely crazy.

The way in which the employee responds to these situations may be influenced by several factors. If he has told his managers and colleagues that he is dyslexic, he will be at a definite advantage in that he may have been able to set up accommodations to reduce the possibility of problems arising. However, even when someone has disclosed his disability, fellow workers may not always show understanding. Patrick described how his immediate boss, who knew about his dyslexia, nevertheless chose to criticize his poor spelling:

> . . . at times my boss would put stuff back on my desk and he'd highlight it in a red pen and he'd circle it and give it back to me. And I said, 'Why are you doing that? You know I'm dyslexic.' I said, 'I'd appreciate it if you would not use a red pen, just use any other colour pen or just let me know.' I used to send him e-mails and they'd be one-to-one e-mails and he used to pick up on it and send them back underlined . . . after about four or five months . . . I started highlighting all his spellings and sending them back to him. And we fell out over it; he wants to discipline me over it. He thought it was inappropriate that I should do it to him.

However, often dyslexic people are quick to find ways of getting support. Patrick, who is very confident in his ability to fulfil the requirements of his position as a safety adviser for a large firm of lift engineers, is aware that he cannot always spot errors in his written work. Part of his responsibilities include writing training courses and sending memos to employees in other branches of the firm; consequently, he has made a casual arrangement with a fellow employee who is happy to proof-read his work:

> It's very personal; he's more or less the same age as me and I explained to him the situation when I first went there and I said, 'I'm terrified, this is going to the directors, can you read it?' He said, 'Yeah, no problem, just send it across.' And now he's just in the habit. That's very, very good, but I've got a good personal relationship with him, which I think I have with most people. And if he's not there, there's two other people I use and I'll send it in to them. I actually send it to the managing director's secretary and I get her to proof-read it if it's going to the directors and I say, 'Don't tell the M.D.'

Creative solutions: the benefits of holistic thinking

Gerber et al. (1992) identified 'learned creativity' as one of the characteristics of highly successful dyslexic adults, i.e. using their strengths for problem-solving and devising compensating strategies to address their weaknesses.

Many dyslexic people thrive in work, particularly where they can put their strengths to effective use. When Pierre chose to become a firefighter 12 years ago, it was because he wanted a job that was intellectually challenging, but relied on mainly practical skills. He was motivated to join the London Fire Brigade because it 'suited the way I think'. He explains:

> For example, if you arrive at the scene of a car wreck, you must make lots of decisions. You need to know where to place the fire engine, you need to be able to make the area safe and you might need to figure out the best way to extract a person from the wreckage. It's true that you learn the procedures of getting from A to B safely, but these don't help you when you have to assess the whole situation. Being a holistic thinker gives me the ability to assess the big picture.

Pierre feels his dyslexia gives him an advantage in terms of his innate ability to see the 'big picture' and make decisions accordingly. Quick and judicious decision-making is obviously crucial since the demands of the job have life and death consequences. Pierre has never disclosed his dyslexia to his colleagues or employers since he fears their reactions. He is concerned that the misconceptions surrounding dyslexia could result in prejudice against him, despite the fact that he has proved his competence on the job. However, he was aware that his dyslexia could become problematic when he had to take down details of addresses and directions received by radio. He knew that a mistake in getting down the correct information could cost a life if the fire engine turned up at the wrong address. His strategy for overcoming this weakness was repeated practice. When his colleagues left the engine for an inspection of a site and he remained at the wheel, he would take down radio calls for other engines. By writing down what he heard and checking on the map to confirm that he had identified the correct street for these calls, he increased his confidence in being able to get down correct information when his engine was requested. After 12 years in the job, Pierre still enjoys the rewards and challenges; his only concern now is that he is limited in pursuing the natural progression to more managerial jobs because of the increase in office work, which he feels would be difficult.

Dyslexic strengths may influence career choice in the same way that weaknesses may discourage individuals from pursuing certain paths. Matthew grew up in Perth, Western Australia, near the sea, but left school at the age of 16:

> I was strongly encouraged to leave. The teachers couldn't understand why I was such a low achiever, yet obviously bright. They saw me as lazy. I had no ambition when I left school; the future looked bleak. All I knew was that I didn't want to be a manual labourer, but there weren't a lot of other choices. When I was 18, I was unemployed but I found out about a 12-week course at a technical college to become a deck hand. I enrolled and loved it; I learned how to splice ropes and wires and make lobster pots. It was so nice to succeed in something that wasn't academic. At the end of the course, I got a job as a fisherman on a fleet in northern Australia specializing in prawn fishing.

Like Pierre, Matthew felt that his holistic approach to problem-solving was a distinct advantage in his career as a fisherman:

> After four years at sea, I took my first written exam and got a skipper's qualification. I loved the work and the life. It was a way of escaping from the academic world where I'd always failed, but it involved using my intelligence. I had to understand the tides and weather systems. I remember my non-dyslexic skipper saying 'To catch prawns, you have to think like a prawn.' But the truth was, you had to be able to understand all the gears and the systems involved in setting up the ropes and traps on the trawler. Learning parrot fashion wouldn't work; when things got into a tangle, I could always sort it out. My ability to see things holistically meant that I could see the rigging all the way through and find out where any problems were in the way the ropes were set up. The challenge was to be diplomatic when I suggested a solution to my skipper – it was easy for me – I could see the whole picture, but he couldn't.

Other creative solutions: turning weaknesses into strengths

The success of dyslexic people may depend on their attitudes to both their weaknesses and their experience of failure. Are the obstacles they encounter 'stumbling blocks' or 'stepping stones'? One of the abilities of many successful dyslexic people is to respond creatively to turn their weaknesses into strengths.

Jenny describes her discovery when she was first teaching:

> I would put my overhead transparencies up and there would be spelling mistakes all the way through and the students would point them out. So I devel-

oped a coping strategy, and that's probably the first time I did. I said, 'That's just a test to see if you're reading properly.' So the next class there wouldn't be any mistakes because I would listen to what they said and they would correct the mistakes. So I started to find ways of coping with my difficulties. And that was the first time I thought, 'Oh, I can get other people to help me.'

Later, as a manager, she developed this further:

> I actually worked with people. That's how I managed. I used other people's skills to support me. I knew what I was good at and I knew what they were good at . . . I was good at delegating and good at using other people's skills.
>
> I also shared all information so everyone knew what I did. So when I went to a meeting, if I didn't understand something, someone else could tell me. When our team went on a teambuilding course, the course leader said he had never met such a good team. And it was all because I shared everything. What I knew, they knew.

She also has strategies to compensate for her weaknesses, particularly in organization; but these increase her effectiveness:

> I've got really good organizational strategies. I use Post-it notes like there's no tomorrow. I put my work on coloured paper. I use highlighter pens. My colleague has taught me to mind-map . . . I have to have everything tidy, otherwise I panic. I suppose in order to control my confusion threshold, I really have to be organized. And if I'm asked to do a task, I do it immediately.

As learning support provision developed, her director offered her the position of head of learning support in the college.

> I had a secretary and I got other people to help me with reports. They would do that for me and I would do something for them . . .
>
> I was really good at my job. I was good at persuading staff – I had a way of getting students [with learning difficulties] on to courses that no one else could. I was very good at getting money because I used to have a lot of ideas – and I could persuade people . . . I can see the whole thing. I use other people to actually put the bits and pieces in but I know the end result. So strategically I can work at quite a high level, but I use the skill of other people to fill in the bits . . . Colleges are only doing now what I did six years ago. I actually saw it [in my head] and I knew it would work.

The notion of delegating responsibility is an effective strategy for success in other jobs as well. Michaela explains how she dealt with her problems with reading and writing as a restaurant manager:

What I'd do is delegate a lot of the work . . . instead of me writing the specials on the board, I would give a waiter or waitress the responsibility and then they'd feel they're gaining something, you know, because their job role is not that interesting but is very mundane, isn't it? So I'd give them extra incentives and special privileges to make . . . their job better, but really it was just me cleverly getting out of not knowing how to spell things. I'd just keep delegating loads of stuff. Delegation was the main word. And it worked. They were happy, they were learning new techniques – I knew how to do these things. It gave them different responsibilities and they liked that. The time would go quicker, the work would be done faster and I'd design incentives so they would get more money doing different things, so they'd make something of it and it would satisfy them as well as satisfy me.

Using other people as a sounding board to check instructions helps Rob overcome his difficulties in processing verbal information quickly:

When I teach Wayne stuff in the kitchen, I always get him to repeat what I've said back to me, and that helps me. I do that, too. In the kitchen, when there's an order and he goes, 'Two linguini, one tagliatelli, one risotto, one calamare and one ravioli,' I would say that all back to him.

In doing this, Rob not only checks that Wayne has understood his instructions, but by hearing information repeated, he is able to check on the effectiveness of his own transmission and reception. The act of 'feeding back' information can overcome many situations where misunderstanding could have disastrous results. Moreover, the auditory reinforcement helps to consolidate the information in the memory.

'Goodness of fit'

Gerber et al. (1992) also identified 'goodness of fit' and the seeking and use of support systems as two key external factors in dyslexic people achieving success at work.

Kay's history demonstrates the importance of the 'fit' or match between the dyslexic person and the employment environment and expectations in creating success for both employer and employee.

I started out working with a kind of neighbourhood development group which was, I think, very creative and I was able to just kind of make my own job and it was people-oriented. And I did very well with that, it was really kind of matching up people with resources.

From there I ended up working with a developer, which was more structured. I remember there was a big joke about how I used to keep my tennis shoes in the filing cabinet. I didn't know what else to do with the filing cabinet. And it took me a long time – I was fairly disorganized, papers would be flying – I mean that's the way I tended to like working, I like to have papers flying and you know kind of be creating a lot of excitement around, and other people just looked at it in total amazement that I could get anything done. And in the process I think, one of the ways I coped – I mean I thought I was coping fine, being disorganized and funny and kind of scatty. And the reality was, other people couldn't deal with me. So I think the way I learned to cope was literally to change the way I was relating to people. I became much more focused, much more organized in terms of – I literally learned how to file, learned how to put paper away. But I remember thinking at the time, you know, it's like I'm some kind of Martian, I have to fit into their system. You know, it wasn't a natural system for me at all.

. . . Another job after that was two years doing market research. And again, I had a lot of trouble. It was numbers-oriented, even though it was on a computer. The creative part of it, going out and dealing with clients, understanding their needs, coming up with creative solutions for what a downtown centre would need in the way of a mix of office or retail – it was really exciting. The part that wasn't exciting was having to write a report and get the numbers right. And inevitably – I mean that's one of the most embarrassing moments when I'd turn in a report and find out that none of the numbers added up on the pages, and in fact I ended up getting fired from that job. And that was I'm sure part of it, just my inability to get a report out.

And I don't know how I coped with that, other than to realize that isn't my natural instinct. Even though I think I've pushed myself into wanting to be organized and efficient and deal with numbers and fit a mould, the reality is I realize that I can't be that kind of market research number-crunching kind of person.

So in fact the next job I took was with the English tourist board doing much more liaison work with consultants . . . [which was] very creative because it was looking at what the local needs were and working with consultants to make sure they came up with creative solutions. And my current job is a little bit of a mix of all of them but again doesn't require any real quantitative experience from me . . .

I much prefer being in a creative career where I can actually match people and resources and come up with something exciting. So in reality what I'm choosing, what experience I have is helping me get into fields where I can be creative as opposed to thinking I have to follow the right path that's going to be a 'success'. Maybe it [dyslexia] has been a great advantage in the sense that I've come to realize that I'm not going to be that kind of high-powered political or even business executive on some level, and in fact, that isn't really what I want to do . . .

I think that I tend to be more creative at work than most people and in some ways I can see how it [dyslexia] is giving me an edge at work because I think I have an ability to take three or four people and their ideas and merge them in a way that everybody's happy. I have a real ability to get everybody kind of moving in the same direction – other people tend to want to just see their own idea and not look at all the other options.

As we have shown, dyslexic people can be valuable employees, with much to contribute. Employers need to be aware that though some dyslexic difficulties seem like incompetence, they need not necessarily be an impediment to doing the job. There is almost always another way of doing something, and, if encouraged, the dyslexic person is likely to find a suitable way. For example, one dyslexic person who could not alphabetize for filing reorganized the filing system using colour coding, which everyone else also found easier to use.

Support from employers and colleagues can encourage creative rather than coping strategies. The most important support that employers and colleagues can offer the dyslexic employee is a willingness to understand the difficulties and find ways around them, while at the same time valuing and making use of the person's strengths and contributions to the job. Exploring solutions to problems and evaluating what is really important for the job can prevent minor difficulties becoming major ones.

Confidence in the dyslexic employee, flexibility and creative thinking will frequently bring about a satisfactory solution to seemingly serious problems. For instance, a supervisor in a nursery was concerned that a dyslexic trainee was unable to spell the children's names to write them on their work. The simple and satisfactory solution to the problem was to use sticky labels pre-printed with the names. (Klein and Sunderland, 1998). Computers, electronic organizers, large wall calendars, diaries and various computer programs can all help. Provision of a laptop for one dyslexic employee meant he could spend the extra time he needed to write reports at home. What is needed for real change is for the non-dyslexic employer or colleague to 'go through the looking-glass' and try to see the situation from the dyslexic person's perspective.

Chapter 7
The dyslexic adult and the learning context

Until relatively recently, there has been a lack of recognition of the fact that dyslexic children grow up to become dyslexic adults. The meagre available energy and resources were invariably concentrated on encouraging diagnosis and appropriate teaching for dyslexic children. When literacy skills were not critical to employability, many undiagnosed dyslexic adults were subsumed within manual trades where they could avoid reading and writing. In Britain during the 1970s and 1980s, there was a developing awareness of and concern about low literacy skills in adults which, coupled with the decline of employment opportunities in the craft and manual trades, led to a campaign to enrol adults in basic education classes. During the early to mid-1980s, tutors in adult basic education in England began to identify dyslexia as a major factor among the increasing number of adults seeking help in these classes. At the same time, media coverage on dyslexia elicited responses from adults who wanted diagnosis and help for themselves, not just their children.

A new framework of provision for the post-16 sector in England is now being established with emphasis on the need to encourage and fund provision for lifelong learning as a means of increasing the employability of young people and adults. Changes in the employment market have resulted in a different employment culture; no longer do individuals enter jobs for life. Ongoing training and education are necessary to ensure that available skills among the workforce are commensurate with the demands of employers. The government recognizes the need for both flexibility of provision and innovative approaches to teaching and learning.

It also set up a working group to advise on ways to support and develop the government's plan for adult basic skills provision. The report of the working group, chaired by Sir Claus Moser, refers to the appalling statistics that an estimated 20 per cent of adults, or roughly seven million, have severe problems with basic skills, that is 'less literacy than is expected from an 11-year-old child' (Moser, 1999). Many of these people are likely to be dyslexic.

In the last 20 to 25 years, two broadly distinct groups of dyslexic adult learners have returned to education. The first group includes those compensated adults whose dyslexic difficulties may appear on the surface to have been overcome; the second is composed of those adults who were largely failed by the educational system and who left school lacking basic literacy skills. For each of these groups, dyslexia has far-reaching, though differing, consequences. Adults who have apparently overcome their difficulties may have achieved levels of academic success in the past that enable them to gain entry into higher education. However, many of their dyslexia-related difficulties surface when they are under pressure from the demands placed on them to perform at higher academic levels. Some adults may actually begin study at postgraduate level before their dyslexia is discovered.

Not all adult returners have a university degree as their goal. Many adults simply want to redress the limitations of their previous educational experience or improve their employability. They may enrol on vocational courses or in basic education classes. The changing needs and demands of society have resulted in the development of new qualifications. However, at the same time, highly practical courses that might attract dyslexic adults place increasing emphasis on written skills. The relatively high-level demands for literacy and numeracy in these courses create obstacles for many dyslexic people. Current government drives to raise the standards of basic skills, though intended to increase opportunities, may actually create more barriers. Literacy and numeracy are rightly issues of access but may serve to exclude rather than include if seen as ends in themselves.

Adults who lack basic literacy skills include those with a variety of learning needs. Some may be barely able to read, while others may be able to read beyond functional level, but may have significant spelling problems. Their difficulties impinge more dramatically in a world where vocational qualifications are demanding more evidence of written language skills.

There are two very important recent developments in education in the UK which have had a significant impact on the increase of dyslexic adults in further and higher education. One is the widened access to higher education; the second is the change in funding in further education to provide specialist diagnosis and support.

The élitist nature of higher education has been challenged by open-door policies that recognize the importance of acknowledging non-traditional qualifications for entry. Further education colleges, which had previously offered primarily vocational courses, have developed access to higher education courses. These offer an alternative route into higher education for mature adults who lack traditional entry qualifications but who bring with them a wealth of life experiences. Many newer universities actively seek to recruit mature students in recognition of this important market of potential students.

To achieve the goal of widening access to people from disadvantaged groups involves considering the needs of people with disabilities, including dyslexia. With the increase of recruitment from the population of mature students, many undiagnosed dyslexic adults have found their way into further and higher education. As educational opportunities increasingly open up to students lacking traditional entry qualifications, more dyslexic adults embark on a variety of courses leading to a wide range of qualifications, from vocational qualifications to university degrees. Although their academic skills may be weak, they often bring with them determination, coupled with maturity and willingness to work hard.

With appropriate support, more and more dyslexic adults are proving their ability to succeed. The report of the National Working Party on Dyslexia in Higher Education (Singleton, 1999) found the overall incidence of dyslexia in the higher education population in the UK in 1996–97 to be 1.35 per cent, with over 40 per cent of those students being diagnosed post-admission. Based on these statistics, the working party concluded that 'the true incidence of dyslexia in higher education in the UK at the present time lies somewhere between 1.2% and 1.5% of all students, i.e. about 20,400–25,500 students in total'. Although these figures represent a huge increase in dyslexic students in higher education, they also point to a dramatic under-representation of dyslexic people relative to the general population, where the incidence is estimated by the British Dyslexia Association to be between four and ten per cent. A possible explanation for this disparity is that those dyslexic students who attend higher education institutions which do not have facilities to organize diagnoses and support are not reflected in the figures. Moreover, it is difficult to know how many dyslexic students do not even consider applying, or simply drop out due to lack of support. The existing figures nonetheless underline the importance of having appropriate support systems in place to encourage retention of those students identified as dyslexic.

A large number of adult returners left school at the statutory leaving age of 15 or 16 and entered employment in a variety of areas. They may have worked and/or raised families, but lack a sense of fulfilment in their lives. They return for many reasons: the need to prove themselves, lack of employment or redundancy, or changes in work expectations. They may be unconfident, even reluctant, students. The re-entry to formal education can be accompanied by a resurfacing of difficulties from earlier schooling, along with feelings of anger and frustration as the realization that their literacy skills are insufficient to demonstrate their level of cognitive and practical functioning.

Gilroy (1995) highlights the contrast between mature dyslexic students and their younger colleagues:

> For a mature student to be newly assessed as dyslexic can be very stressful; old fears and negative thoughts well up from the past, there is often anger at past neglect, there are worries about being 'disabled', about implications for children, for careers. These students . . . contrast with a newly emerging group of 18-year-olds who have benefited from the 1981 Education Act, been assessed at a young age and who have grown up with the knowledge that they are dyslexic. They seek help with their studies but do not suffer the deep-rooted anxieties of these other students.

The other significant development has been the introduction of specific funding for supporting students with learning difficulties and disabilities in further education colleges. For the first time ever in the post-16 sector, colleges were required by law 'to have regard' to the requirements of students with learning difficulties and disabilities

(Further and Higher Education Act, 1992). Students with disabilities, including dyslexic students, were no longer Cinderellas, but were invited to the ball – and given money for the ballgown. This had a tremendous impact on the development of provision and support for dyslexic students and more particularly on the availability of a diagnostic assessment for those who had never been assessed. As a result, more low-achieving young people and adults from working-class and ethnic minority backgrounds on vocational courses have been identified and given support. This has enabled them to achieve and, in some cases, to progress to higher education.

The Act also led to the setting up of a committee under Professor John Tomlinson to investigate provision for students with learning difficulties and/or disabilities and to advise the government on whether the new legal requirements were being satisfied. The committee's report, called *Inclusive Learning* (HMSO, 1996) has helped to set the agenda for post-16 education. Inclusiveness, or the notion that what is available to one member of a society should be available to all its members, fits well with the emphasis on widening participation, making it incumbent upon institutions to identify the learning needs of groups of people previously excluded from mainstream provision. This has also led to a rapid expansion in courses to train teaching staff to diagnose and support dyslexic students.

In setting up the new post-16 framework, the government is changing the structure of funding to include community and work-based training on the same basis as colleges. It is acknowledging the need for 'flexible and innovative approaches' (*Learning to Succeed*, DfEE 1999) in order to attract those who have previously been excluded from education. This certainly includes many dyslexic adults.

A truly inclusive model demands not only specialist support but an understanding of the institution's role in supporting students, from the classroom teacher to library staff and curriculum managers. This means a concerted staff development strategy to involve all staff in the support of dyslexic students.

Defining the challenges

In addition to the changes in access, funding and the design of new qualifications, there have also been changes in the approach to teaching and learning to accommodate increasing numbers of students and evolving educational goals. The traditional model of lectures, seminars and tutorials is gradually being replaced by emphasis on group work activities, independent learning and computer-based courses. These changing approaches to course delivery pose different challenges to the dyslexic learner from those encountered in more traditional models. In some cases, the dyslexic learning style may be advantageous and students may find that some of their holistic strengths become a valuable resource. Graham describes what he sees as the benefits of his dyslexia for his degree course in business:

> . . . I'm studying corporate strategy, which is putting all the elements of my course together, like marketing, finance, business applications, accountancy . . . sort of working out strategies for companies. To me this is very simple, working out how or what went wrong. I think that's something to do with my dyslexia, 'cos I get this really broad picture when looking at something. I can see everybody else is really struggling with it. I'm quite happy with things like that. And also, the creative things in marketing, creative ideas, I'm really good at those.

These changes with more and more emphasis on the individual learner also present challenges to teachers and lecturers to ensure that each student can learn effectively and achieve individual and vocational goals. This means developing approaches to teaching that appeal to the wide variety of learning styles of all their students, dyslexic and non-dyslexic alike.

It is important to recognize that, frequently, strategies and approaches that are beneficial for dyslexic adults also suit the needs of many non-dyslexic students. It is therefore not always necessary to consider a separate approach to teaching the dyslexic learner. However, a crucial distinction between dyslexic students and their non-dyslexic peers is that the latter will probably manage regardless of how they are taught, whereas dyslexic learners may very well fail if the teaching does not suit their learning style.

As a general rule, dyslexic students learn best when material is presented in a multi-sensory way. Having visual props such as overhead transparencies, diagrams and flow charts will help students who find it difficult to take in information primarily through auditory channels. If these are made available as photocopies prior to the lecture, the dyslexic student will find it easier to process the information that is being presented orally. Similarly, a student who finds it difficult to process visual information will benefit from more auditory input; discussions may help to consolidate new information and ideas. Many students find that their learning is enhanced when tactile and kinaesthetic strategies are employed. For example, students may find that acting out situations or case studies through role-play helps them to commit information to their long-term memories. The greater the variety of ways in which information is presented, the more likely it will be that effective learning will take place.

Traditional ways of presenting information usually conform to the way in which teachers themselves learn best, but do not take into account the cross-section of students in their classrooms. In recollecting his experiences at school, Graham's views of his teachers indicate an insight into this conflict between teaching and learning styles:

> I could understand that the problem was theirs a lot of the time and not mine; I would understand that if I was taught differently, I would have understood. I felt that they weren't good teachers. I've tried to bring that out more in the last couple of years, when people try to teach me something. I don't look at it as a problem that I can't learn. I try to look at it as the fact that they can't teach me.

Other students, who become more aware of their own learning preferences, actively seek out teachers whose teaching style coincides with their learning style. Roberta, a kinaesthetic learner, avoided subjects that were predominantly lecture-based and chose a course that had mostly laboratory classes. She understood that her own learning would be enhanced primarily through practical activities and discussion rather than by lectures.

There is a need to shift the responsibility for previous educational failure from the learners themselves to their teachers. This change in attitudes can have a significant effect on students' self-esteem. Many adults who have not succeeded within the educational system blame themselves for their failure. However, if the onus is placed on teachers to teach in a way that enables students to learn, individual students can begin to view the problem as one in which the system has failed them, rather than accept that the failure was their fault. This change in emphasis can be instrumental in allowing the adult student to re-enter education with a positive outlook.

In response to the widening access to further and higher education, all teachers need to re-evaluate their approach to teaching to accommodate larger numbers of students with a wider range of individual needs. Traditional models are no longer viable. The emphasis is more and more on the individual learner. For example, in further education every student has an individual learning plan and institutions are expected to show that individual needs are being met.

The learning style of dyslexic students is commonly characterized by holistic, non-linear, often visual thinking. Tasks involving sequencing are often problematic. Academic success, in contrast, requires well-organized, logically ordered written work with clear sentence structure and accurate spelling. Moreover, complex reading skills are required both in academic pursuits and vocational areas. Tracking difficulties may create problems in following a line of print or correctly identifying a word. The person's eye may 'jump' on the page, resulting in misreading. This can lead to misinterpreted questions and/or difficulty in understanding texts. One student misread an economics question as ' . . . explain the flow in this argument'. The student copied the question on to a separate piece of paper to bring to her session with her support tutor. After a frustrating hour, both realized that the question in its existing form was not possible to answer. Had the tutor seen the original, it would most likely have been clear where the problem lay. In fact, the question asked the student to ' . . . explain the *flaw* in this argument'.

Because of their dyslexia, students face problems when their written work is assessed. Weak proof-reading, caused by difficulties in 'spotting' errors, may easily be misinterpreted as laziness or lack of concern. Time and again students report their frustration when they receive comments suggesting that they did not proof-read their work. They may have checked it four or five times, but simply could not 'see' their errors.

Note-taking is another challenge for dyslexic students. Poor handwriting and short-term memory deficits may lead to inaccurate note-taking. Most find it very difficult to listen and write at the same time, and spelling difficulties may exacerbate the problems. They may need copies of notes from the tutor or another student, to learn a mind-mapping approach or to use tapes as back-up.

Difficulties organizing work and managing time are further taxed by the demands of working to a deadline and juggling assignments. The fact that several assignments may all fall due at the same time makes it extremely difficult to prioritize and organize the workload.

Writing under timed conditions creates great stress and may result in confused expression and inadequate answers. Reading difficulties may also be exacerbated under stress.

Although by no means an exhaustive list, this overview explains why a dyslexic student's true ability is often not demonstrated. However, teachers themselves may present the greatest challenge as they may not understand the nature of the dyslexic student's difficulties and therefore do not know how to help. For instance, one student was unable to understand his error in a maths problems even though the tutor tried to explain it. The tutor was not able to understand that the student could not 'pick up' from where he made his error, but needed to go back to the beginning and go through all the steps again. Dyslexic students are also often bewildered by expectations that are implicit. They need to have the conventions and expectations for essays, exams and assignments made explicit. For example, a student on a jewellery course could not understand what her tutor meant when he asked her to 'develop' her design. Her support tutor suggested she ask the tutor to show her an example of 'developing a design' as none of his verbal explanations made sense to her.

Assessing achievement

One of the obstacles to success in the academic environment for many dyslexic students is the difficulty in demonstrating their knowledge within conventional academic expectations. Dyslexic difficulties are intensified under stress: both slow processing and poor short-term memory make it particularly difficult to produce work under time-constrained conditions such as examinations. In recognition of this fact, many examination boards and colleges and universities offer dyslexic students extra time (usually between 10 and 15 minutes per hour) to 'level the playing field' with their non-dyslexic peers. However, although extra time may suffice for many students, it does not overcome the problems experienced by others, who may be disadvantaged by an assessment system that demands the very skills with which they struggle. To obtain a fair basis of assessment, institutions must look at individual needs and make arrangements accordingly.

For example, students who have persistent reading difficulties may fail an examination simply because they misread the questions, not because they lacked knowledge of the subject. Students who have visual processing difficulties may be helped by having examination scripts printed in a larger font or on coloured paper. Others find it necessary to hear the questions read aloud, either on tape or by a reader. Indeed, in recognition of the reading difficulties experienced by many adults, the Department of Vehicle Licensing allows prospective drivers to have a taped version of the multiple choice questions required to pass the theory part of the driving test.

Students with severe spelling or handwriting problems are disadvantaged either because they cannot produce a script using the words they want or write legibly. One tutor was so shocked by the illegible scrawl that was submitted by a law student that she asked him to read his script aloud to her. Her impression of the student's excellent understanding and knowledge of the subject was confirmed when she heard his answers; had she not given him the chance to read to her, she would have had to fail him. In subsequent examinations, he was allowed to dictate his answers onto tape for transcription by an audio-typist. Other accommodations for such students might include the use of a word processor, dictation to an amanuensis who scribes the student's words, or examination by *viva voce*, that is, an oral examination. However, these accommodations often require developing a different set of skills, such as good keyboard skills or the ability to dictate ideas in 'written' form, and may need practice before being recommended.

Interestingly, research has shown an average increase of 13.5 per cent in correct responses on examinations using computer-based assessment. The research at the University of Derby suggests that when information is presented in large font, with one item presented at a time, candidates can overcome many of the problems associated with traditional multiple choice tests, which are particularly non-friendly for dyslexic students (Constantine, 2000).

For some students who are disadvantaged by examination assessments, one solution is to enrol for classes that have different methods of assessment. However, even coursework-based assessment may disadvantage dyslexic students, who find it difficult to express their ideas in writing. Errors in spelling, syntax and punctuation, coupled with word omissions, poor organization and weak expression all contribute to limiting the ability of students to demonstrate their knowledge and potential. There is often a marked discrepancy between what the student knows and what he is able to communicate in writing. For example, many students flourish in an environment that encourages them to produce visual representations to demonstrate their creative thinking. Cooper's research (1996) with vocational students in further education involved classifying them in terms of their location on two dimensions of thinking, a verbal-visual axis and a holistic-sequential axis. He identified learners who were dominantly visual and holistic as being particularly disadvantaged by the fact that

> their learning performances are often misinterpreted by teachers. Their learning tends to happen when the picture falls into place, rather than as a product of measurable effort . . . The disadvantage is particularly evident in the assessment process.
>
> (Cooper, 1996)

It is therefore important to consider alternative forms of assessment for such students.

Art and design students often present excellent three-dimensional models through which they can demonstrate a wealth of knowledge. Other students can prove their problem-solving skills and subject understanding through producing videos, diagrams or posters and offering oral presentations to show their understanding of concepts being assessed. Students on vocational courses may be able to produce excellent examples of their work, but may not succeed on written examinations. Ed, for example, was a creative painter and decorator with skills in producing complex artistic effects. He had never, however, attained the qualification he required because he was unable to read the questions on a written examination. To ensure that society is not denied the rich contributions of dyslexic adults, it is essential to devise new forms of assessment which offer a fair basis on which to judge individual talents and achievements.

Competence-based portfolios are used increasingly to offer candidates an opportunity to demonstrate their skills in more varied ways than traditional examinations and essays. However, at the same time, efforts to obtain 'parity' between vocational and academic qualifications have resulted in more emphasis on written assessment. Opportunities for work-based assessments of theory need to be valued and seen as equally valid to more traditional assessments. For instance, one group of trainees was assessed on theory in their workplace by talking through the reasons for their decisions as they demonstrated a procedure.

Group assignments

Increasingly, many courses require students to work in groups and submit coursework in the form of a group presentation or combined written assignment. This poses interesting challenges for the dyslexic learner who may be both advantaged and disadvantaged by the demands of group work. On the positive side, if dyslexic students are prepared to share the fact of their dyslexia with their peers, they may benefit from being able to 'volunteer' to take on those tasks that appeal to their strengths. For example, they may be very competent in researching and gathering information, particularly if this involves contacting people or organizations by telephone or in person. Many dyslexic students have excellent 'people skills' which enable them to organize and possibly chair group meetings. They may feel comfortable contributing to group discussions about the topic or suggesting ways of approaching tasks. Often the creative, 'right-brained' attack on the subject may shed a different light on the way in which the project is tackled. A holistic view may provide other group members with new insights to explore. If dyslexic adults offer to work in areas that reflect their strengths, they may also be able to ask other members of the group to take on aspects of the assignment with which they are less confident. For example, another student may act as the scribe for group meetings, taking and distributing notes. Someone might volunteer to proof-read for the dyslexic student, thus relieving the pressure caused by worry about poor spelling, punctuation and written expression.

Although many dyslexic people rely on their strong verbal skills, they may have difficulties in finding a space to be heard in group discussions. Sarah was a dyslexic social work student who had difficulty with visual and auditory processing. She was highly articulate and presented her thoughts orally in a coherent, well-expressed fashion. It therefore came as a surprise to her tutor when she indicated that she found it extremely difficult to enter into discussions in a group. Sarah explained:

> It takes me time to digest what people are saying when there are several people talking. I find that by the time I have processed what has been said and figured out what I wanted to say, the conversation has moved on and it is no longer possible to get my foot in the door.

These problems are exacerbated when several people talk at once. Andy explained his frustrations at entering group discussions:

> I have difficulty in groups detecting when to speak. I don't seem to be able to hear the changes in tone. When I speak to one person I feel I may rely more on the visual clues rather than the vocal ones.

The issue for such students is not comprehension, but rather speed of processing. They are usually fine in one-to-one discussions or in class when there is a pause after each person has spoken, but in group situations the rapidity of incoming information results in delayed processing. They may also find it difficult to handle auditory information when it is being received from several directions at once. This is often the case when students sit in classrooms and try to process discussions from people seated in front of and behind them. Some students find it easier to assimilate information if they sit at the front, others at the back of the room. Jean explained:

> I don't have to concentrate so hard if I sit at the back – I can just sit back and let all the words come to me.

Other people develop a strategy to address this problem which may be perceived as an irritating response. They may constantly say 'Pardon' or 'Excuse me' as a means of getting information repeated, when it appears that they have actually heard what was said. The strategy serves as a delaying tactic to allow the information received to be processed. Unfortunately, it may be misinterpreted as a failure to pay attention and can be annoying to others. Anastasia, a Greek student, was so distressed by her inability to process auditory information correctly, that she always took her boyfriend with her when she had to understand 'important' information, such as from the bank, the tax office, the doctor or her tutors. Without him, she could never be sure that she had correctly interpreted what was being said. Interestingly, this was nothing to do with the fact that she was a non-native English speaker. On the contrary, she had the same problem in all four languages she spoke (Greek, English, Spanish and French).

Some dyslexic students may find group assignments daunting. Their complaints may be partly for the same reasons as those of their non-dyslexic colleagues, namely the fact that some group members are unreliable and do not carry their weight in the division of labour. However, the educational rationale for assigning group work may be precisely because it mirrors 'real life' situations and teaches participants how to deal with the challenges of being a good team member. In addition to these general concerns, the pace at which the group works may frustrate the dyslexic individual. Many, if not most, dyslexic adults need to spend considerably more time than their peers to produce work that reflects their knowledge and understanding. For this reason, it is essential that they spread out their work and do not leave it until the last minute. Unfortunately, other students are often not as disciplined or organized and can often 'get by' with last-minute efforts. This can be disastrous for the dyslexic student, who needs to meet at regular intervals to collate work and discuss the next steps. Michaela comments:

> I feel angry because I want to get it all done and everyone else wants to leave it to the last minute. I find this really annoying. A lot of my friends feel they produce better work when they're under pressure, but I can't work like that. I often take the lead in group work; I can organize people, but the problem is to try to get them to produce the work.

The dyslexic student needs assignments to be broken down into manageable chunks and this may not be consistent with the working style of the rest of the group.

Another drawback to group work for dyslexic students is the forced exposure of their weaknesses to their peers. Students who are not embarrassed by their dyslexia may feel comfortable about confiding their weaknesses and may offer to contribute in areas where they feel confident. However, such students have generally known about their dyslexia for many years and have learned how to accommodate their difficulties. Recently diagnosed mature students may remain reluctant to share their problems with other students. They may feel a sense of embarrassment, or fear the response of others. They may perceive a stigma attached to the label or may simply feel ashamed of the visible signs such as poor spelling or difficulty taking down written information. When working on individual assignments, these students may have developed adequate coping strategies, but the group pressure to 'perform' publicly makes it difficult for them to hide their weaknesses. If teachers are aware of these issues, they can suggest solutions. They might, for example, make group assignments optional (for all students). If the assignments are a mandatory course requirement, the teacher might try to discuss the situation with the dyslexic student and place her in a group with students who will be sensitive and offer appropriate support. Opportunities for dyslexic students to work together can also be helpful, as these reduce the stress of having to perform before others and offer chances both to share strategies and to feel less isolated.

Impact of technology

Another major change in education today is the role of technology in both teaching and learning. For some dyslexic students, technological advances have provided the necessary help to enable them to succeed in academic spheres and to compete from an equal vantage point. Computer technology can offer dramatic support to students who might never have succeeded academically in the pre-technology age. For many adults, the emergence from the 'dark ages' to a new 'technological age' offers hope for circumventing the technical hitches that previously made it impossible to communicate effectively in writing. It also demands a new range of skills and ways of thinking that may suit the dyslexic cognitive style.

Many dyslexic people have a natural affinity for computers. Nevertheless, those who are gifted in their abilities with computing may struggle with using language to express themselves. Neil was self-educated in computer programming and problem-solving. When his successful business was purchased by a larger company, he decided to take advantage of his new-found economic freedom to return to study, enrolling on an HND in computer studies. After the first year of this two-year course, he was invited to progress – on to a Master's degree course! His sophisticated knowledge and insights into computers were so astounding that his lecturers felt he would be wasting his time studying at an undergraduate level. The MSc facilitated more personal growth and development as he was encouraged to pursue an independent project. However, in spite of completing his MSc, Neil continued to struggle with basic literacy skills.

There is a range of computer 'solutions' which might address the difficulties students encounter in academic performance. Dyslexic students are hampered by a lack of technical or secretarial (transcription) skills, rather than limited knowledge or understanding that might affect content. Although dyslexic people may also have problems with composition, these are not necessarily dyslexia related. In other words, all students, dyslexic or not, may find the content of a subject challenging, but the non-dyslexic student will usually have an advantage over his dyslexic peer in that he will not have to expend energy worrying about the technical skills of writing. However, some specific composition problems for dyslexic individuals may occur as a result of general sequencing difficulties which create organizational chaos. Another area affecting composition may be expressive language difficulties, manifested in problems with word retrieval or awkward use of language.

According to Nicolson and Fawcett (1990), 'dyslexic reading and writing performance appears more effortful, more prone to error, and more easily disrupted than normal performance'. They hypothesize that dyslexic individuals fail to automatize the subskills necessary for fluency in reading and writing. This hypothesis could explain the fact that many dyslexic people feel defeated by the size of the task of simultaneously being able to think and write down their ideas. As one dyslexic student put it, 'Ideas just explode in my head, but I can't get them down on paper.' The transcription skills that non-dyslexic writers take for granted (e.g. spelling, punctuation, paragraphing, and handwriting) constantly interfere with the thought process; these are the very skills the dyslexic writer has been unable to automatize. Frank Smith (1982) argues that the transcription and composition skills involved in writing are conflicting tasks that compete for the writer's attention. He suggests that this competition can be the source of writing difficulties. The battles between composing and transcribing must be resolved if dyslexic students are to be judged on an even footing with their non-dyslexic peers. Technology certainly provides a key to overcoming many of the transcription problems faced by the dyslexic adult.

Word processing

Word processing has revolutionized the writing process, allowing all writers the freedom to draft and redraft without the physically laborious task of rewriting or retyping. The ease with which the writer can delete, move, 'copy and paste' text encourages the attainment of precision in expression and more effective organisation. Moreover, clear and immediate visual feedback supports students who might otherwise have given up in despair; spellchecker and thesaurus facilities make it easier for dyslexic writers to experiment with expanding their vocabulary. Changes to the colour of the screen or size or type of font may aid some students to read and thus check their work more easily.

However, word processing is not necessarily the panacea that it is purported to be. Set against its many advantages is the need to learn a new set of skills, both in an operational sense (e.g. how to open, save and organize files, how to edit, design layout, etc.), and in terms of motor skills (manipulating a mouse and mastering use of the keyboard). Technophobia may make these tasks daunting for the adult learner. David had a computer for two years before confessing to his tutor that he rewrote several drafts of each essay by hand before typing it on the computer. When asked whether he used the cut, copy and paste facilities on the computer, he admitted ignorance. In fact, he was struggling with the basics of keyboard skills and had no knowledge of the range of functions that the computer could offer. As illustrated by David's case, the notion of a computer as an 'answer to the dyslexic student's prayers' may raise unrealistic hopes unless appropriate training is available.

In addition, lecturers are often less sympathetic to dyslexic difficulties when students have produced work on a word processor. They may assume that a spellchecker will eliminate all spelling errors. In fact, the spellchecker may be unable to offer a correct alternative to a highlighted error or the student may not see a difference between the alternative presented and the original attempt (e.g. 'actualy' and 'actually'). Moreover, students with weak word recognition may mistakenly choose the wrong word from a list of options; this can result in the type of error that unwittingly befell one student, whose sentence related to 'scarred cows wondering about India' when her intention was to write about 'sacred cows wandering about India.'

Isobel describes her discovery of the limitations of spellcheckers:

I did an essay about psychologists. Because the computer gives you choices, I
chose 'physiologist' since the shape [of the word] was the same. So each time I
wanted to say 'psychologist', I chose 'physiologist.' I just saw it as the word I was
looking for. When the essay came back, the tutor asked me to look up the difference between a psychologist and a physiologist – I still didn't know why she was
asking, since when I looked back, it still looked right. So the computer doesn't
solve spelling problems.

The word processor cannot pick up common dyslexic problems such
as word omissions, inappropriately used vocabulary or punctuation
errors. Some of these problems may be even more apparent in a
word-processed text, since the commonly used strategy of covering
up poor spelling and confused punctuation by poor handwriting is
no longer available. Thus, a beautifully presented piece of work may
be returned with highly critical and soul-destroying comments.

Many word processing programs contain built-in grammar checks
that highlight possible errors in syntax. Unfortunately, they assume an
existing knowledge of rules of grammar that would allow the user to
judge the accuracy of the query raised to determine whether to
accept the suggested change. This is often confusing for the dyslexic
user, who may have limited knowledge about grammatical terms and
conventions. The result may be that the writer agrees the change
simply because the computer has made the suggestion, but this can
be disastrous, possibly resulting in a less well-constructed sentence
than the original. One student commented, 'I just fiddle around with
the green lines until they go away – then I know it's OK.' Students
must be warned about these inherent dangers and advised not to use
the grammar check if they are unsure about its recommendations.

However, the word processor can transform the work of students
with handwriting difficulties. Where the student previously had to
concentrate on forming letters, he is now free to attend to what he
wants to say. For many such students, using a keyboard allows them to
express themselves adequately for the first time. The difference in the
quality of their work can be so extreme as to be almost unrecognizable.

Screen readers

A screen reader, such as *Keystone* or *Read and Write Texthelp*, encourages the use of multi-sensory strategies. These programs, which read

aloud text from the screen, assist the dyslexic writer to hear errors, such as inappropriate choice of vocabulary (a correctly spelled but misused word, e.g. 'quiet' instead of 'quite'), word omissions, and awkward sentence structure. All too often, these errors are not picked up through conventional proof-reading since the student sees what was intended, rather than what actually appears on the paper. However, employing both visual and auditory cues can often alleviate this difficulty. *Texthelp* has many other useful features, including text enlargement and in-built spellchecker. The program's facility to read aloud the options offered by the spellchecker makes it less likely that the user will select an inappropriate word. Students are also helped to identify poor punctuation when they can hear their work read aloud. Finally the use of speech synthesis is a significant contribution to independence, as it is possible to hear one's own work as often as necessary without having to rely on another person to read it aloud. Thus, for students whose preferred learning modality is auditory, speech synthesis is a considerable bonus.

Anne sings the praises of *Texthelp* and the liberation of using a computer:

> I use him [*Texthelp*] for punctuation, spelling mistakes. He'll read back a sentence to me and I'll think, well, no, that's grammatically incorrect or that's not how I would say it, so you learn to rearrange sentences. And just the actual invention of the computer – the first time I sat down at a computer and was able to use the computer at the speed at which my mind goes . . . It's just wonderful. [With writing] I felt that my hand could never keep up.

Screen readers can be invaluable for helping students to identify errors and thus improve their writing skills. They may also address the needs of students with poor reading skills, including those whose reading problems stem from Scotopic Sensitivity (or Meares-Irlen) Syndrome (SSS). Individuals with SSS generally suffer from light sensitivity and find that reading causes extreme fatigue, resulting largely from distorted perception of print (Irlen, 1991). When screen readers are used together with a scanner, text can be scanned into the computer and then read aloud; many students find that this facility improves their comprehension. Moreover, some students have reported significant improvements in their reading skills as a result of the multi-sensory input gained from simultaneously hearing and seeing the text. Freedom to adapt the screen colour and font size also helps to reduce those errors resulting from unstable visual perception. Text-enlarging facilities limit the range of words appearing on screen, thus facilitating accuracy in reading.

Not everyone, however, adapts easily to the use of a screen reader. Kaptan, a dyslexic information technology student, gave *Texthelp* a rating of eight on a scale of ten. Despite his positive overall reaction, he points out that, 'It also has some drawbacks . . . the synthetic voice is irritating at first, but it grows on you eventually.' Some students have difficulty discriminating between the sounds, especially since the 'voice' relies on phonetic pronunciation. Students with weak auditory discrimination may prefer to read the text aloud themselves.

Another helpful tool for students with poor reading skills is the Reading Pen, which scans a word from the printed page, displays it on the pen's self-contained screen, and reads the word aloud. It can offer definitions, display syllables and spell out the word letter-by-letter. Although this is not a useful aid for a student struggling to read extensive text, it is particularly valuable to someone like Rob who needs help decoding the occasional word. He comments about its value in figuring out unfamiliar words in recipes which he must read for his job as a chef:

> The pen is a great thing. It gets you past that little bit, because that's the stage I'm at. I'm at the stage where I can read, but I get stuck, so then I just use the pen. I get a lot more confidence when I use the pen – my lifesaver.

Planning programmes

The creative, holistic approach employed by 'global thinkers', along with weakness in sequencing, can hinder their ability to present a cogent, linear argument, a crucial ingredient of academic success. Feedback on their writing may indicate that the ideas appear to be there, but the order is muddled and it is difficult to follow the line of reasoning. For such students, software programs that help with planning and organizing may be useful. One such program, *Inspiration*, enables users to produce a mind-map of their ideas, which can then be reorganized and, if necessary, presented in linear fashion to help organize the flow of writing. The ability to 'brainstorm' ideas before structuring the essay ensures that the learner can get down ideas without fear of forgetting them and can then determine what is or is not relevant.

Study skills software

Dyslexic students who are fortunate enough to be diagnosed and given learning support may find that new approaches to their learning that address their individual strengths can greatly improve their academic performance. However, learning support is additional to existing study, placing demands on the student to assimilate new approaches to learning at the same time as concentrating on learning their subject. Moreover, dyslexic students need to overlearn; that is, their learning of new skills and information must be reviewed and reinforced over and over again to ensure the transfer to long-term memory. It is therefore extremely helpful for individuals to review learning strategies as often as possible and at their own pace. *Wordswork* is a software package designed to help dyslexic students to address their study skills. It is based on a learning-styles approach to improving learning skills and encourages users to identify their own learning strengths. Through a series of interactive exercises it engages learners in tasks to help them practise the strategies presented. Although aimed at adults, the program does not assume knowledge. It therefore provides teaching in basic skills, such as how to use an apostrophe correctly, as well as more sophisticated study skills including examination revision and essay writing strategies. All material presented on screen is also offered in voice-overs, ensuring that the program is truly multi-sensory and accessible even to those people who are not proficient readers.

The use of word processing and enhancement software – including speech synthesis, planning, and study skills programs – can yield increased independence and improved writing and reading skills for many dyslexic adults. Recommendations for computer use should acknowledge the need to develop the essential motor skills, including mouse control and keyboard proficiency. Students with a reasonable level of competence in these areas can then explore available software to improve their academic skills, but the importance of initial technology training and continued support if necessary should not be overlooked.

Voice recognition systems and the severely dyslexic student

What of the student whose difficulties are so severe that the achievement of basic word-processing skills is an unrealistic goal? Students with severe motor or auditory processing skills may have persistent spelling or handwriting difficulties that seriously impede their ability to commit their thoughts to paper. They may also find it difficult to develop the necessary keyboard and mouse skills, resulting in an enormous time lag between their thoughts and their ability to convey them on paper. For some dyslexic students, the difficulty and seeming futility of the task stops them from even wanting to write. The main option previously available to such students is the use of an amanuensis to enable them to vocalize their thoughts and have someone else scribe their words. This time-consuming and disheartening strategy implies total dependence on another person. Using a dictaphone is a modification of this approach and relies on subsequent transcription by an audio-typist, often resulting in considerable delay between composing the thoughts and receiving visual feedback. Severe spelling difficulties may mean that any changes in the original dictation must be sent back to the audio-typist to correct. The laborious and expensive nature of this process may result in accepting the first draft as 'good enough,' which means the student's full potential is not realized.

John is an example of a student who achieved independence through voice recognition software. He left school at 14, unable to read or write. He eventually taught himself to read, but his severe spelling difficulties seemed insurmountable. During the 1980s adult literacy campaign, John was encouraged to return to study in the hope that he could overcome his difficulties. In his mid-20s, he was diagnosed as dyslexic by a dyslexia-trained adult literacy tutor who encouraged him to pursue an access course. When he progressed to a degree course, he found the demands of higher education exceedingly difficult to meet. However, he developed a sophisticated strategy for using his considerable oral strengths to dictate ideas for subsequent transcription. John also became interested in computers and developed the technical skills to manipulate text on the screen, allowing him to edit text that the audio-typist produced on disk. Unfortunately, although he could delete, cut and paste and move text, he remained unable to alter his original writing significantly unless he had someone to help him spell new words. A spellchecker was of little use; it served only to highlight the incorrectly spelled words that John could easily identify himself. But his bizarre spelling patterns were too unusual for the spellchecker to offer a reasonable alternative. John's determination and newly-discovered optimism led him to believe that one day technology would advance to the stage where it would be possible to speak directly to a computer and have the dictated words appear in print.

To John's delight, that day arrived, and he discovered true independence. Voice recognition software allows the user to dictate words that then appear on the screen. One main advantage of this software is the writer's emancipation from worrying about how to spell words. Once the computer is trained to recognize the user's particular pronunciation, it will always spell words correctly. However, if the user doesn't ensure that the initial computer selection is the correct match for the voiced word, the computer will always respond incorrectly to a particular utterance.

There are several possible solutions to this catch-22 situation. The user can read text into the computer, correcting incorrect guesses by referring to the printed version. Alternatively, reading into the computer from relevant books or other printed matter can 'train' a wider vocabulary. The more words that are trained into the computer's memory, the better the computer's guessing mechanism becomes, and the fewer errors it will make. Some people find problems training the computer because of the need to read aloud large portions of text accurately, which can result in frustration. A specialist dyslexia tutor working with students on vocational courses has been helping students to train the computer through producing their coursework on it.

In John's case, a support tutor provided the necessary checks to ensure that he was not training the computer with the wrong words. After regular sessions, the tutor commented, 'As John's voice files developed, there became less and less of a need for me to intervene and point out errors. By the end of the first term, John was confidently using speech recognition independently with only minimal support.' John successfully completed his degree and continued to use voice recognition software in his subsequent job.

Voice recognition technology (VRT) may be seen as a kind of 'scaffold' that allows the person to experience the act of writing and then to develop further skills. Emma found that seeing her words in print gave her the desire and incentive to write:

> When I wanted to write, I first had to remember which letter I needed, what it looked like, and how it joined to the next letter. I also had to remember the correct spelling rule for each word in order to spell. The computer freed me to read and write, free from stress. It puts me in a relaxed state so I don't have to worry about phonics and spelling rules. So, my vision returned – I made a bond between my vision and language. I could then write from my thought – there was a connection between what was in my head and what's on paper. Once I had done that, I could pick up a pen and write more easily. It also helped me to read and improved my grammar and spelling.

Many people who provide advice on technology for dyslexic adults encourage the use of VRT. However, not all dyslexic adults have the necessary motivation to persevere with these programs. If there is great difficulty writing thoughts on paper, the incentive to master the technology is great and success is likely. Although the software has become considerably more sophisticated and much more affordable than it was in the early 1990s, it still presents obstacles for smooth use. Ironically, the need to focus on each word as it is spoken creates an emphasis on transcription skills at the possible expense of composition skills. Many dyslexic learners find it difficult to hold their thoughts in short-term memory while diverting attention to ensure the correct input by voice recognition programs. Kaptan was eager to try a VRT program since he believed it would facilitate his ability to get his thoughts on paper. However, he found the amount of time and energy needed to train the program extremely frustrating. In the end, he abandoned it in favour of word processing.

Several of these obstacles were reported by Sanderson (1999) in work with six dyslexic students at Nottingham University. In contrast to Sanderson's experiences, Litten (1999) recorded successful use of VRT among 14–15-year-old dyslexics who used *DragonDictate Classic* in conjunction with the text-reading program *Keystone*. Litten's observations suggest that the combined use of the two programs overcomes many of the initial training problems. Similar success is reported at a further education college with basic skills students who also used *DragonDictate Classic* and *Keystone*. It may be that, as the software becomes increasingly simple to use, more 'moderately' dyslexic adults will find it helpful. At the moment, however, it seems that many dyslexic adults are attracted to the concept, but still find the reality of using voice recognition somewhat daunting. Perhaps the answer lies in a different approach to training the students to use the software.

Is technology 'The answer?'

To what extent is computer technology 'the answer' for adult dyslexic students? The degree to which limitations in technical skills inhibit composition skills varies along a continuum ranging from mild interference to major impediment. The means of intervention must be decided by the nature of the student's difficulty.

Clearly no spellchecker is going to resolve all the spelling problems presented by dyslexic writers, and reliance on its use can promote a false sense of security. Successful use of computers requires the development of new skills, some of which require excellent motor integration. The demands of academic study make it difficult to devote the necessary time to acquiring these skills. Mark had training in computer skills at the beginning of his Master's degree course. However, he found it impossible to devote the time necessary to develop these at the same time as studying. Upon completion of his training, he reported:

> The computer teaching slotted into place after I finished the MA. The pressure of the MA, coupled with my dyslexia and labour-intensive obsessional learning style, meant that, try as I might, I just could not integrate new word processing skills while I was engaged in academic study. Instead I became anxious and developed something of a computer phobia. But now it's gone, as I really enjoy word processing. Looking back, this has taught me a lot about the weaknesses and strengths of my personal learning style.

However, in spite of these drawbacks, the revolution in computer technology has opened doors for adults who previously had no chance of achieving independence in reading and writing at a level commensurate with their intellectual or oral abilities. The availability of a tool to perform the transcription aspects of writing allows more energy to be devoted to content. This means the dyslexic writer is placed on a more equal footing with non-dyslexic peers. Clear and attractive presentation affords a pride in written work that may not previously have been possible for someone with poor handwriting and spelling. Tools such as spellcheckers and the thesaurus can liberate expression and improve vocabulary skills. The facility to gain a multi-sensory input through the use of text readers reinforces the very strategies that dyslexic learners are encouraged to employ. The use of VRT clearly overcomes many transcription problems faced by severely dyslexic students who possess strong oral skills. Study skills and planning programs can encourage learner autonomy. Mark comments on his newly developing computer skills:

> I find that even having modest computer skills is empowering and liberating, as I can transcend some of my dyslexic learning problems and get greater enjoyment from academic and creative writing.

Another feature of computers to which many dyslexic people respond positively is the visual-graphic aspect. Using visual representations can help with maths, organizational planning and presentations, as it reflects the way many dyslexic people naturally think. Designing graphics on the computer can be done quickly, saving the student with motor difficulties from the tedium of having to measure and draw accurately and neatly.

On balance, then, if proper advice and appropriate support are made available, technology may provide the tools to enable independence for dyslexic learners. These adults have made a commitment to succeed, either in education or in the workplace; it remains the challenge of educators and employers to help them achieve this goal.

Chapter 8
Supporting dyslexic learners: remediation or remedy?

Many adult students report having had remedial help at school, usually to little avail. There are countless tales of students who were put into remedial classes or in the bottom stream where they felt out of place. Mark sums up his school experiences, which echo those of many other adults:

> Everyone was saying, why isn't he functioning? Why can't he just sit down and concentrate on spelling? And they said 'cos I read more, my spelling would come. For me reading wasn't a problem. If anything, I was held back because I was always kept in the bottom group. I was really left in a very unusual situation with a group of slow learners for years. I was reading books that were way ahead of my years. I remember reading *1984* when I was quite young. People were amazed then because I was supposed to be quite stupid . . . it was very bizarre and I felt very lopsided.

Others describe remedial classes generally as 'more of the same'. Jackie recalls:

> When I went to senior school, we had remedial help for the first year. I could read, I could do joined-up writing, but my reading was poor, my spelling was poor. And all we done, we used to have these cards that would have four words. We used to have to read them, sound it out, spell it and then put it into four different sentences and then we had to go write it, so they could check our handwriting. And that's all we did. So, while everyone else was sitting in an English class, learning English, I was sitting doing spelling and sounds.
> *Did working on those sounds help you?*
> No, I don't know whether it helped me then, but now it hasn't helped me because sound is my biggest problem, because I always got taught to spell how it sounds. But when you start getting silent letters, I just haven't got a clue and it just doesn't work with me. It was just a complete waste of time. OK, if I'd been a little bit slow, then maybe it would have helped me, but where I was actually

dyslexic, it just did nothing for me. It just confused me. I mean, everything which they tried to do which they thought was right for me, turned out to be wrong for me.

Dyslexic adults often attribute the frustration they experienced at school to teaching methods that did not match their learning styles. Michael was diagnosed in his early 20s when he enrolled in basic education classes. He left school with no exams, barely able to read a tabloid newspaper and with poor writing skills. Four years later, for his first essay at university, he wrote about his experience in remedial classes:

> I became part of the 'hardcore'. By 'hardcore' I mean we were put there in the first year and were still there in the fifth . . . The separation of these classes reinforced the stigma of backwardness. If only some thought was given to the needs of the members of these classes, how things could have been different! The question 'Why are they not learning?' was never asked. Conventional methods of teaching had failed us, but they were still embodied in these classes: spelling tests, reading aloud, writing out spelling rules. Different people need different strategies to learn – it is just a matter of finding which one.

This experience of 'more of the same' coupled with continuing failure or limited progress year after year creates frustration and contributes to low self-esteem, but there may be even more damaging consequences. Emma was given specialist help after being diagnosed at age 11. She describes how being taught phonics had a destructive effect on her ability to visualize:

> It was like a TV channel that had the plug pulled. It went black inside my head. I can't visualize and concentrate on phonics or remember a spelling rule at the same time – it's a different way of thinking. Even if learning phonics raises your reading age it takes away what may be the most important thing in your ability to achieve in life. It's like a duck; you can clip its wings and it may be able to waddle around on land, but it will never be able to fly. Only when I let go of what I'd been taught and connected my vision to language could I begin to express myself in language.

The processing problems of dyslexic people are neurological and developmental. However, what can be developed neurologically at six with regard, for example, to discriminating or segmenting sounds cannot be as easily developed at 16 or 60. Attempts to 'remediate' thus often founder. The learning support teacher who tries to teach adults using phonics and rules or worksheets, word lists or exercises usually finds students become bored, frustrated and even stop attending. Several of our students report experiences in adult literacy classes which mirrored their school experiences. Jean comments:

> I went to adult literacy classes, which was fine, but I couldn't write down what they asked me to because I couldn't spell and they weren't teaching me to spell.

Adults have immediate needs and particular purposes and contexts for developing literacy skills, such as writing job applications, taking messages or reading to their children. There may be specific job-related reading or writing tasks which teaching must address. Emphasis on phonic skills or spelling rules will not meet these needs as dyslexic learners do not easily generalize. Rather, they learn best when learning is contextualized and relevant. Adults' time is precious; teachers need to acknowledge and respect this.

It is usually ineffective to try to remediate weaknesses. For example, attempts to teach phonic skills to adults with auditory processing difficulties usually fall (quite literally) on 'deaf' ears. Students report that they can't 'hear' the sounds of the words and therefore cannot match them to the appropriate letters for spelling and reading. Working on visual and lexical ways of 'seeing' words can help students to find non-phonic ways to remember spelling and increase word recognition skills. This can help them to develop a sense of *mastery*, which they get from finding their *own* strategies for remembering and from discovering that they can use their strengths to learn and to circumvent their weaknesses.

Although there are a lot of anecdotal claims about the effectiveness of different teaching interventions with dyslexic learners, well-documented studies are hard to find. Most existing studies are primarily child based and relate mainly to teaching reading. However, Brooks and Weeks (1998) conducted a study comparing different methods of teaching spelling to three groups: 14-year-old slow learners, 14-year-old dyslexic learners, and a spelling-age matched control group. The results indicated that spelling performance increased when children were taught according to their preferred cognitive styles. Their research confirms that traditional remedial models, which emphasize overcoming weaknesses, are not as effective as those models that capitalize on strengths. The idea that there is one 'best approach' is challenged by their findings. It is particularly important to evaluate the appropriateness of teaching methods for adults in light of their maturity as well as their goals. Their natural approaches to general problem-solving in their lives may be transferable to their studies. Individuals actually learn best when strategies match their learning style.

Teaching to the learner's style

Dyslexic students are not 'typical learners'. They challenge existing assumptions about learning and compel teachers to address differences in learning styles. It is important for teachers and learners alike to appreciate learning styles and how people learn. A learning-styles model is intrinsically related to an inclusive approach to teaching and learning, as its premise is that learners are not 'good' or 'poor' but different. By identifying their preferred modes of learning, students can begin to use their strengths to develop effective learning strategies. Often, students are unconsciously aware of how they learn and it is simply necessary to raise their level of consciousness to validate these strategies. Linda found the concept of focusing on her strengths a revolutionary idea:

> As someone who's just been diagnosed as dyslexic, I'm finding it really interesting because I'm beginning to understand that multi-sensory learning is the key. We can't change the way our brain operates. All we really can do is learn skills to cope with it. I'm finding it really useful to think about using my visual strengths.

It is fascinating to observe how quickly adult learners can improve their self-image and show demonstrable progress when teaching responds to their needs. An interior design student reported that she had to insist that her lecturers demonstrate physically to her what they were describing; when told that this was because she was most likely a kinaesthetic learner, she replied:

> Do you mean that I could have been taught like this in the past? I spent my childhood being sent to an educational therapist who insisted that the only reason I couldn't succeed in school was because of my poor behaviour.

Affirmation of ability may be the key to opening the door to successful learning. Certainly, the negative feelings created by the attitude 'I can't do it' often become the basis of a self-fulfilling prophecy. A learning-styles approach replaces the deficit model which underlies remedial teaching. Encouraging learners to see that people learn in different ways and to find out how they learn best creates a positive framework for developing effective learning strategies. The use of a learning-style questionnaire (such as in Klein and Millar, 1990, or Morgan and Abrahams, 1999) can stimulate discussion about, and exploration of, individual strategies and strengths. This can help students to let go of past failure and instil confidence in their ability to learn.

It is therefore crucial for students to experience immediate or nearly immediate success. Embarking on a structured spelling programme which gives quick, tangible results, even with students in higher education, may be a good basis on which to build a support programme. It also enables students to discover and evaluate the effectiveness of methods for learning that suit their cognitive style. Students may be using learning approaches which do not actually match their learning style. This can be the result of having been taught in a particular way to the exclusion of other approaches. For example, some students rely totally on phonetic approaches to spelling, but may actually have significant auditory-processing weak-nesses, resulting in bizarre misspellings. These students need to be shown visual strategies to help remember the correct spelling. Emma notes that other dyslexic adults whom she teaches often claim they cannot visualize. She believes this ability is frequently blocked by the way they were taught. When the stress is removed, often through the use of voice recognition technology, their ability to visualize usually returns, often accompanied by amazement and tears.

Unfortunately, teachers too often complain that a learning-styles approach won't work with 'their students', particularly those on lower-level vocational courses or in basic skills classes. Our experi-ence has shown that not only is this not true, but often students' own grasp of the approach and their creative responses can be humbling to the teacher. Some of the best and most effective tutors are those who are open to learning from their students. The interaction between tutor and student can be mutually advantageous and tutors can pass on successful learning strategies to other students.

One basic education tutor describes working with one of her students who relied heavily on mnemonics. For example, to learn the spelling of 'measurement', the student said:

Mea sure ment – it's like 'sea', but it's not 'shore', I 'meant' 'sure.'

The tutor goes on to describe the student's method:

This was his idea after we had discussed the 'sure' part of the word. He recites this each time he spells it and it works. He has problems with straightforward visualization and as he is engrossed in fantasy books and war games, the more fantastic and bizarre a mnemonic, the better it works. I point out the problem areas and suggest possible connections; Ron invents the rest.

Another tutor who confesses to being 'very strongly left-brained and finding it difficult to empathize with a right-brained style' describes her work with Cathy who was working towards a basic education qualification (Wordpower Level 1) and writing her life story:

The first word she chose to experiment with was 'autobiography.' We broke it down into:

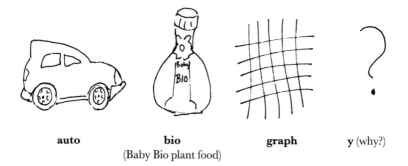

auto	bio	graph	y (why?)
	(Baby Bio plant food)		

Figure 1

Cathy took to this immediately and, with the help of a volunteer, had a go at some more words. Just watching her, I could see that she was remembering so much better than she had been before, and she tried to describe to me how the system worked for her. As usual, I was totally bewildered – as bewildered as she had been when trying to sound out words.

I then showed her how to use different bright colours to highlight areas of the words she found difficult. From then on there was no looking back. Cathy evolved her own technique for learning new words based mainly on colours, and is tackling with confidence amazingly long Latin flower names and will be starting a BTEC National Diploma in floristry next term.

Cathy herself writes about using coloured pens:

> I was amazed at the effect this has on me as I was able to break up a word using different pens, which made the word become clear for me to understand. Now there is no stopping me.

Whatever their strengths and weaknesses, one of the common features of dyslexic learners is their need to have a strong personal connection to their learning. Eileen is a case in point. She had a very poor visual memory for words and relied on sounding out, so silent letters caused great problems. To learn spellings, she developed a system of mnemonics based on her life, particularly related to her flat and the food she ate. For instance, the word '*kitchen*' represented silent 'k's. The word 'knife' was thus remembered as: '*kitchen* n-i-f-e', whereas 'knuckles' had two '*kitchens*'. Words like 'anaesthetic' also caused difficulties as did most vowel sequences or short unaccented vowels which could not be remembered by sound alone. Consequently, 'an**ae**sthetic' was recalled by using '*apple*' and '*egg*' which was what she had for breakfast, and in that order. The relevance of the mnemonic was vital; for example, she wouldn't use '*orange*' for the letter 'o' because she never ate oranges.

Another student used her visualizing strengths to avoid having to sequence letters and sounds. So for 'pyramid' she pictured the pyramid (see Figure 2a).

She then imagined a P at the top; the stem of the 'P' made an upside down 'Y' with the pyramid (see Figure 2b). Finally she visualised a ram inside the pyramid with an 'ID' tag around its neck (see Figure 2c).

For learning to be effective, students need to select words from their own writing rather than lists out of context. Generalizations about spelling can best be developed from a student's own words, where meaningful links can be made (see Klein and Millar, 1990). If the student is not using the word and doesn't actively want to learn it, the teaching is unlikely to succeed.

In teaching adults with poor literacy skills, it is important to use an approach that is holistic, builds on strengths and is contextualized. Helping students to find effective spelling strategies is not just about teaching spelling. For instance, many students who are unable to use phonics to decode words may be helped with reading through learn-

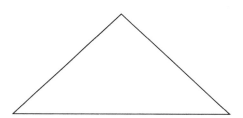

Figure 2a A pyramid

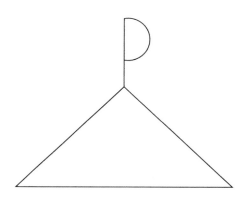

Figure 2b ...with a 'P' at the top

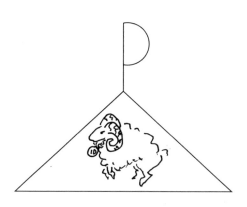

Figure 2c ... and a ram with an 'ID' tag

ing to spell. Developing visual and lexical strategies for remembering spellings improves word recognition. One specialist tutor in a further education college taught a dyslexic non-reader to read solely through working on his spelling. A language experience approach can be extended by having the student learn the spellings generated and dictating them back to the student. Gradually the words and sentences create enough of a bank of words for the student to begin to write independently as well as to recognize the words in written texts. Other multi-sensory materials may be used but the key to success is that the words are meaningful to the individual.

The teaching of handwriting skills may be introduced along with a structured, individualized spelling programme. By practising frequently joined groups of letters, such as 'ing' and 'ght', the student's motor memory may be reinforced, which can aid the development of automatic spelling and writing.

The discovery of strategies that suit their own learning style and the acknowledgement that people learn in different ways, enable these students not only to achieve, but to gain confidence in themselves as learners. Those teaching dyslexic adults need to take a diagnostic approach to their teaching and relate the strategies employed to the student's strengths and weaknesses. They also need to check the effectiveness of strategies and if one is not working, to try another. The dyslexic person needs to *own* the strategy or it will not be effective in the long term and will increase disaffection and reinforce low self-esteem. If teachers persist with a method that doesn't seem to be working or does not result in a positive response from the learner, the teaching and learning situation is doomed to fail.

Lisa found her experience of learning altered from the first week at university when she attended a session that focused on learning styles:

> Just being diagnosed dyslexic changed my learning . . . learning how to take notes and little bubble diagrams that I learned in freshers' week . . . that was wonderful. That was really the start of me being able to take notes, using mindmaps. Learning support made a great difference . . . you thought about how you were doing it and what suited you best and what suited the teacher best may not have necessarily been your preference. It was great to see things in that light. I learned how to use my auditory strengths. I found myself a study partner who's absolutely brilliant at reading. She explains what she's picked up; I talk to her about it and I understand them better when she tells me what the problems are. We've worked very well as a team.

The following comments from students describe some of the benefits of understanding how they learn and ways to improve their learning:

Isobel

It sort of revolutionized my study because before I felt that you had to read, read, read – explore text visually before you could write an essay. But now, I listen, I tape lectures so that I can listen to them again and again and pick up bits that I would miss because I'm so worried about spelling something right or writing things down. All of the knowledge of understanding how I learn has helped me to better my work and to better my study in many ways.

Luke

I make spidergrams. When I get a question, I rewrite it in my own words – why use all these complicated words? I put it in simpler words, then I put answers to the questions that I know already, and sometimes I'm quite shocked by how much I already know.

Anne

I know that I pick things up through my hearing so therefore, if I was in a lecture, I would always sit at the front. Now that's not because I want to be teacher's pet, but I know if I sit at the back, my eyes start to wander and I don't listen to what's going on. So therefore by sitting at the front, I am putting all my concentration on my hearing. You take very few notes, you take the main points down and do spider maps – that's another thing that I've learnt to do and it just enhances your learning ability.

Although I was never aware of it, I think that's the way that I've learnt all the time. I've always enjoyed listening rather than watching things. I think as I've gone on, I've tried to use my visual skills and tried to build them up, although I'm never going to be perfect at that and I'm better on the auditory side. I listen to tapes, tape my lectures and use the computer to read back my essays.

Supporting learning: learning to learn

Dyslexic adults, many of whom are undiagnosed, participate in education at all levels. Those who are unaware of their dyslexia are particularly found in basic skills classes where there is often a lack of knowledge of dyslexia and untested assumptions about why adults lack basic skills despite having been through the education system. It is important that basic skills tutors have an understanding of dyslexia, including how to identify it and how to teach dyslexic learners. There should also be some tutors within all basic skills provision who have specialist dyslexia training in both diagnosing and teaching dyslexic adults.

The need to be taught by specialist tutors was stressed by the dyslexic adults who responded to a consultation for the working group looking into the basic skills needs of adults with learning difficulties and/or disabilities (DfEE, 2000). The respondents also wanted classes exclusive to dyslexic learners, as many found their previous experience in adult basic skills classes unsatisfactory.

In further and higher education, provision for dyslexic learners is primarily offered as learning support. The learning support model may differ from the student's previous educational experiences in several ways. Perhaps most importantly, the emphasis is on teaching the student *how* to learn rather than focusing on content.

Any skill associated with improving learning can be addressed in learning support using course-related materials as the basis for skills development. Brinckerhoff et al. (1993) argue that 'the learning-strategies approach is based on the assumption that students with learning disabilities are strategy deficient, unable to spontaneously tap the strategies they need'.

One important characteristic of learning support is that the onus is on the student to provide material; in the successful learning support relationship, the student controls the session and uses the tutor primarily as a resource rather than as a repository of knowledge. The student–tutor relationship therefore becomes more balanced and egalitarian than traditional student-teacher roles. For example, in working on a structured spelling programme, it is import-ant to use words from the student's own writing. When lists of words are suggested by the tutor, the learning is less effective and not retained. One basic skills tutor who had been having excellent success with a student decided to move from using words from the student's writing to a list following a specific spelling rule because she thought it would be helpful. The next week the student had failed to retain the spellings and explained that he preferred learning his 'own words'. The tutor, a quick learner, realized the importance of making the learning relevant to the student.

Individual support should focus on agreed priorities. However, the urgency of getting an assignment completed may dominate the session. In working out an overall plan for support, the tutor and student may target reading, writing, spelling and maths, or aspects of all four. In addition, there may be general issues, such as managing time and organizational skills. Some students may also need to develop strategies for non-academic aspects of their study. For example, an art student studying weaving had problems keeping track of the sequences involved. Another, a potter, needed to learn to recognize and retain the numbering system for glazes. For Isobel, learning support helped with:

> . . . organization and getting organized, giving myself prior deadlines so that I can then come here to show you before I have to hand it in. This means it gets done. It's making me do things before they're due, which means that I'm not stressed – I don't make so many silly mistakes.

In the learning support relationship, students may feel their weaknesses are exposed. Some students may be unwilling to bring in written work for several weeks until they feel they can trust the tutor and overcome the fear that they will be laughed at or criticized. Individual support sessions can be crucial in terms of increasing an adult's self-esteem. Having a tutor who offers encouragement rather than criticism, who provides honest appraisal of strengths as well as weaknesses and who 'believes' in the student may be the most important affirmation of the person's decision to return to education. In spite of motivation, the negative feelings associated with past experiences can easily undermine efforts. A student who was feeling particularly negative about her chances of succeeding on her course continually complained to the tutor, 'I can't do it.' Finally, the tutor wrote a 'guarantee' on a post-it note that simply stated, 'You WILL finish your degree.' The student put this in the front of her diary and said that every time she doubted herself, she referred back to it. The significant fact here was that someone whom she trusted and respected believed in her.

The ability of many dyslexic adults to articulate their ideas and thoughts orally can conceal their weak literacy skills. Support tutors may find it difficult to hide their surprise when they see the discrepancy between what the student is able to articulate orally and what is presented on paper. The student must be encouraged to show written work, but the response from the tutor must be positive if a trusting relationship is to be developed. On the other hand, the tutor must be careful to offer honest feedback. To gain trust, it is important to acknowledge the reality of the student's difficulties. Students will know immediately if tutors are condescending. It does not help them to be told their spelling is 'not that bad' or for the tutor to be over-effusive. Clear feedback on how to improve and, most importantly, strategies that the student can see working will build confidence and maintain enthusiasm. Untactful criticism could rekindle past flames and leave the student feeling crushed. Students must perceive their learning support sessions as completely different from past learning experiences. Michaela makes sure to inform each new support tutor who works with her to use any colour other than red to highlight errors in her work:

> The red pen . . . at school they used to put red pen over everything. In the end, I started writing in red, so then it didn't look so bad. Good tactic, because then my friends didn't think I was as thick as they [the teachers] were making out I was. But now I need to make sure that I never see red pens again – any other colour, but not red.

Strategies for individual support

Multi-sensory approaches are known to work best with dyslexic learners. Although all students may benefit from multi-sensory strategies for learning, dyslexic students must take advantage of as many ways as possible to transmit information to the long-term memory. Lorraine's understanding of the importance of multi-sensory learning helped in her examination revision:

> When I was revising, I read into a dictaphone a lot and played back what I had read. At the same time, I put some aromatherapy oils under my nose so that I could associate what I was revising with a smell. Then in the exam I had a tissue with the essential oil relating to that exam. It really helped me remember what I'd learnt.

By keeping in mind the learning style of the student, the tutor can help students explore strategies that appeal to their strengths. Discussion of the student's preferred mode of learning can result in creative means of reinforcing learning or overcoming obstacles to retention of information. A student who learned best through visual and kinaesthetic modalities discovered that she could remember the different characters in a case study by designing some board game characters from magazine pictures mounted on cardboard. Bringing the characters to life in this fashion helped her both to remember the different roles each played as well as to consolidate the main issues of the case.

James, a biology student, has great difficulty remembering facts. His examination results rarely reflect his knowledge of the subject, simply because he finds that his mind 'goes blank' when under pressure. By placing large posters of coloured drawings of different body systems in varying rooms in his home, he was able to improve his recall. For example, he put a large labelled drawing of the respiratory system on the wall by his exercise bicycle and a poster of the digestive system in the bathroom. James found that when he entered the examination hall, he was able to visualize the rooms in his house and recreate the pictures he had placed on the walls.

Ongoing discussions about the reasons for trying particular strategies help to develop students' awareness of their learning and encourage them to attempt new approaches. For example, Roberta had quite severe auditory processing difficulties which affected her pronunciation and spelling, causing embarrassment when she had to give oral presentations. Her weak short-term memory meant that she often forgot what she wanted to say and the anxiety of having to give a presentation to the class exacerbated these problems. However, her understanding of herself as a kinaesthetic-visual learner enabled her to use these strengths to overcome her weaknesses. She was not very artistic, but could draw comical stick figures which helped her to remember specific theorists or characters in case studies. She used coloured paper and a variety of coloured pens and highlighters but, more importantly, found that making collages helped her to commit her ideas to her long-term memory. The act of finding pictures in magazines, cutting them out and pasting them on to large poster-sized paper reinforced her learning. Although time consuming, she actually enjoyed the challenge of creating imaginative and fanciful collages. Moreover, she was able to use her posters as prompts for her talk. Gaining control helped to overcome her considerable anxiety and to reduce her stammer.

Michaela's difficulties with visual processing make it very difficult for her to read. She describes how lighting affects her reading:

> This type of light, this fluorescent light – I've been told that I'm allergic to it. It makes rivers down the pages. It makes the white really glare out and the black letters sort of blend into each other, when I try to read in this light.

During learning support sessions, a range of strategies were explored to help Michaela address her difficulties, known as Scotopic Sensitivity Syndrome (SSS) or Meares-Irlen Syndrome. She was encouraged to keep a journal of her reading habits to discover the optimum conditions for her. After one week, she reported her observations:

> If I have a different type of light, there's much less strain; it's much more relaxing for me to read. Or if I put something like a blue plastic overlay over the page, it's much better. But the thing that surprised me most was that I can read for almost twenty minutes [before the distortions start appearing] if I read in the morning with natural light. I've now changed my whole study routine so that I don't try to read at night.

In addition to helping students discover creative strategies using their strengths, the support tutor may also provide a 'scaffold' to help students develop strategies to deal more directly with specific weaknesses. Vygotsky defines scaffolding as a technique used by teachers to enable learners to achieve at a higher level or to complete tasks that they cannot do unaided: 'help which will enable a learner to accomplish a task which they would not have been quite able to manage on their own . . . [and] which is intended to bring the learner closer to a state of competence which will enable them eventually to complete such a task on their own', the aim being 'a greater level of independent competence as a result of the scaffolding experience' (Mercer, 1994).

To be effective, the support tutor needs to be diagnostic in her approach. For example, expressive language difficulties may underlie the writing problems of some students. They may need structured work on oral language, including developing precision of expression and expanding vocabulary. Those with motor integration difficulties, however, may need the tutor to scribe their ideas while they speak, or learn to dictate on to tape and write from their dictations. Lorraine found that having a scribe enabled her to focus on her ideas:

> So much effort of my brain power is taken up with forming the words, the sentences, the paragraphs, etc., which other people do automatically. The reason why my expression is weak is because half of my energy has gone into the writing and I've lost the main crux of the argument. Being able to dictate it makes it so much easier.

Another student found she had to dictate to herself, that is say the words aloud before she wrote them. She said, 'I know it sounds weird but that's the only way I can be sure that what I want to say gets down on the paper.'

Since dyslexic students tend not to learn from rules, it is necessary to identify many examples of the same thing to help the learner generalize. For example, dyslexic adults can usually offer a 'definition' of a sentence which they 'learned' at school. They may say, 'A sentence is a complete thought and begins with a capital letter and ends with a full stop.' However, these words do not transfer to the individual's own writing and may have no real meaning for the student. One student decided that a 'complete thought' was approximately ten words long and consequently punctuated every tenth word with a full stop.

The use of modelling to demonstrate how to improve a particular problem, such as sentence structure or paragraphing, is a powerful example of scaffolding. By providing an example of a well-constructed sentence or paragraph conveying the same information that was intended in the original piece of writing, the student can begin to absorb the subtle reasons why her own expression may be weak. Ideally, the tutor can then point out the next sentence/paragraph where a similar pattern is apparent and ask the student to offer her own correction. Luke, who was studying for an A level in economics was concerned about the negative feedback he received on his essays. His support tutor was able to point to an awkward sentence, model a clearer way of expressing the same ideas and then point to another similarly structured sentence. After several examples, Luke began to see that he was simply trying to express too many ideas in one sentence and that by separating his thoughts into two sentences his writing became much clearer.

Tutors need to separate their responses to the content from reactions to the presentation of ideas. Indeed, if the content is muddled by poor expression, it might be useful to say, 'I'm not clear what you're saying here, although the ideas you're discussing seem interesting.' Through careful questioning, the tutor can elicit information from the student ('What I was trying to say was . . .') which might then be scribed by the tutor. The tutor might read aloud an unclear passage and ask the student how she thinks that sounds. Often, the auditory input will allow the student to hear when written expression is unclear. If the tutor wants to highlight a particular problem, such as word omissions, she might select sentences in which a word has been left out, read them aloud and ask the student to identify what sounds wrong.

Stephen's support tutor asked him to read aloud a poorly expressed section of his essay and was surprised to hear him read words that were not actually on the page. He also read as if he had punctuated correctly, though he had omitted the punctuation marks. When the tutor read his piece, he realized that his writing didn't make sense and became aware of the need to proof-read more carefully.

The next step for Stephen's tutor was to use error analysis marking, a good example of a scaffolding technique. This consists of using an agreed code (e.g. 'G' for grammar, 'P' for punctuation, 'Sp' for spelling, 'O' for word omission, 'SS' for sentence structure, etc.) to identify the nature of the error appearing on a particular line. The student then tries to locate and correct the error. If it is a frequently made error (e.g. 'as' for 'has'), the student will usually be able to pick it out quite quickly and self-correct. This approach encourages the student to engage in proof-reading (a task generally avoided by many dyslexic writers) and to develop skills of self-correction. If the student is unable to see where the error lies, the tutor can point out the mistake and explain how to correct it.

Another scaffolding strategy that tutors can employ is the use of 'writing frames', which were originally developed for young children but are effective for learners of all ages and levels (Lewis and Wray, 1996). Giving the structure and language for a particular genre, for example a procedure, a discussion essay or a piece of persuasive writing, enables learners to unpack the features of the genre and replicate it for themselves. This is particularly effective for dyslexic writers because it makes the conventions explicit and provides a means of structuring their thoughts. A writing frame can also be a useful tool for overcoming problems with using linking words.

The technique of 'kernelling' sentences can help students understand how to develop complex sentences from simple 'kernel' ideas (Shaughnessy, 1977). Through encouraging the embedding of adjectives, adverbs and clauses into simple basic sentences, students gain insights into the grammatical structure of language as well as develop a functional understanding of punctuation marks. This building up from the simple to the complex suits the dyslexic learner more than an analytic approach.

Finally, support sessions can address difficulties that students encounter with their reading. In addition to problems of decoding text, many students have difficulties with comprehension. A scaffolding strategy for helping students to become more active readers and to improve their comprehension is PQ4R. This involves previewing the text, raising questions, and then reading, reflecting, reciting and reviewing to check on understanding and retention of material. Tutors might also help students to explore other resources, such as videotapes, books on audiotape, and simpler texts in order to familiarize themselves with the vocabulary and issues before trying to read a more difficult text.

The use of imagery can also help to improve reading comprehension. Encouraging students' attempts to describe verbally what they read, first in sentences, then in paragraphs, can aid visualization and develop an alternative way to hold words in the memory. Making visual diagrams, drawings and mind-maps can help readers identify and use the structure of what they are reading to help extract specific information as well as general understanding of a particular type of writing or 'genre'. Mind-mapping (Buzan, 1993) is a technique that many dyslexic learners adopt wholeheartedly. It not only helps students to take notes from lectures or meetings and to plan writing, but also to access and remember information from texts and other resources. Directed interactive activities with texts such as giving 'titles' or headings to paragraphs or having to arrange cut-up sections of text can help students to engage with the meaning and structure of a text (Fowler, 1997).

The support tutor needs to be clear that she is acting as a 'scaffolder' and not a 'crutch'. Scaffolding is removed as the learner takes on more and more of the task successfully. A frequent criticism levelled by those who are unfamiliar with learning support is that the support tutor is 'doing the work' for the student by acting as an editor or proofreader. In some cases, this is voiced as a criticism; on the other hand, subject tutors have been known to suggest to dyslexic students that they should take their work to a support tutor to get it 'corrected'. In training courses for specialist tutors run by the authors, one of the most challenging tasks is to help prospective tutors to distinguish between what is 'editing' and what is 'teaching'. The support tutor has a limited time to spend with the student, usually one or two hours per week at the most. During this brief period, there are many goals to achieve. The primary aim is to teach the student skills that will ultimately lead to learner autonomy. This certainly cannot be achieved if the tutor concentrates primarily on correcting the written work presented by the student. On the contrary, the evidence is that students will not internalize new learning if their work is simply edited. The tutor must at all times be clear about his or her teaching aims.

Using groups

Although it is important that dyslexic students have opportunities for at least some individual support, many study strategies can be taught to dyslexic adults in small groups. For some purposes, the group has advantages over the one-to-one model and may be less threatening to those students who feel safer when they can avoid exposing their weaknesses. Groups are obviously less resource-intensive and, consequently, can serve more students. Brinckerhoff et al. (1993) describe several functions that can be served by support groups. They suggest the use of 'different themes to focus the group activities (e.g. disability self-awareness, study skills, job readiness or job seeking). Reiff et al. (1997) stress the importance of support groups for helping students to learn from each other.

For Janet and many others, the opportunity to meet with other dyslexic adults was a life saver. Attending special classes for dyslexic adults, she met others and began to find out she wasn't unique. As Helen, also part of that group, remembers:

> Out of the class, we all started to talk – you used to have trouble getting rid of us
> . . . I used to think I was the only person that had trouble with the time until I
> met Janet.

Group sessions can demystify some of the confusion that adults have about the nature of dyslexia (see Morgan, 1996). Differences in past experiences and recency of diagnosis may contribute to varying degrees of understanding about dyslexia. Those with more understanding may help those with less. Moreover, mixed groups consisting of people who were diagnosed at different stages in their lives may offer newly diagnosed adults opportunities to meet and identify with those who have achieved.

Dinklage (1991) argues that support groups provide a vehicle for dyslexic students to make sense of their experiences through shared information: 'Such a group enables them to become experts in their own learning process and, incidentally, if there are non-dyslexic leaders of this group, to educate them as well.'

Group sessions might focus on understanding how memory works and how to improve recall. Stimulating group members to think about how they approach their learning and memory tasks may serve to raise their consciousness about ways to develop these areas. Group sessions may also be a useful arena to share multi-sensory strategies, which students can try out and discuss. The use of holistic approaches such as mind-maps can be explored, as can the value of using visual reinforcement through colour, pictures, cartoons, etc. Auditory learning approaches such as the use of tape recorders, study groups for discussion, and verbalizing thoughts for taping or for someone to scribe are examples of strategies that can be presented in a group situation.

Dyslexic people tend to have a poor sense of 'audience' when they write. The use of peer editing can help to improve and develop their writing. In one group, a student who could produce only half a page of writing presented a short piece of writing about photography, a keen interest of hers. Through questioning and comments, others in the group were able to help her understand how to expand and develop her writing. The following week she brought in a six-page piece.

One of the drawbacks of teaching dyslexic students in groups is the difficulty of establishing a group dynamic. Since students may be diagnosed at any point during the academic year, there may be a constantly changing attendance in group sessions. Students will be at different points in their levels of confidence as well as their knowledge about successful strategies. While more established group members may initiate newly identified ones, they may also inadvertently intimidate less confident students. Veronica found the experience of attending a study skills group for dyslexic students quite daunting:

> I went to my dyslexia support group on Thursday nights. We just learned differ-
> ent techniques, like spelling and mind-maps. I did it for about two years, but I
> actually just couldn't take it. I still felt stupid, because I felt like the others could
> do their work, and I'm still struggling and I'm with dyslexics! I just couldn't take
> it, so I left.

On the other hand, the group helped Michaela to overcome her feelings of isolation:

> What I find extremely helpful is we all meet up once a week and meet other
> people with the same problems. Because sometimes, I've been pulling my hair
> out, thinking, why did I come to university – I can't handle this. But then when
> I come to the group, I meet other people who have the same problems and they
> say, don't worry, you could try this or this, and I feel relieved. I'm glad I've
> come along and I've met other people and I don't feel alone like I did at school,
> where I was the only one with the so-called 'problem'.

When deciding upon the best type of intervention for a dyslexic
adult, the individual's personal preferences must always be considered. Some adults feel quite uncomfortable in group situations and
much prefer receiving one-to-one tuition from a specialist tutor who
understands how best to teach them. Others find that meeting fellow
dyslexic adults enables them to gain confidence through hearing
about other people's experiences. There is no golden rule that
applies to all dyslexic adults; their needs are as unique and special as
their individual profiles, and each person must be assessed and
advised accordingly.

The role of the subject tutor

Dyslexic students need to 'overlearn'. They are inductive learners
who may need many concrete experiences before they can generalize about the conventions of language. It is not sufficient for the
support tutor to explain a point of grammar, correct a spelling error,
restructure a sentence or point out how to correct punctuation and
then assume that this information will be assimilated as new knowledge. It may be necessary to go over the same point several weeks in
a row using different contexts or examples, until the student can
demonstrate evidence of having internalized the new learning.
Asking the student to explain the point using her own words
gives the tutor the opportunity to check whether there is ongoing
confusion.

Dyslexic students do not generally benefit from much of the feedback that their well-intentioned lecturers provide on their written work. Non-dyslexic students may find it useful to see a spelling error corrected and may be able to make a mental note to record the corrected spelling in their visual memory. However, the dyslexic student needs to devote dedicated time and conscious intent to learning the spelling. There may be a multitude of errors in a piece of written work submitted by a dyslexic student; it can only be disheartening to get the work back covered in corrections or with comments about poor spelling, grammar, punctuation and sentence structure. The student knows these problems exist, but simply pointing them out will not remedy the situation. What she needs to know is how to correct them. Following are some responses from a group of dyslexic undergraduates who were asked to discuss their feelings about feedback received from their subject tutors:

Michaela
So many times I get work back saying 'Improve your sentence structure, your spelling, etc.' And I try, but that's my problem, my spelling, my reading, my sentence structure. That's how my dyslexia affects me. So I've spent hours on this essay, and they say, 'Have you just done this the night before?'

Anne
The standard length of a tutorial is fifteen minutes, if you're lucky. An extra five minutes would help because they hand you the feedback form and expect you to read it there and then. I can never absorb their comments, especially if I'm trying to read with someone watching over my shoulder.

Linda
The problem is that tutors need to understand what dyslexia is. Unfortunately, I've had terribly negative responses on my feedback sheets. Comments like 'I wish you'd look at your spelling' are demoralizing, especially if you've reread it five times and it looks fine to you.

Bob
I want teachers just to look at the content of my work. I don't want them to mark me up because I'm dyslexic. In the real world, everyone's spelling isn't perfect. I just want them to be more aware.

The same group of students was asked to suggest ways in which mainstream lecturers could improve the learning experience for dyslexic students. Their reactions included the following:

- Offer constructive comments, not sarcasm like 'Haven't you got a dictionary?' Something constructive, emphasizing the positive things as well as saying what was wrong with the work.
- Write the correct spellings (for specialist vocabulary and names) on the board.
- Provide notes in advance of the lecture.
- Use colour and diagrams on overhead transparencies.
- Make sample past papers available for examination revision.
- Provide advanced reading lists, including secondary readings.
- Offer feedback on the content of work, not the spelling, etc.
- Clarify meaning of essay questions by being approachable and willing to talk to students.
- Try to be more understanding.

The discussion among these students emphasized that many of their requests would benefit all students and not just the dyslexic students in the class. Our experience confirms that dyslexic adults can succeed in education at all levels if they are taught in a way that meets their needs. Students themselves, as well as support and subject tutors, must understand the importance of recognizing and teaching to different learning styles. The words of the educator, Grace Fernald (1943) are still relevant today:

> There are many ways of accomplishing a given result. To suppose there is just one way of doing anything shows a failure to understand the psychology of learning.

Chapter 9
From basic literacy to university and beyond: a longitudinal case study

Throughout this book, we have explored the experiences of a range of dyslexic adults across a spectrum of life situations. Most of the adults we mention have spoken freely about how their past and present experiences have affected them in their work, academic and personal lives. The current chapter presents a case study of a 53-year-old man, who has been known to the authors over a period of 14 years. His views of his own struggles and his development both in self-confidence and in specific literacy skills have been the subject of a series of interviews held over the past ten years, with the most recent interview taking place five years after the completion of his university degree. Although his story is not necessarily typical, it raises several issues that appear to be of common concern to many adults who have grown up in ignorance of the reason for their academic struggles. We hope that through sharing Martin's story, we shall be able to highlight some of the common threads as well as to isolate the unique qualities of his experiences.

Background

Martin B. was born in 1946, the eldest child in a family of five children. He grew up in London, where he and his three brothers and sister all attended a local school in Kings Cross, a deprived inner-city area. Family life was fraught; Martin described his father as an alcoholic who often spent his weekly wages on alcohol and had little involvement in the family. Mr. B. had been trained as a gas fitter, but lost several jobs due to his drink problem. He worked in several other areas, including as a butcher and, for quite a long time, as a postal employee. In fact he had aspirations for his eldest son to follow him in this area:

> My father just didn't realize I couldn't read and write; I just couldn't work in the post office. I would have loved to go to the post, but they wouldn't take me . . . so, yes he had expectations, he just didn't know that I couldn't do it.'

Martin is aware that the social and economic conditions surrounding his childhood had a considerable effect on his schooling. He described the insights he gained during his first year at university when, during his studies of sociology, he learned about Peter Townsend's analysis of poverty in 1960s Britain:

> . . . [the government] failed me, because we were one of the small pocket groups that were living in poverty and when you're living in poverty like that, there's too many other worries about where the money's coming from. So that took over a lot of concerns and [was more important than] expectations of children.

During the 1950s and 1960s there was little awareness of dyslexia among teachers and the economic concerns of many working-class families took precedence over those about their children's academic achievement. There was also, and continues to be, an attitude that 'teachers know best' and therefore, if a child was not succeeding at school, the parents often placed the blame on the child rather than on the system.

Martin's mother was kept busy trying to make meagre ends meet to provide for the needs of her five children. Her ability to become involved with their schoolwork was hampered by her own difficulties with reading and writing, which Martin says were shared by all his siblings. Interestingly, the only family member who did not have literacy problems was the father, but his involvement with his children was limited.

Despite the difficult circumstances at home, Martin and his siblings all attended school regularly. In fact, Martin's memories of school are generally positive:

> I enjoyed school throughout because I enjoyed learning. That's why I eventually went back into study.

His frustration at school was created by his limited reading and writing skills, but he never saw these as a reflection of his intelligence. On the contrary, Martin saw himself as being very bright in subject areas such as history, geography and maths, but couldn't explain why he was struggling with reading and writing. However, he never internalized the labels of 'thick, lazy and stupid' with which so many other dyslexic adults have grappled. In reflecting on why he left school at 15, Martin says:

> I felt the school system had failed me. I felt I was very bright in most subjects but my reading and writing wasn't very good, so I didn't see much point in carrying on. It felt like a door was shut in my face.

Interestingly, his self-esteem does not seem to have been seriously damaged by his school experiences, largely because he was able to blame the system and not himself for his limited academic success. This is unusual in our experience, since most adults who did not receive the benefit of assessment until years after leaving school report low self-esteem connected to the internalization of negative labels. Many adults acknowledge that underneath they didn't believe that they were 'stupid, lazy or thick' but found it difficult to shed the stigma that was attached to those labels.

In retrospect, Martin recalls some early indicators of dyslexia during his childhood. He remembers being unable to tell the time at age 8:

> The teacher used to always ask me to tell the time, before people had watches. When I came back [from checking the clock] I used to say to a friend, 'One hand's this way and the other hand's that way – what's that?' Then I'd go and tell the teacher. So I knew at eight or nine that I was having problems that other kids didn't have. But if you look at it, even at that age, I also would find an alternative way around to overcome that problem. I would see the visual image of the clock and describe it back to a friend and then he'd translate it into the spoken word.

He also recalls his constant struggles with trying to read. At age 13, his classroom was located in the school library and he wistfully recalls 'sitting in this classroom amongst all these books that I couldn't read'. This frustration was compounded when, in his final year, he was given a prize on prize day. When asked what the prize was for, Martin replied:

> I think they finally gave me something for trying so hard, basically. It was a consolation for not teaching me to read and write, I suppose. I just don't know.

Unfortunately, to add insult to injury, the prize was an adventure book, which Martin has to this day never read:

> The chap who got second prize was given a set of craftsmen's chisels and tools. Now I would have loved them because I could have done something with them.

Life post-school

Despite his enjoyment of learning, Martin left school at the age of 15, barely able to read and write. A teacher who had taken an interest in him towards the end of his schooling suggested that he might like to stay on. However, he saw very little point in remaining in a system that was offering no support for his literacy difficulties. Moreover, as the eldest son he felt a responsibility to contribute financially to the family.

The Jobcentre sent him to a firm that made medical instruments. There he received training and remained in the same company for nine years until he was made redundant. He subsequently gained employment in another business making medical instruments, where he stayed until he was once again made redundant 17 years later. He acknowledges that there was some degree of satisfaction in this work, as it was a skilled craftsman's trade in which he had the pleasure of creating the entire instrument, from beginning to end. However, in common with many other dyslexic adults who feel frustrated and angry by being denied options, Martin states:

> What stopped me ever liking the job was because I was not there because I wanted to be there; I was there because I couldn't choose the jobs I wanted.

This lack of options is a theme we have explored in Chapter 5. As a result of his ongoing weakness in reading and writing, Martin decided to return to education in 1984 when he learned from his brother about adult literacy classes. The main incentive to attend these classes was the fact that he had been asked to be the best man at a friend's wedding and he was terrified about having to read telegrams aloud.

So I thought I'd go along – I started in January; the wedding was at the end of February. I thought, 'Great, I'll learn to read and write in a month!' Of course, 15 years later, I still have problems with reading and writing.

Literacy classes as a stepping stone to further education

When Martin began attending literacy classes, he was aware of the limitations that his reading difficulties posed. He relied heavily on context to access meaning from print. His initial motivation to attend literacy classes to improve his reading was that he could not decode unfamiliar names. This was the challenge that the prospect of being best man confronted him with:

> . . . what concerned me was names and street names; I had no clues either side of it. If I couldn't read that name, I had no way of making a guess. . . I had a car, so I read car manuals, but fortunately they had a lot of diagrams. I had also read the Highway Code.

Much to Martin's disappointment, however, the approach to teaching him reading in literacy classes seemed to him to be based on the same methods that had been used at school. He was extremely frustrated by the emphasis on phonics, because he couldn't process the sounds he was being taught:

> When I went to school, I wanted to learn and I worked very hard, but the standard teaching methods did not work then and they weren't working now. There were teachers who started giving me the sounds of vowels. This was what happened in secondary school when I was in a low group for reading; they tried to teach me the sounds of vowels and I just couldn't make any sense of it at all. [The phonic approach] literally confused me. When I said I can't hear the sounds, they kind of implied you must be deaf.

Martin persevered, however, but became increasingly frustrated. He acknowledges that the basic education tutors were extremely positive and encouraging, but felt this attitude was exactly the same as he had encountered in his school days:

> What they told me at school on my reports was that 'He tries hard; he's a late developer, it will come, it will come.' And now they were saying to me, 'Calm down and relax, it will come.' I mean, I've done a university degree now, and I still have reading and writing problems!

A piece of his writing from this time demonstrates both the struggle he was experiencing as well as the emotional impact that his difficulties caused:

13 May 1985

Fear

Over the years I have been afraid of many things From the fear of water, and till I learned how to swim, The fear of the dark when I was a child, I'm over that fear. The fear of not being able to read and spell properly, this I am overcoming slowly as I improve my spelling and reading am still afraid of the unknown and that covers a big area. I must admit I panic easy. easily.

Another sample of Martin's writing produced after attending literacy classes for approximately one year, gives evidence of his optimism for the year 1985. His goals at that time were clearly work orientated, even though no specific career goals were mentioned.

1985

I am looking forward to 1985, I think it will be a good year for me, I know we say that every year. This coming year I have great hopes and ambition to do well in my English classes, and I am confidence that I will do well. In 1985 I would like to see a change in the Government, to a caring and more understanding Government, I think we all wish this would happen. I would also like to see full employment. I myself would like to change my job, and get a job which is a clearer and more enjoy one, with more pay and shorterhours. I know I am being very, ambitious, but my motto is, aim high and hope for the best.

Note that both of the examples of Martin's written work are final versions, completed after considerable attention devoted to finding correct spellings. There are indications that he is able to express himself clearly in written form, but struggles with handwriting and gets confused with certain word endings – e.g. 'confidence', 'enjoy'. These problems persisted throughout his university years.

In 1986, two years after beginning literacy classes, Martin met a tutor who had recently been trained in conducting assessments of dyslexic adults. She diagnosed dyslexia and Martin was offered tuition from her in a small group with three other dyslexic adults. His goals at the time remained vocationally related:

30 March 1986

ILEA

From education I personally want a sufficient educa-tion for me to cope well in with this modern world.
To bread this down into more detail, to cope means an education which will allow me to get a job I would like to do.
I would like to be able to read and understand what I am reading quicker then I do now.

At this time, Martin began an access to higher education course and attended support classes for specific help with his dyslexia. Prior to the diagnosis, he felt irritated by the fact that literacy skills were being taught through the use of material that was beneath his level of intellectual interest. Once he embarked on the access course, he felt more intellectually stimulated by the content of the work and appreciated the fact that he was improving his literacy skills, albeit slowly, through addressing the assignments for his course. His initial frustration highlights the importance of ensuring that all learning materials used with adults are appropriate to their intellectual interests. Moreover, it is crucial for teachers and employers of dyslexic adults to recognize that low literacy levels do not necessarily indicate low intellectual ability. Unfortunately, there is still a common tendency to correlate poor spelling with low intelligence.

Martin's reaction to diagnosis was a mixed one; initially, he wasn't sure that he believed the tutor, but he felt the positive outcome of diagnosis was that he was transferred into a dyslexia support class where the teaching was more tailored to his needs. He also appreciated gaining a clearer insight into the nature of his difficulties:

> When I got diagnosed as being dyslexic, I was told that this is a problem you'll have. You'll learn skills to cope with it, but it won't go away. I suppose before that, I always had an end goal that I was going to be able to read and write fluently; when I was diagnosed, you then knew this problem was always going to be with you. Well, I have learned ways to cope.

Perhaps most importantly of all, Martin felt that the main benefit of diagnosis was that it gave him access to the type of support he needed while enabling him to discover his own learning style.

Learning style

Since his original diagnosis at age 38, Martin has developed considerable understanding of how his strengths and weaknesses affect his learning. He is acutely aware of the optimum conditions for him to concentrate and process new information and has developed a bank of strategies that enable him to achieve his learning goals. He recognizes his need to work by himself in absolute quiet with no distractions; any background noise seriously interferes with his learning. Martin found one of the advantages of attending learning support classes was that he could be taught in 'small classes with no noise'. He also acknowledges the need to take frequent breaks from reading or writing tasks to enable him time to reflect on and process information.

Martin's insights into his strengths and weaknesses go a long way to inform his approach to learning:

> My problems are with auditory processing, so that's my weakness. My strengths are visual. I need to see things. I also need to kind of act things out . . . sometimes I would just need to go for a walk, and then when I came back, I would understand it.

This kinaesthetic approach to learning was observed by one of Martin's support tutors, who often watched him pacing up and down with his eyes closed and his hand on his forehead while he was trying to find the words to articulate his ideas.

Visual strategies that Martin employs in his academic work include mind-maps and colour coding:

> Ideas come out for me in a jumble, so I brainstorm it as it comes, then structure
> it after. If I try to do more than one thing at a time, if I have to think of the ideas
> and structure them at the same time, within ten minutes, my brain is so tired, I
> can't do anything. With mind-mapping, you just write it down as it comes and
> worry about what's relevant and what's not afterwards.

Martin also developed increasing confidence in his spelling after embarking on a structured spelling programme in which he negotiated with his tutor to find the strategies that best suited him:

> Breaking words into syllables would be a waste of time for me. In my [diagnos-
> tic] report, it said I was missing out the middle [of words]. That was useful to
> know. In the beginning stages, I used to miss out the endings, but I now think
> this is better. I now know to look in the middle. I find it useful to break spelling
> down into smaller bits, using words with patterns, like 'ight'. Also knowing the
> root of a word is useful.

Support through further and higher education

Martin worked with a series of support tutors over the period from 1986 when he was first diagnosed until 1995 when he completed his degree – a BA (Hons) in Social Policy for which he received an Upper Second Class. When he first attended specialist support sessions during the time he was on his access course, he presented as a highly organized, but extremely demanding student. As he began to feel that his tutors understood his learning needs, he relaxed and became less demanding. By the time he had finished his degree, Martin's tutor was aware of his increased confidence; although he was always a serious student, he learned to enjoy his sessions and could joke with his learning support tutor.

He always brought work to his sessions; he was punctual and focused and would ask his tutor to assist him with very specific tasks. Support sessions often consisted of helping him to structure a plan for an essay from a brainstorm, which he presented in the form of a mind-map. Subsequent sessions might be devoted to addressing spelling, grammar, or sentence structure problems which manifested themselves in his written work. The nature of the sessions was always determined by the work he brought in, but certain patterns of diffi-culty emerged, such as grammatical confusions over 'has' and 'as' or 'was' and 'were'. Some of these problems were related to his use of verbal syntax; others were due to difficulties with auditory processing and the fact that Martin could not actually discriminate subtle distinctions between two words.

Visual strategies were employed as much as possible to appeal to his strengths, and the use of highlighting and colour coding proved very beneficial. For example, he would highlight text to isolate main points in his reading and would colour code the highlighting with areas of interest he had identified in his mind-map. Another strategy that Martin found helpful was for the tutor to identify the type of error made in his written work by using error analysis marking (an agreed code in the margin). He would then go through his written work in the tutor's presence and try to locate where his errors were and self-correct, when possible. Through repeated work on the same type of error, he became increasingly competent in self-checking and self-correcting and his written skills gradually improved. An excerpt from an essay written towards the end of his access course attests to his improving ability to express sophisticated ideas in written form:

19/2/89

Why did Marx believe that "what the bourgeoisie produces is its own gravediggers. Its fall and the victory of the proletariat are equally inevitable."

This essay is going to explore why Karl Marx believes that "what the bourgeoisie produces is its own gravediggers. Its fall and the victory of the proleta-riat are equally inevitable." You must bear in mind, that Marx wrote this quotation in 1848, the same year as the French Revolution, perhaps believing, revolution would spread through out Europe. Also in 1848 the bourgeoisie industrial revolution was in full gear, and the consequ-ence of this revolution, Marx believe,would leave the proletariat with no choice, but to rebel against the bourgeoisie. I will   go on to discuss the consequence of this revolution in more detail, showing how it united a labouring class, and how this unity would be their strength to rise up against the bourgeoisie. I will also explain how the bourgeoisie unwittingly furnished them with the weapons to fight for emancipation, and how exploitation, and alienation at work, would be causes for revolution.

In 1990, six years after returning to adult literacy classes and four years after first being diagnosed as dyslexic, Martin embarked on a degree course in policy studies. Perhaps the difficulty that most hindered Martin's progress was the slow speed at which he processed information and was able to produce work. His dedication and determination were absolute; there was no question about his ability to understand and synthesize the intellectual concepts to which he was being exposed. But the extremely slow pace at which he worked made it unlikely that he would be able to succeed at degree level. Fortunately, the support tutor acted as an advocate on his behalf and helped him arrange to extend his three year degree over four years, so that the course load for each semester could be reduced to a more manageable level. Martin successfully completed his degree in 1994.

Life beyond degree level

To demonstrate support for Martin's outstanding achievement of attaining his degree ten years after returning to basic literacy classes, his support tutor decided to surprise him by attending his graduation ceremony. However, the surprise was reversed – Martin wasn't there! The tutor was quite amazed, since she expected that the ceremony would mark his achievement and he would surely want the formal recognition it afforded. However, when questioned about it several weeks later, Martin explained that his goal had never been the degree; rather it had been to gain the education that he had missed out in his youth. He felt that he had achieved that aim, and did not need a piece of paper to prove it. The tutor had to acknowledge that she had projected her own values in assessing the significance to him of the ceremony.

Martin left university and began the task of job hunting. He spent considerable time writing a *curriculum vitae* only to discover that most prospective employers requested the submission of an application form. Although Martin didn't have clear career goals, he was interested in getting involved in some sort of welfare work. No suitable jobs presented themselves and the Jobcentre suggested that he might like to enrol for a National Vocational Qualification (NVQ) in care work. He thought this seemed like a good idea since it provided a possible entrée to work through some on-the-job training in a placement with the elderly. Martin did not tell the NVQ tutors that he was dyslexic:

> I left university and I decided I was not going to be dyslexic. I think you feel you've achieved more if you can do it without saying you're dyslexic.

As a result of his placement, he was offered a permanent job where he has remained for the past three years. He enjoys the work, but has several conflicts:

> Ninety per cent of the time I enjoy the work. I actually gain quite a lot from it personally. But it's not that high a paid job, and I could be doing more, and I know it. They wanted me to move up to a senior position but, the more you go up, the more you go away from [working with] the actual people; you just go into the administrative side. I know this is going to be more stressful, so what's the point? But I also know that because of the dyslexia problem, I'm running away from it. [I know] my strengths are in the area of working with people. If I'm going to work in the admin, I'm going into my weaknesses. It's just, you know, I've got a university degree.

There seems to be a conflict in that, although the degree was never the goal, he still feels he should be doing more with the qualifications he has achieved.

The symbolic significance of a degree has also created a conflict in Martin's self-identity. While at university, his cultural and social as well as academic horizons were broadened and he 'felt [he] was between two classes'. He described feeling that his working-class friends could not understand his newly found interests in the arts, theatre, classical music and ballet, but he feared that his middle-class friends could never truly accept him because of his working-class roots. Now he seems clearer as to his position:

> Oh, I'm still working class. The degree has equipped me, empowered me, to be out there. I can go and get what I need now. My new skills have given me confidence . . .

Overall, he is extremely positive about the impact his recent education has had on his life:

> It's broadened my horizons and helped me cope and have a better lifestyle than I would have had if I didn't go to university. And I achieved a lot; that's the same with everybody, dyslexic or non-dyslexic. There's more to my life . . .

[education] opened many doors. It will still be a struggle, but I'm not worried about the struggle and the effort I will have to put into it. I can accept that.

Dyslexia defined and its impact on Martin's life

At the age of 53, with the benefit of 15 years distance since first entering adult education, Martin appears considerably more confident, relaxed and happy than when the authors first met him. He still finds it embarrassing to be dyslexic, but is more open about discussing his difficulties with friends:

> What I say to them is dyslexia is not just about reading and writing. It's all forms of processing . . . I define it from how the problems affect me. I tell them that spelling is a problem for me; reading's not really a difficult problem except if words are taken out of context, like street signs or maybe an odd word in a restaurant. Sometimes I can't read the words in the restaurant, so I just fall back and order my normal fish or something. There's also definitely a problem pronouncing words, and I tell them I'm easily distracted. But then I start to add the good bits. First of all, it's what I am and if they're friends of mine, then they must like that part anyway. Also it makes me more sensitive to other people with disabilities.

His current employers do not know he is dyslexic and he feels they would not understand if he were to inform them now. However, their lack of awareness makes him uncomfortable and he would definitely tell any future employer about his difficulties:

> I want to be somewhere where they do know that I'm dyslexic and they'll take me on from that basis. The reason for that is I'm not hiding anything.

Martin feels that his career choices are limited by his weaknesses, rather than influenced by his strengths, but he is nonetheless aware that he has chosen care work because he works well with people.

Martin is clear about the many ways in which dyslexia affects his life, but has developed excellent coping strategies. Shortly after beginning his access course, he wrote the following:

4/10/86

Myself

I am 5ft 4 ins in height, ~~underweight~~ underweight at 8 stone well I think I am.

I am a man of 39 years with short greying hair.

I was born in London of a family of five children of which I am the oldest.

I have one sister.

I walk with a limp because of a motor bike accident in 1966

I am a great worrier and a loyal person to friends and family.

I am single.

I live with two of my brothers in a flat in Camden Town.

I left school at 15 years of age not knowing what to do with my life so I went into jobs I did not like.

Work has been like that ever since.

I like to go abroad for my holiday if I can. I would not like to go on a holiday on my own.

I do not smoke, but I do drink too much at times, and then I talk too much.

I have had my friends for a long time and they are used to me talking too much when I have had a drink.

I remember being asked to write about myself at school, and sitting in the class room for an hours and not being able to write anything.

It pleases me to now be able to write about myself; it should I have improved.

His final statement in this piece reflects the beginning of his improving self-image.

Thirteen years later, he recognizes that his education has enabled him to feel generally more self-confident. Significant changes in his life include having the confidence to travel abroad to non-English speaking countries, to go to foreign films with subtitles, to write personal letters or leave a note for a friend:

> What are little goals for some people are quite big goals for me – quite big achievements.

In retrospect, five years post-university, Martin states:

> I've achieved a lot and there's more to achieve; there's more that will be
> achieved.

He comments that the teacher who suggested he was a 'late
developer' was right, but now he feels equipped to catch up on many
of the areas in his life that he missed out on in the past:

> I sometimes feel I'm like someone in their late 20s or early 30s; I'm at that stage
> of life, socially and career-wise.

Clearly Martin, like many other dyslexic adults, has come a long way
on the road to literacy and his new found skills have equipped him to
open many previously closed doors.

Part III
Turning Points

Chapter 10
Dyslexia in the twenty-first century

Many traditional fairy tales have an ironic twist at the end when the older, supposedly brighter sons fail to solve the riddle, win the princess or save the kingdom – but the ultimate success goes to the unconventional approach of the youngest son, the so-called 'stupid' one. The non-dyslexic view of dyslexia as a 'deficit' mirrors the arrogance of the older sons in these tales; perhaps we can all benefit from seeing the world through more than one perspective and recognizing that unconventional, lateral approaches to problem-solving may be the way forward in the twenty-first century.

Developments in technology are not only rapidly opening pathways for researching, diagnosing, teaching and supporting dyslexic adults, but changing our world and the required skills and talents necessary for success. Instant global communication has widened our viewpoints. Our vision of society is evolving to one that respects and values diversity and is more inclusive, one that accepts responsibility for ensuring that whatever is available for some people is made accessible to all.

We face some urgent decisions regarding the implications of a truly inclusive society; we must examine our commitment to diversity and decide how best to nourish it.

Changes in the education system

The implications of inclusiveness are many and profound for the dyslexic person as well as for those with other disabilities. In his introduction to *Inclusive Learning* (HMSO, 1996), Tomlinson states that:

> We want to avoid a viewpoint which locates the difficulty or deficit with the student and focus instead on the capacity of the educational institution to respond to the individual learner's requirement . . . There is a world of difference between, on the one hand, offering courses of education and then giving some students who have learning difficulties some additional human or physical aids to gain access to those courses, and, on the other hand, redesigning the very processes of learning, assessment and organization so as to fit the objectives and learning styles of the students.

Only the second option can claim to be inclusive:

> By 'inclusive learning' therefore, we mean the greatest degree of match or fit between the individual learner's requirements and the provision that is made for them.

The idea of inclusiveness supports a model of difference rather than of disability, and requires that we abandon perceptions of deficits as well as the labelling of 'unsuccessful' learners as 'failures'. Instead we must question our basic assumptions of how learners should learn. These underlie our perceptions of learners within the education system and the larger culture. There are judgements about the 'right' way to teach; and worse, beliefs about 'right' ways to assess learning, namely through written examinations.

We are at a crossroads in education. On the one hand, attempts to widen access have resulted in an increased range of vocational qualifications and better basic skills support, including specialist dyslexia support. On the other hand, anxieties to establish and maintain standards and ensure parity among qualifications have resulted in increasing demands for written assessment. Candidates must demonstrate their 'key' skills, which include written English and maths. This continues to disadvantage dyslexic students, whose written skills may never be at the same level as their other skills, resulting in underachievement of potential.

The emphasis on achieving qualifications has increased, while unconventional routes into both vocational and professional careers have dwindled. Many dyslexic adults have achieved success only through demonstrating their 'real life' skills in the workplace. Others, who have taken a vocational route and now have their own businesses, admit that they succeeded only because they were able to avoid or 'get by' with the minimum in written examinations. In future, will they be more rather than less likely to be excluded? Will they continue to be judged on their weaknesses rather than their strengths? We do not devalue the abilities of those who cannot draw – why demean those who cannot spell? We seem to have confused the importance of teaching children and adults to read, write and spell as a way of giving them access to information, ideas and opportunities with seeing these skills as an end in themselves, removed from a context.

Are we putting too much emphasis on reading and writing and sequential thinking? Do we as a society adequately value intuitive and visual-spatial talents – especially among those who lack the required verbal skills? Do we foster and reward the range of 'intelligences', as Gardner (1983) calls them? Is it time for us to think about a 'multi-intelligence' society as well as a multi-cultural one?

We need to recognize a range of cognitive and learning styles and address these, allowing for people to learn and achieve in different ways and not be labelled as poor or failing learners simply because they cannot make sense of phonics, sit still and listen for long periods of time or 'deploy neat penmanship', as one dyslexic man put it.

The demands of a rapidly changing world and an overabundance of information imply a need to shift the emphasis of the curriculum from content to process, from cognition to metacognition, from 'learning' to 'learning how to learn'. Helping individuals discover and learn through their own preferred learning style creates independent and confident learners who can maximize their strengths and minimize the effects of their weaknesses.

A further change in the curriculum is the increasing use of visual images and models and awareness of their positive impact on learning. The ability to create visual materials is becoming as essential as that of creating written ones, and some educationalists emphasize that visual literacy skills are as important as reading and writing skills. Rake (1999), for instance, suggests that visuals help students improve comprehension and that creating visual materials aids communication, so the more students understand visual elements, the more they will be able to use this 'language'. This shift may offer dyslexic students more opportunities to develop and gain recognition for their strengths within the education system.

One of the most well-entrenched beliefs from the Victorian era is the idea of the classroom as *the* setting where learning takes place. However, this is finally being re-examined. Concern about the large numbers of adults and young people who leave the education system and do not return is forcing new thinking about ways to take learning out of the 'classroom'. The changes in the curriculum for 16–19 - year-olds in Britain are in part a response to the need to shift learning and opportunities to gain qualifications more to the workplace, a change that would well suit those dyslexic learners who learn best in context. Hugh Pitman, Chairman of the Association of Learning Providers affirms the value of work-based education:

> The work-based method of preparing young people and adults for employment opportunities, and upskilling and developing them within their careers, has proved beyond any doubt to be the most successful and cost-effective system in existence.
>
> (Pitman, 2000)

These changes are also part of a continuing move towards a more flexible curriculum where academic and vocational subjects are integrated, and there are opportunities to create more individualized learning packages. What is also needed is a flexible model of assessment to ensure individual potential is realized. The assumption that the only valid standard is performance in a written exam is difficult to shift.

In fact, there is frequently a mismatch between what employers want and what the examination system provides. Hall et al. (1999) found that employers and employees felt that GCSE maths and English were not directly relevant to work. Aldrich (2000) suggests that 'the precise relationship between educational achievement and employment levels remains elusive. Today, as in the past, education often serves to keep people out of the labour market rather than prepare them for it.'

Ten years ago, Walter Frey (1990), himself an engineer, wrote that the current school system was depriving the US of innovative engineers by screening out 'right-brain-dominant' and/or dyslexic people. He suggested that 'a significant proportion' of engineers, most of whom graduated before 1960 and were among the innovators who 'developed semiconductor electronics and computers, lasers, optical communications, satellite communications – and put a man on the moon', were 'right-brain-dominant' or dyslexic. He believes that the system is now screening out these potential innovators because they struggle with an education system that is 'so strongly left-brained and memory oriented'. It seems the best engineers are those who can visualize whole systems and thus identify likely problems and solutions. New qualifications rely heavily on sequential thinking, along with more stringent reading and writing demands; these, he claimed, were weeding out many of the most talented, who were also dyslexic.

A recent report (TES, 2000) notes the low pass rates and poor retention on many further education college engineering courses. These results are mainly due to poor performance of 16–18 year old students on foundation and intermediate level courses who are struggling with the 'heavy amount of portfolio work required'. In some departments 'up to 90% of Level 2 students need some form of additional support'.

This perspective is also reinforced by Peter Fowler (2000), who runs a multimedia design programme at the Liverpool John Moores University. He set up the course, aimed at art and design graduates, because his own work was expanding and he was unable to find people with 'the skills we knew were central – the combination of a design sensibility with competence in the relevant software packages'. Since 1991, his students have formed two companies and there are others who are working in twos or threes or as sole traders. Together they employ more than 200 people. Their earning potential is enormous, with many having realistic chances of becoming millionaires. Yet a high percentage are dyslexic, some profoundly so. Fowler expresses his concern that:

> there is no connection between what we are doing and the rest of the education system. Those we employ and those who, as a result, are succeeding so brilliantly, were rarely 'discovered' during their conventional schooling.

He goes on to say:

> The non-alignment between the accidental success of those who have worked for us, and the educational system as a whole is alarming. Here we have a bunch of kids, a world of wealth and fun before them, who almost certainly would do no better in school today than when they were there.

Another rapidly developing initiative to take learning out of the classroom is the setting up of the National Grid and University for

Industry to develop learning online. This is another way of learning that suits many dyslexic people who respond well to computers and are attracted to the visual and interactive opportunities of the internet. The potential for flexibility and variation for individual learning packages online is likely to necessitate new thinking about qualifications, making them as individual as the learning itself. This could offer dyslexic people the chance to be judged on what they can do, rather than on what they cannot.

Even in universities, the bastions of tradition, changes in funding for students with disabilities, including dyslexia, now mean that dyslexic learners can access the technological and learning support they need to fulfil academic requirements. The fact that students can now receive funding to support part-time study may enable increasing numbers of dyslexic students to pursue degrees, since they can work at a pace that suits their processing style. David, who was a highly successful dancer and choreographer and had set up his own modern dance company which toured the world, returned to education at the age of 35. He summed up the feelings of many dyslexic adults when he said:

> I've proved myself physically; now I want the chance to develop the bit that never got a chance – I want to gain an education.

New courses and opportunities in higher education will enable more people like David to realize their dreams.

Changes in the world of work

The work 'place', like the classroom, is also in transit. Many people now operate from home and in 'cyberspace'. The need for rapid communication is replacing the need for formal communication. E-mails, text messages and mobile phones demand less formality, with less emphasis on accurate spelling and punctuation. Voice recognition technology is improving rapidly, and devices such as 'reading pens' are likely to become commonplace. Computers can do calculations, analyze and compare data. As Iain Arnison, a 27-year-old severely dyslexic lecturer in multimedia and internet applications at John Moores University, asks:

> Why do we need to be taught mental arithmetic when we have calculators? Why do we need to read text when computers can read it for us? Why do we

even need to write when the latest dictation software can take down our words as we speak?

(Bowers, 2000)

Employers now seek many qualities other than literacy skills. Creativity is of great importance in a highly competitive changing economy, as is the ability to solve problems and to relate to people. The complexity of information and multi-dimensional tasks common in twenty-first century jobs demand considerable team-work. Fowler notes that one of the qualities of the successful dyslexic individuals in his unit is their ease in working in teams. Teamwork both values and respects diversity. One of its advantages is that members of a team can contribute their strengths, and each person does not need to be good at everything. Someone else may do the writing, for instance, or do any research involving texts, while the dyslexic person makes other contributions.

Shifts in the educational curriculum are mirroring changes in work where there is a rise in service jobs and fast-growing areas of communications technology and graphic design, for example, in designing websites and software. These changes may enable dyslexic people to capitalize on their strengths by finding employment that 'fits' their cognitive style, or by setting up their own companies. We may even find that dyslexic people are at the heart of the revolution in technology and work.

Technology and dyslexia

Technology may have more direct effects on dyslexic individuals, changing the way dyslexia is identified and treated. Genetic research as well as research on brain organization is also expanding rapidly. The genetic links established by Fagerheim et al. (1999) suggest the future possibility of an objective diagnosis of dyslexia and the future likelihood of using brain scans to identify it at a very early stage. This would overcome the considerable controversies that currently exist, including the doubts of sceptics about the very existence of dyslexia.

New technology is also offering possibilities for working with the brain's plasticity to change its organization. This raises important ethical questions as many dyslexic people are glad their brains are 'wired' differently and do not want to be 'cured'. However, it also suggests that there may be neuro-based techniques to deal with some of the worst problems of dyslexia.

From her research, Tallal, co-director of the Center for Molecular and Behavioural Neuroscience at Rutgers University (Begley, 2000), believes that in many people dyslexia stems from a neurological difference which affects the ability to process sounds rapidly. Her computer-based programme, *Fast ForWord*, achieves what cannot be done by the human voice; it is designed to alter the duration and amplitude of sounds and thus 'retrain' the brain to discriminate sounds and distinguish rapid sound changes. Results with 25,000 children have shown that after 6–8 weeks of training, 90 per cent progressed one and a half to two years in reading. Tallal also claims good results with an adult version of her programme. Her colleague, Merzenich, believes that exploitation of brain plasticity will lead to 'neuroscience-based education. In 10–15 years this will be everywhere, and every school will be able to deliver help based on brain plasticity.'

Challenges of the twenty-first century: a different kind of thinking?

The modern problems in science and industry are more and more complex and rely increasingly on understanding complex systems and the ability to visualize. The success of dyslexic people in graphic design and multi-media has already been mentioned. This success in part depends on the ability to find design solutions that 'enable users to access vast amounts of material' (Fowler, 2000). The lines are blurring between science and art. Fowler emphasizes the importance of acknowledging that we live 'in different times'.

As West (1992) suggests, 'Voluminous data from satellites and other automated sources overwhelms traditional methods of analysis.' Graphics systems that focus on a 'visual representation of the whole rather than the parts are inherently better suited to dealing with such complex phenomena'. West asserts:

> What is so surprising and so hard for people to understand is that we're dealing with a different kind of intelligence. The problems of molecular biology, for example, are to do with how the surface shapes of viruses interact, how strings of genetic markers roll up and wrap around themselves.'

(Price, 1996)

He goes on to describe a dyslexic designer who designs memory chips for an advanced graphics system:

> He can see the circuit design in many dimensions, and the patterns and rhythm of the data coursing through the memory chips. His ability to predict bottlenecks is based entirely on visualization. There's no way of doing it using existing mathematical/design theory.

The intention of this book has been not only to help professionals and others better to understand and support their dyslexic colleagues, employees and students, but also to learn to value and make better use of the contributions dyslexic people can make to enlarge and enrich our world by looking at it from their perspective. Karen, an Interior Design student, found reading and writing extremely difficult. She relied heavily on her partner to read aloud the texts she needed for her course. In the course of her diagnostic interview, she revealed her deep shame and embarrassment about her poor literacy skills. When asked if she had ever used a computer, she replied, 'Oh, computers. Of course I've used them. I build them.' When the tutor expressed her amazement at such skill, Karen responded, 'But that's easy.' Like West (1992), we believe that when we understand that 'for some, the "easy things" are difficult, but the "hard things" are easy, then we may find that we are surrounded by much more talent than we could have imagined'.

We leave you with another Nasruddin story:

> The Khan of Samarkand said to Nasruddin one day, 'Reasonable people always see things in the same way.'
>
> 'That is the trouble with reasonable people,' said Nasruddin. 'They include at least some people who always see only one of two possibilities.'
>
> The next day Nasruddin rode through town on his donkey, facing its tail. He arrived at the palace and requested the Khan to ask his advisers what they had just seen. They all said, 'A man riding back to front on a donkey.'
>
> 'That is exactly my point,' said Nasruddin. 'They did not notice that perhaps it was me who was right and the donkey the wrong way round.'
>
> (adapted from Shah, 1968)

References

Aldrich R (2000) A happy marriage? Times Educational Supplement: 5 May.

Alm J, Andersson J (1995) Reading and Writing Difficulties at Prisons in the County of Uppsala. Uppsala: National Labour Market Board of Sweden.

Antonoff J (1995) Juvenile Justice, Dyslexia and Other Learning Disabilities.

Appleyard D (1997) The art of being dyslexic. Independent Education 27.02.97.

Arkell H (1977) Introduction to Dyslexia. London: Helen Arkell Dyslexia Centre.

Baddeley A (1986) Working Memory. Oxford: Clarendon Press.

Beaton A, McDougall S, Singleton C (1997) Humpty Dumpty grows up? Diagnosing dyslexia in adulthood. Journal of Research in Reading, Special Issue: Dyslexia in Literate Adults 20(1): 1–6.

Beech J, Singleton C (1997) The Psychological Assessment of Reading. London and New York: Routledge.

Begley S (2000) Rewiring your gray matter. Newsweek: 1 Jan.

Boden C, Brodener DA (1999) Visual processing of verbal and non-visual stimuli in adolescents with reading disabilities. Journal of Learning Disabilities 32(1): 58–71.

Bowers S (2000) Modern visions and the old school of thought. The Guardian: 29 Feb.

BPS (1999) Dyslexia, Literacy and Psychological Assessment: Report by the working party of the Division of Educational and Child Psychology of The British Psychological Society.

Brinckerhoff L, Shaw S, McGuire J. (1993) Promoting Postsecondary Education for Students with Learning Disabilities: A Handbook for Practitioners. Austin, Texas: Pro-Ed.

Brooks PL, Weeks SAJ (1998) A comparison of the responses of dyslexic, slow learning and control children to different strategies for teaching spellings. Dyslexia 4(4): 212–22.

Butterfield A (1996) Are most adults in literacy classes dyslexic or learning disabled? Unpublished MA thesis. Birkbeck College, Department of Applied Linguistics, University of London.

Buzan T (1993) The Mind Map Book: Radiant Thinking. London: BBC Books.

Cline T, Reason R (1993) Specific learning difficulties (dyslexia): equal opportunities issues. British Journal of Special Education 20(1): 30–34.

Constantine A (2000) Computers mightier than the pen in tests. Times Educational Supplement: 2 June.

Cooper R (1996) Identifying real differences in thinking and learning styles. The National Journal of Vocational Education: Assessment Matters 2: 3–5.

Cooper R (1997) Initial assessment: responding to learning styles. Assessment Matters, Autumn. (Reprinted in The Skill Journal 62: Nov 1998.)

Coyle P (1996) What dyslexic lawyers confront when they read or write. The Lawyer's Magazine – American Bar Association Journal 82, September.

Critchley M (1970) The Dyslexic Child. Springfield, IL: Charles C Thomas.

Davis R (1994) The Gift of Dyslexia. Burlingame: Ability Workshop Press.

DfEE (1994) Code of Practice on the Identification and Assessment of Special Educational Needs. London: DfE.

DfE (1999) Learning to Succeed. London: DfEE.

DfE (2000) Freedom to Learn: Basic Skills for Learners with Learning Difficulties and/or Disabilities. London: DfEE.

Dinklage KT (1991) Counseling the learning disabled college student. Journal of College Student Psychotherapy 5(3): 3–27.

Dyslexia: Symptoms – a Video about Dyslexia. Manchester Adult Education Services.

Dyson L (1996) The experiences of families of children with learning disabilities: parental stress, family functioning and sibling self-concept. Journal of Learning Disabilities 29(3): 280–286.

Edwards J (1994). The Scars of Dyslexia. London: Cassell.

Everatt J, Steffart B, Smythe I (1999) An eye for the unusual: creative thinking in dyslexic adults. Dyslexia 5(1): 28–47.

Fagerheim T, Raeymakers P, Tonnessen FE, Pedersen M, Tranebjaerg L, Lubs HA (1999) A new gene (DYX3) for dyslexia is located on chromosome 2. Journal of Medical Genetics 36(9): 664–69.

Fernald G (1943) Remedial Techniques in Basic School Subjects. McGraw-Hill.

Feuerstein R, Miller R, Rand Y, Jensen M (1981) Can Evolving Techniques Better Measure Cognitive Change? The Journal of Special Education 15 (2): 201–19.

Fink R (1995) Successful dyslexics: a constructivist study of passionate interest reading. Journal of Adolescent and Adult Literacy 39: 4.

Fink R (1998) Literacy development in successful men and women with dyslexia. Annals of Dyslexia 48: 311–46.

Fowler E (1997) Developing independent readers in basic skills. Basic Skills Agency Journal, April/May: 16–19.

Fowler P (2000) Dreaming in colour. The Guardian, 29 Feb.

Frey W (1990) Schools miss out on dyslexic engineers. IEEE Spectrum, December.

Frith U (1999) Paradoxes in the definition of dyslexia. Dyslexia 5(4): 155–77.

Galaburda A (1990) Neuroscience issues in dyslexia. Paper presented to the Orton Society Annual Conference.

Galaburda A (1999) Developmental dyslexia: a multilevel syndrome. Dyslexia 5(4): 183–92.

Gardner H (1983) Frames of Mind: the Theory of Multiple Intelligences. New York: Basic Books.

Gates HL Jnr (1996) Belafonte's balancing act. The New Yorker: 2 Sept.

Gerber P, Ginsberg R, Reiff H (1992) Identifying alterable patterns in employment for highly successful adults with learning disabilities. Journal of Learning Disabilities 25(8): 475–87.

Geva E (1999) Issues in the assessment of reading disabilities in children who are work-
    ing in their second language: beliefs and research evidence. Paper presented at the
    BDA International Conference, Manchester, June.
Gilroy D (1995) Stress factors in the college student. In Miles TR, Varma V, (Eds)
    Dyslexia and Stress. London: Whurr Publishers.
Greenbaum B, Graham S, Scales W (1996) Adults with learning disabilities: occupation-
    al and social status after college. Journal of Learning Disabilities 29(2): 167–73.
Hales G 1995). Stress factors in the workplace. In Miles TR, Varma V (1995) Dyslexia
    and Stress. London: Whurr Publishers.
Hall I, Hardman F, Smith F, Taverner S (1999) The relevance of GCSE mathematics
    and English as preparation for employment. Journal of Vocational Education and
    Training, vol 51, no 2, pp 283–304.
Hammersley M (1994) Introducing ethnography. In Graddol D, Maybin J, Stierer B,
    (Eds) Researching Language and Literacy in Social Context. Clevedon:
    Multilingual Publishers Ltd. in association with the Open University.
Hammill D (1990) On defining learning disabilities: an emerging consensus. Journal of
    Learning Disabilities 23: 84.
Hampshire S (1981) Susan's Story. London: Sidgwick and Jackson.
Hanley J (1997) Reading and spelling impairments in undergraduate students with
    developmental dyslexia. Journal of Research in Reading (Special Issue: Dyslexia in
    Literate Adults) 20(1): 22–23.
Hinshelwood J (1917) Congenital Word Blindness. London: H.K. Lewis.
HMSO (1996) Inclusive Learning: Report of the Learning Difficulties and/or
    Disabilities Committee. London: HMSO.
International Dyslexia Association (2000) Web address: www.interdys.org
Irlen H (1991) Reading by the Colors. New York: Avery.
Kirk J, Reid G (2000) An examination of the relationship between dyslexia and offend-
    ing in young people and the implications for the training system. University of
    Edinburgh.
Klein C (1992) Final Report – National Development Project: Developing Learning
    Support for Students with Specific learning Difficulties. London: Basic Skills
    Agency.
Klein C (1993) Diagnosing Dyslexia: a Guide to the Assessment of Adults with Specific
    Learning Difficulties. London: The Basic Skills Agency.
Klein C (1998) Dyslexia and Offending: Intervention for Change – Final Report on the
    Dyspel Pilot Project. London Action Trust.
Klein C, Millar R (1990) Unscrambling Spelling. London: Hodder and Stoughton.
Klein C, Sunderland H (1998) SOLOTEC Dyslexia Good Practice Guide. London
    Language and Literacy Unit.
Klein H (1985) The assessment and management of some persisting language difficulties
    in the learning disabled. In Snowling M (Ed) Children's Written Language
    Difficulties. Windsor: NFER-Nelson.
Krupska M, Klein C (1995), Demystifying Dyslexia: Raising Awareness and Developing
    Support for Dyslexic Young People and Adults. London Language and Literacy
    Unit.
Lewis M, Wray D (1996) Writing Frames: scaffolding childrens' non-fiction writing.
    University of Reading: Reading and Language Information Centre.

Litten M (1999) Introducing voice recognition software to dyslexic users in a specialist school. Dyslexia 5(2): 118–21.

McLoughlin D, Fitzgibbon G, Young V (1994). Adult Dyslexia: Assessment, Counselling and Training. London: Whurr Publishers.

Mercer N (1994) Neo-Vygotskian theory and classroom education. In Stierer B, Maybin J, (Eds) Language, Literacy and Learning in Educational Practice. Open University Press.

Miles TR (1993) Dyslexia: The Pattern of Difficulties (2nd edition). London: Whurr Publishers.

Miles TR, Varma V (1995) Dyslexia and Stress. London: Whurr Publishers.

Mitchell C (1984) Case Studies in Ellen R. Ethnographic research: a guide to general conduct, p. 237–241. London: Academic Press.

Morgan E (1996) Mapping an understanding of dyslexia. Dyslexia 2: 209–11.

Morgan E, Abrahams B (1999) Wordwork: a CD-Rom of Study Strategies for Dyslexic Adults. London: Alphabetics, Ltd.

Morgan E, Rooney M (1997) Can dyslexic students be trained as teachers? Support for Learning: Journal of the National Association for Special Educational Needs. 12(1): 28–31.

Morgan W (1996) Dyslexic offenders. The Magistrate Magazine 52(4): 84–86.

Moser C (1999) A Fresh Start: Improving literacy and numeracy. Report of working group chaired by Sir Claus Moser. London: DfEE.

Nicolson RI, Fawcett AJ (1990) Automaticity: a new framework for dyslexia research? Cognition 33: 159–82.

Pitman H (2000) We are the future. The Guardian, 25 April.

Preston M (1996) Four Times Harder: Six Case Studies of Students with Dyslexia in Higher Education. Birmingham: The Question Publishing Company.

Price E (1996) The skill that dares not spell its name. The Evening Standard: 4 June.

Pumfrey P, Reason R (1991) Specific Learning Difficulties (Dyslexia): Challenges and Responses. London: NFER-Routledge.

Rack J (1997) Issues in the assessment of developmental dyslexia in adults. Journal of Research in Reading 20(1): 66–76.

Radford T, Woodward W (2000) Proof that knowledge is good for the brain. The Guardian: 14 Mar.

Rake, G (1999) Teaching visual literacy in a multimedia age. TechTrends 43(4): 14–18.

Reid G, Kirk J (2000) Adult Dyslexia for Employment, Practice and Training (ADEPT) Project Report, Employment Service.

Reiff HB, Gerber P, Ginsberg R (1993) Definitions of learning disabilities from adults with learning disabilities: the insiders' perspectives. Learning Disability Quarterly 16: 114–25.

Reiff HB, Gerber P, Ginsberg R. (1997) Exceeding Expectations: Successful Adults with Learning Disabilities. Austin, Texas: Pro-Ed.

Riddick B (1996) Living with Dyslexia. London and New York: Routledge.

Sanderson A (1999). Voice recognition software: a panacea for dyslexic learners or a frustrating hindrance? Dyslexia 5(2): 113–18.

Saunders R (1995) Stress factors within the family. In Miles TR, Varma V (Eds) Dyslexia and Stress. London: Whurr Publishers.

Shah I (1964) The Sufis. London: Jonathan Cape.

Shah I (1968) Caravan of Dreams. The Octagon Press.

Shaughnessy MP (1977) Errors and Expectations: a Guide for the Teachers of Basic Writing. New York: Oxford University Press.

Shaywitz S (1996) Dyslexia. Scientific American, November: 78–86.

Shaywitz S, Towle V, Keese D, Shaywitz B (1990) Prevalence of dyslexia in boys and girls in an epidemiological sample. Journal of the American Medical Association 181: 143–57.

Siegel, Himel (1998) Socio-economic status, age, and the classification of dyslexics and poor readers: the dangers of using IQ scores in the definition of reading disability. Dyslexia 4(2): 90–104.

Singleton CH (1999) Dyslexia in Higher Education: policy, provision and practice. (Report of the National Working Party on Dyslexia in Higher Education.) Hull: University of Hull, on behalf of the Higher Education Funding Councils of England and Scotland.

Smith F (1982) Writing and the Writer. London: Heinemann.

Smith S (1991) Succeeding Against the Odds. New York: Jeremy P. Tarcher/Perigee Books.

Snowling M (1987) Dyslexia: A Cognitive Developmental Perspective. Oxford: Blackwell.

Snowling M, Nation K, Moxham P, Gallagher A, Frith U (1997) Phonological processing skills of dyslexic students in higher education: a preliminary report. Journal of Research in Reading (Special Issue: Dyslexia in Literate Adults) 20(1): 31–41.

Springer S, Deutsch G (1998) Right Brain, Left Brain: Perspectives from Cognitive Neuroscience. New York: W H Freeman and Co (5th edn).

Stanovich KE (1991) Discrepancy definitions of reading disability: has intelligence led us astray? Reading Research Quarterly 26: 7–29.

Stanovich KE (1996) Towards a more inclusive definition of dyslexia. Dyslexia 2(3): 154–66.

Stein J, Talcott J (1999) Impaired neuronal timing in developmental dyslexia – the magnocellular hypothesis. Dyslexia 5(2): 59–78.

Sunderland H (1998) Diagnosing dyslexia in adult students learning English as an additional language. Unpublished MA thesis. Thames Valley University, Dept. of English Language Teaching.

Sunderland H, Klein C, Savinson R, Partridge T (1997) Dyslexia and the Bilingual Learner: Assessing and Teaching Adults and Young People who Speak English as an Additional Language. London Language and Literacy Unit

TES (2000), Engineer Courses 'not up to scratch', Times Educational Supplement: Further Education Focus p.iii 4th February.

Tur-Kaspa H, Weisel A, Segev L (1998) Attributions for feelings of loneliness of students with learning disabilities. Learning Disabilities Research and Practice 13(2): 89–94.

Turney B (1997) I'm Still Standing. Winchester: Waterside Press.

Turner M (1997) Psychological Assessment of Dyslexia. London: Whurr Publishers.

Warren J (1999) How I won my battle against dyslexia (interview with Richard Branson). The Express, 23 July.

Wertheim C, Vogel S, Brulle A (1998) Students with learning disabilities in teacher education programs. Annals of Dyslexia 48: 293–309.

West T (1991) In the Mind's Eye. New York: Prometheus Books.

West T (1992) A future of reversals: dyslexic talents in a world of computer visualization. Annals of Dyslexia 42.

Wilkins A (1995) Visual Stress. Oxford: Oxford University Press.

Wszeborowska-Lipinska B (1998) Non-verbal problem-solving and learning styles in developmental dyslexia. Unpublished paper. (University of Gdansk, Poland: Royal Society Visiting Research Fellow 1997/98, University of Hull.)

Zabell C, Everatt J (2000) The Dyslexia Handbook 2000. Reading: The British Dyslexia Association.

Zephaniah B (1999) Final word. The Teacher, May. London: NUT.

Index

213

school *v.* work performance 102
Scotopic Sensitivity Syndrome (SSS)
    149, 171
screen readers 148–50
self-correction 173, 189
self-esteem 57, 82–3, 182, 192
    and age of diagnosis 50–2, 62
    influence of dyslexia on 49, 50, 51,
        74
semantic coding 13
sequencing difficulties 16, 18, 138, 146
severity, of dyslexia 49
shopping, getting change 71
short-term memory 14, 15, 66, 114
siblings 75
    sibling relationships 80, 90–1
social class 54–7
social life 67, 70
social skills 79, 82–3
social work, as a career 112–16
    appropriate support from supervi-
        sors 114–16
software, *see* computers; technology in
        education; voice recognition tech-
        nology; word-processing
solicitors/lawyers 102, 121–2
spatial rotation tests 11
specialist tutors, importance of 167
speech/voice synthesis technology
        16–17, 19–20, 149
spellchecker software 147–8, 152–3,
        155, 155–6
spelling 32
    as means to reading 163–5
    phonetic approaches to 161
    rules, difficulty with 15, 16
    strategies for 161–5, 188
    teaching methods 159–60, 161, 167
spelling analysis 39
spelling tests 25
spidergrams/spider maps 166
strengths 6
    focusing on 160
    gift of dyslexia 4, 6, 8–12
    research into 8
    turning weaknesses into 126–8
stress

exacerbating dyslexic difficulties
        63–65
    parents' 92
    visual stress 30
    stress factors, for families 49
stubbornness 87, 92–3
students
    dyslexic *v.* non-dyslexic 136
    group assignments 136, 142–5
    mature students 133, 134
    student–tutor relationship 167,
        168–9
study skills software 151
subject tutors 177–9
supervision, in social work 114–16
support 57–63, 77
    from employers and colleagues 124,
        130
    for learning 166–9
    parental involvement 90
    support strategies 169–75
support groups 175–7
support tutors 171, 172–5, 188–90
    editing *v.* teaching 175
synthesis 7
    v. analysis 4, 204–5

teaching
    learning-styles model 160
    see also teaching as a career; teaching
        styles; tutors
teaching as a career 108–12
    arguments against 110
    arguments for 109–10
    coping strategies 111, 126–7
    disclosure of disability 119
    suitability for 110–11
teaching styles
    conflict with learning styles 137
    teaching to learning styles 11, 16,
        160–6
teamwork 127, 203
technology and dyslexia 203–4
    in the work place 202–3
technology in education 145–56
    computers 145–6, 156, 202
    planning software 150

Please remember that this is a library book, and that it belongs only temporarily to each person who uses it. Be considerate. Do not write in this, or any, library book.